Mistaking Africa

Mistaking Africa

Curiosities and Inventions of the American Mind

Curtis A. Keim
Moravian College

Westview Press
A Member of the Perseus Books Group

Published in 1999 in the United States of America by Westview Press, 5500 Central Avenue, Boulder, Colorado 80301-2877, and in the United Kingdom by Westview Press, 12 Hid's Copse Road, Cumnor Hill, Oxford OX2 9JJ

Library of Congress Cataloging-in-Publication Data
Keim, Curtis A.
Mistaking Africa: curiosities and inventions of the American mind / Curtis A. Keim.
p. cm.
Includes bibliographical references (p.) and index.
ISBN 0-8133-3508-6 (hardcover).—ISBN 0-8133-3509-4 (paperback)
1. Africa—Foreign public opinion, American. 2. Public opinion—United States. I. Title.
DT38.7.K45 1999
960—dc21 99-21972
CIP

The paper used in this publication meets the requirements of the American National Standard for Permanence of Paper for Printed Library Materials Z39.48-1984.

10 9 8 7 6 5 4 3 2 1

To Karen

Contents

Preface

I teach about Africa at a small liberal arts college where students are required to take one non-Western culture course. Most frequently, therefore, my students study Africa because of the requirement, and they will most likely never take another non-Western course. I have a mere fourteen weeks to interest and inform, and to build a foundation for further exploration and concern. This is indeed a privilege and a challenge.

Over the years that I have been teaching such survey courses, I have found that students' ability to approach the continent is deeply influenced by American stereotypes about Africa. Many students filter accurate information through their inaccurate stereotypes, thus making my teaching less effective than I would like. Therefore, I now take time at the beginning of every course to discuss our heritage of ideas about Africa. I ask students to explore what our stereotypes are, how we have acquired them, where they appear in our culture, and why they persist. As each course proceeds, I find places where students can pause to think about how our stereotypes relate to the topics at hand. I have written this book for students and others who are just beginning to consider how we commonly misperceive and misrepresent Africa.

Africanist scholars have extensively described and criticized American stereotypes about modern Africa. They have had the most obvious success in improving K–12 textbooks, children's literature, and news reporting, but their studies apply to numerous areas of American culture. Thus, I have been able to rely on experts in many fields for both ideas and examples. My own contribution is original only in the sense that I have attempted to gather ideas into one place and in a form accessible to undergraduate college and university students.

I hope that other teachers of Africa will find this book useful. As I wrote, I tried to keep in mind that individual chapters might be used separately or omitted, depending on a teacher's time constraints and purposes, and I therefore attempted to write each one so it stands by itself. I also sought to make each chapter (with a couple of exceptions) brief enough that teachers can assign two or three chapters per class period when there is a need to move quickly to content about Africa itself.

Some faculty might want to use this book to construct an entire introductory course around American or Western perspectives on Africa. This book could serve as an anchor for examining the many available materials that illustrate Western views, whether they be Joseph Conrad's *Heart of Darkness* or *The Lion King*. Class readings and projects for this type of course will interest a variety of students, who can explore how Africa is treated in television news, newspapers, nature programs, movies, novels, churches, advertising, books by travelers to Africa, and museum exhibits. They can also interview Africans or people who have traveled to Africa as tourists or missionaries, on business, or otherwise.

As I wrote this book, I was aware that many readers other than college and university students might wish to consider how Americans have perceived and misperceived Africa. I hope that this book will be of general use, perhaps to those who report on African affairs, travel to Africa, host African guests, study cross-cultural communications, or teach grades K–12.

Curtis A. Keim

Acknowledgments

I thank the many friends and colleagues who contributed to this book. I am especially grateful to Steven Adams, Robert Mayer, Doris Schatt-Schneider, Donald St. John, David Waas, and James West, who read chapters or the entire draft. I also thank my colleagues who discussed ideas with me and suggested sources, including Patricia Alden, Clarke Chapman, May Collins, Dennis Glew, James Green, Hwa Yol Jung, Frank Kuserk, Phillip Lapansky, Jill MacDougal, William Scott, Robert Steelman, Robert Stinson, Louis Tremaine, and Stanley Yoder. At Moravian College Reeves Library, Bonnie Falla, Dorothy Glew, and Linda LaPoint helped generously with my queries, and Deborah Gaspar and Nancy Strobel quickly tracked down materials the library did not own.

Students also played an important role in the completion of the text. My Africa classes generously shared their perceptions and misperceptions of Africa. They also read and commented on various chapters and drafts and several contributed examples of popular images of Africa. Christina Szoke, a student assistant in the history department at Moravian College, helped locate books and verify sources and citations. She also read and commented on a draft. Sarah Soden became my part-time assistant over the summer of 1998. She was sponsored by Moravian College's SOAR program, which gives superior students opportunities to do research with faculty. Sarah read drafts, tracked down books and articles, wrote portions of Chapter 10, and found many examples of ways that Africa is used in popular culture. Sarah also interested her mother in the project. For several months, Marie Soden sent packets with ads or articles that she had come across in her reading. Both Sarah and her mother have my heartfelt thanks for their interest and aid.

Special appreciation goes to Ann West, my sister, who helped me as agent, editor, and cheerleader. At Westview Press, I thank Laura Parsons and Jennifer Chen, acquisitions editors, and Norman Ware, copy editor. Most of all, I thank my wife, Karen, and my son, Nathan, for innumerable acts of kindness and support, for their good advice, and for sharing my interest in Africa and how we view Africa.

C. A. K.

Mistaking Africa

Part One

Introduction

1

Changing Our Mind About Africa

Most of us who are Americans know little about Africa. We might have studied Africa for a few weeks in school or glanced occasionally at newspaper headlines about Rwanda, Congo, or South Africa, but rarely have we actually thought seriously about Africa. And if we do want to learn about Africa, it is difficult to find ample and accurate information in our popular media such as television and newspapers. Africa and its people are simply a marginal part of American consciousness.

Africa is, however, very much a part of the American subconscious. Ironically, even though we know little about Africa, we carry strong mental images of the continent. Once you begin to notice, you will find that Africa appears in the American public space quite frequently. Although it may not figure often in the news, it appears in advertising, movies, amusement parks, cartoons, and many other corners of our society. And although most Americans do not possess many facts about Africa, we do know certain general truths about the continent. We know, for example, that Africans live in tribes. And we know that Africa is a place of famine, disease, poverty, coups, and large wild animals.

General images are useful and perhaps necessary for our collective consciousness. We can't know everything about the world, so we have to lump some things into big categories that are convenient if lacking detail. Life is too short for most of us to become experts on more than a couple of subjects. Thus, these images help us to organize Africa's place in our collective mind. A war in Congo? Ah yes, that's more of the "African trouble" category. Elephants being used in a commercial? Yes, wouldn't it be fun to have an elephant wash your car. There are lots of large animals living in the wilds of Africa, aren't there?

If general categories are reasonably accurate, they help us navigate our complex world. If, however, they are inaccurate, these categories can be both dangerous and exploitative. If, for example, we are wrong about Africa's supposed insignificance, we will be blindsided by political, environmental, or even medical events that affect how we survive. Or, if we think of Africa only as a place of trouble, a large zoo, or a storehouse of strategic minerals rather than as a place where real people live real lives, we will likely be willing to exploit the continent for our own purposes. France's former president, François Mitterrand, demonstrated this possibility graphically when, speaking to his staff in the early 1990s about Rwanda, he noted that "in some countries, genocide is not really important."[1] Although in the short term the exploitation of Africa might help France or us, in the long term the planet's society and environment will pay dearly for our failure to care.

Speaking "African"

Anyone who wants to study Africa in depth needs to learn an African language, because language is the major key to understanding how people mentally organize the world around them. Likewise, anyone who wants to understand Americans must examine the words Americans know and use. You can begin to discover American ideas about Africa by trying some free association with the word *Africa*. Ask yourself what words come to mind when you hear *Africa*. Note that this is not the time to "clean up your act" and impress yourself with your political correctness. You are searching for the words your society has given you to describe Africa, some of which will seem positive, some negative, and some neutral.

My students have helped me create lists of words that come to mind during such an exercise. Within a few minutes, a class frequently generates thirty or forty words that Americans associate with Africa. *Native, hut, warrior, shield, tribe, savage, cannibals, jungle, Pygmy, pagan, voodoo,* and *witch doctor* are commonly associated with "traditional" Africa. "Tourism words" include *safari, wild animals, elephant, lion,* and *pyramid*. There are also "news words," including *coup, poverty, ignorance, drought, famine, tragedy,* and *tribalism*. And then there is a group of "change words" (indicating Western-induced change), such as *development, foreign aid, peacekeeping,* and *missionary*. Occasionally, the really honest person will come up with "racist words" they have heard, like *spear chucker* or *jungle bunny*.

Although some American words might be positive—*kinship, wisdom,* or *homeland*—the overwhelming impression gained by studying American language about Africa seems to be that Africa is a primitive place, full of trouble and wild animals, and in need of our help. A recent survey by a major American museum on popular perceptions of Africa found many widely held misconceptions such as the following: Africa is just one large country; Africa is all jungle; Africans share a single culture, language, and religion; Africans live in "grass huts"; Africans mainly hunt animals for their subsistence; and Africa has no significant history.

If you think you have escaped these concepts, you are either extraordinarily lucky or you are easily able to fool yourself. The messages that perpetuate such impressions pervade American culture. They are ideas that have deep roots in American history as well as strong branches that entwine our daily lives. In our history, white America once did not even consider Africans to be equal as humans! By comparison, today's understanding is positively enlightened. Yet historical misperception, ignorance, stereotype, and myth still cast shadows upon our thinking. Once you begin to look for them, you will see inaccurate portrayals of Africa in which the blatant old images are reproduced in more subtle, modernized versions. In fact, it is a worthwhile exercise to ask yourself where the words listed above have come from. Home? School? Church? Friends? Television? Newspapers? Magazines? Movies? Books? Amusement parks? It is difficult to get complete and balanced views of Africa in everyday American life. This topic will be discussed further in Chapter 2, "How We Learn."

This book investigates the histories of our inaccurate and stereotypical words and ideas and suggests alternatives. For example, Africans are sometimes referred to in everyday America as "natives." You may or may not think that *native* is a negative word, but its use is a legacy of the colonial period in Africa when words were weapons employed by outsiders to keep Africans in their places. In the first part of the twentieth century, most Americans believed that Africans could be (indeed, *should* be) subjugated because they were primitives, natives. The problem is not the term itself, however. The first dictionary definition of *native* is someone who belongs originally to a place. Thus, "He is a native of Boston" is a neutral and acceptable use of the word. We also use *native* in a positive political way in the phrase "Native American," which implies that an "American Indian" has rights and connections that go beyond those belonging to the rest of us who are more recent immigrants. But the term "African native" evokes a negative connotation, whether intended or not, that is a holdover from its colonial meaning of "primitive," "savage," or "unenlightened." It is interesting to ask why we can think of Africans as natives, but never the Chinese. The answer is that we have long thought of Africans as primitive and Chinese as civilized. Today, even when we do not intend to insult Africans, we have these leftover phrases and connotations that get in the way of conceiving of Africans as real people like ourselves.

You can get around the "African native" and "native African" problem in a number of ways. For example, if you are referring to an African living in a rural area, you can say "a rural African." If you mean someone who is an inhabitant of Africa, just say "an African." If you mean someone who belongs to the Kikuyu ethnic group, use the words "a Kikuyu." These phrases are more precise and therefore less likely to create images that evoke stereotypes. And, to escape even a hint of insult, you might avoid the use of phrases like "He is a native of Cape Town," which in most other contexts would be neutral but in the African context might elicit musings on whether you have spoken the word in the stereotypical manner.

The Use and Misuse of Stereotypes

In an ideal world, we would abandon our stereotypes about Africa and learn to deal with Africans as they really are. Human cognition does not allow this, however. Everybody stereotypes. And we do it about practically everything. The reason for this is, first of all, that we are biologically wired to try to make sense of reality, even when it makes no particular sense. Whether through science, history, literature, religion, or whatever, humans strive to understand and categorize what is in front of them. In fact, *not* trying to understand apparent reality is so extraordinary that Buddhism, as one example, has made a philosophy out of it. Buddhism's attempt to experience the "is-ness" of reality directly, without thought, promises liberation from ordinary human consciousness and suffering, but such salvation is sought only by a few. Most of us will continue our attempts to make sense of the reality in front of us.

We also stereotype because it is virtually impossible to know everything that is going on in reality, and therefore we are bound to make our judgments on partial information. Like the proverbial blind men and the elephant, we each take our separate, limited experiences and extrapolate to make sense of the whole. Moreover, we often use ideas provided by our culture instead of investigating things for ourselves. If our culture has a premade picture of reality for us, we are likely to accept it. One way to think about this is to invert "seeing is believing," making it "believing is seeing." Once we "know" something through our culture, we tend to fit new information into the old categories rather than change the system of categorization.

To say that we inevitably use stereotypes is really to say that we use mental models to think about reality. But the word "stereotype" also implies that our models are so limiting that they deform reality in ways that are offensive, dangerous, or ridiculous. Thus we need to strive to make our mental models as accurate as possible. We should, for example, study African art, history, literature, philosophy, politics, culture, and the like so we can differentiate between Africans. We should also ask ourselves whether we cling to inaccurate models of Africa because they shore up our self-image or allow us to do things that would be otherwise unthinkable.

Below are brief discussions that explore different reasons for the persistence of our misconceptions about Africa. Later in the book there are extended discussions of many of these topics.

Leftover Racism and Exploitation

During much of American history, racism and exploitation of Africa have been considered acceptable to a large majority of Americans. Although we never ruled colonies in Africa, Americans did enslave Africans and maintain both a slavery system and segregation. Moreover, we profited from our businesses in Africa, sent missionaries to change African culture, and did not protest the colonization undertaken by Europeans. This exploitation of Africa, whether direct or indirect, required thinking about Africans as inferiors. In other words, our culture has had a lot of practice, hundreds of years of it, in constructing Africa as inferior. The legacy is obvious in the words and ideas that we call to mind when we hear the word *Africa*.

Our legacy of negativity poses a question. Can we attribute a major portion of our modern stereotypes about Africa to the fact that we just haven't gotten around to changing the myths we inherited from our racist and imperialist past? Perhaps we no longer need most of these myths, but they persist because only a few decades have passed since the end of the colonial period and a similarly brief period since the passage of the American Civil Rights Act. A few decades in cultural history is really only a moment in time because cultures have momentum and are slow to change direction. Perhaps our myths about Africa are dying, but slowly.

Support for this view comes from the fact that African independence and the civil rights movement have made it unacceptable for news reporters and commentators to use the most blatantly negative of the words we once associated with race and with Africa. Likewise, schoolbooks are vastly improved in their treatment of Africa. One could argue that with greater sensitivity to the issue and more time, Americans will change. To put this idea another way, shouldn't we give Americans the benefit of doubt and assume that most people do not consciously intend to exploit or misrepresent Africa? I believe that we should.

Current Racism

I am assuming that most readers are not intentionally racist, because such people probably wouldn't read this kind of book. But we have to take account of the connection between our stereotypes about Africa and current racism in America. I do not need to argue that racism is still alive in

America. The most derogatory American images of Africa are so obviously racist that they can no longer appear in public spaces, and therefore we must conclude that they persist because we learn them in the more private aspects of our lives, from family and friends, and often through jokes or offhand comments. Unfortunately, such private racism is difficult to eradicate because continuing efforts like this book can do little for those who would not seriously consider them. Others of us, perhaps most of us, are a different kind of racist, for although we truly want to believe that all humans are equal, we entertain undercurrents of racist doubt in our minds that make us susceptible to more subtle myths about Africa. It is this "real but unintentional" racism that concerns us here, because a deeper consideration of the issues can help us see Africans more clearly.

It would be incorrect, however, to say that all or even most of the public stereotypes about Africa come from unintentional racism. First, each of us has negative stereotypes about others that are not racist. Second, not all of our stereotypes about Africa are negative. *Inaccuracy and insensitivity are not necessarily racist, even when they have racist roots and produce racist results.* This is a fine distinction to make, especially if you are a victim, but it seems a necessary distinction if we are to help decent, willing people to see Africa in new ways.

Current Exploitation

We also perpetuate negative myths about Africa because they help us maintain dominance over Africans. From our perspective in America, it is difficult for us to see how globally influential our country actually is. In simple terms, we are a superpower. To wield this kind of might and still think of ourselves as good people, we need powerful myths. Whereas, in the past, the myth of the racial inferiority of Africans was the major justification for Western control of Africans, now cultural inferiority is a more likely reason. Our news media, for example, are much more likely to inform us about African failures than African successes. And the successes we do hear about tend to demonstrate that our own perspectives on reality are correct. It doesn't take much imagination to figure out that modern Americans who deal with Africa—bureaucrats, aid workers, businesspeople, missionaries, and others—might have an interest in describing Africa in ways that justify the importance of their own work.

Entertainment

If Africa were portrayed as being "just like us," it would be quite uninteresting. "Man bites dog" sells more papers than "Dog bites man." The word *exotic* describes the point; exotic portrays African culture as excitingly different. Usually this is at the expense of African culture, an extraordinary portion of which is removed from its everyday context in a way that allows us to believe that the wider culture itself is wholly extraordinary. Movies and novels thrive on this sort of thing. In his book *American Ways,* Gary Althen describes an international student who was misled by myths about exotic America. He came to America after watching American movies and expected to find a lot of women ready for sexual activity with him. Actually, he found them, but it took him nearly two years to figure out that such easy women were also marginal and often disturbed and that more desirable women were not so readily available.[2]

I will provide African examples in later chapters, but give a first illustration here. A recent issue of *National Geographic* included a short article on the gold of the current Asantehene, Otumfuo Opoku Ware II, king of the Asante people in Ghana.[3] Ten beautiful photographs show the gold clothing and ornaments of the Asantehene, his court, and his relatives. But there is almost no effort to tell us how all of this fits into the life of the Asante or of the modern country of Ghana. Presumably, *National Geographic* does not intend to portray Africans in stereotypical ways. Without (con)text, however, the reader might think almost anything.

This is exoticism. Exoticism portrays only a portion of a culture and allows the imagination to use stereotypes to fill in the missing pieces. Most frequently, when we supply the missing pieces, we extrapolate that other people are more different from us than they are similar. We can too easily sustain our myths about Africans and believe that words such as *mysterious* and *the dark continent* actually apply to Africa.

Self-Definition

Sometimes we use other people, including Africans, as a mirror. We want to know about them so we can know about ourselves. This very human activity accounts at least partially for our interest in people-watching in parks, sitcoms on television, movies, literature, history, and many other cultural phenomena. Yet this is a tricky business. For example, we know that people who spend a lot of time watching soap operas begin to conceive of the world as a soap opera and themselves as characters. And those who watch the local evening news feel that life is much more violent and chaotic than it really is.

In the case of Africa, we might say that many of us want Africans to be a bit savage so we can feel more satisfied with our own lot in life. The *Loony Toons* announcer on the Cartoon Network puts it well: "Without nuts like these, the rest of us look crazy." Perhaps you have never thought of Bugs, Daffy, and Elmer as therapists, but doesn't Africa often serve the same function? If we focus on ourselves without comparison to others, don't we look pretty messed up? But if we can see that others are poorer, less educated, or more chaotic, then it is easier to believe that we are fine despite our problems. To put it differently, we can't be rich without the poor, developed without the underdeveloped, saved without the sinner, normal without the abnormal, civilized without the uncivilized, and so forth. Sometimes students tell me that they believe the reason they are required to study other cultures in college is to demonstrate how good we have it in America.

Our culture is especially susceptible to this kind of thinking because of the way we conceive of time. Our idea of time as a continuum from the past to the future—rather than, for example, as a circle returning to a golden age of the past—is embodied in our concept of progress. For us, progress generally means going forward, moving on, getting over it, improving ourselves, growing up, and a whole collection of other images implying that the past is negative and the future is positive. Of course, if we believe this to be true, then we will expect reality to substantiate the belief. Indeed, one way we perceive African reality reveals this way of thinking. We see African community life as basic, but impossible to *return to* in our own communities. And tribalism is something we have *gotten beyond*. It wouldn't help to find much of use in Africa, because that would contradict our understanding of progress.

The same is true for the way we understand nature. Although we might believe abstractly in the balance of nature, or might desire that our lives resemble a peaceable-kingdom painting where friendly lions and lambs coexist, we have been more likely to see our lives in *dog-eat-dog* terms that conform to the *law of the jungle*. Africa can be a useful metaphor to help understand that jungle and our own place in it. Africa as the prototypical jungle is useful as a myth to substantiate our view of daily life as a jungle we escape from when we go home at night.

Positive myths about Africa also serve Western self-definition. Those who are dissatisfied with modern American life might construct Africa to present viable alternatives. Some might search African customs for a more natural way to live. Some might look to Africa for a less racist culture. Some, specifically African Americans, might be looking for their idealized personal and cultural roots.

Stereotypes over Time

As Europeans spread across the world from the 1400s onward, they had to make sense of the new peoples and places they encountered. Over time, and for reasons explained elsewhere in this book, Africans and Africa became representative of extreme "otherness." They were not the only representatives of difference, of course, because there were also Aborigines, Native Americans, and so forth. But Africa certainly became a primary symbol that Europeans and white Americans used to express difference. Even black Americans found Africa's difference useful at times.

This is not all bad because, indeed, there is a great deal of difference between African and Western cultures. Moreover, we know that humans tend to think symbolically, so it is natural that Africa should stand for something, rather than nothing, in our minds. The real problem has been that using Africa as a *symbol* of difference has meant that the continent has been treated as an object. As an object, Africa is described and manipulated, but Africans cannot speak for themselves or make comments on who *we* are.

Fortunately, with each passing decade, Americans have been treating Africans with less prejudice. Perhaps we are in the midst of a real exit, however slow, from the myths of primitive Africa. Indeed, we cannot afford such myths. Africa, by its shear size, population, resources, and modernization, will play an increasingly important role in the world, whether for good or ill, and will have to be taken seriously. Our long-term interest, in our shrinking world, is to understand Africa in as unbiased a fashion as possible.

The point is not that an accurate and whole picture of Africa will be totally positive. Indeed, such a claim would be a continuation of our stereotyping. What we should strive for is a view of Africa as a continent full of real people, both like us and not like us, similar and different. On the surface this seems easy: "It's a small world after all!" "Why can't we just get along?" "All we need is love!" "Just leave them alone." But these stereotypical, facile solutions don't automatically work in the real world. As you will see in the pages that follow, seeing others as fully human without desiring to change them into ourselves is exceedingly difficult. It may be, however, the only thing that will make our home—the planet—a safe place to live.

A Word About Words

Before we go any further, a warning is in order. As I wrote this text, I realized that some of the words I use regularly are problematic. For example, the word *Africa* is used incorrectly throughout the book, because I mean "Africa south of the Sahara." This is a problem that might be helped by replacing all occurrences of *Africa* with *sub-Saharan Africa*. However, reading would be awkward and the change would not solve the problem entirely: For example, not all sub-Saharan Africans are the subjects of the stereotypes discussed in this book, assuming that we consider the millions of European Africans in South Africa, Zimbabwe, Kenya, and elsewhere to be "real" Africans. Following the example of other scholars, I have opted to use the convenient expression "Africa" instead of a more accurate term. I am assuming that readers will understand what is meant and will fill in missing qualifiers where needed.

Likewise, terms such as *Westerners* and *Americans,* and the pronouns *we* and *our,* are frequently distortions of the truth. There is, you will agree, no such thing as an average American, just as there is no such thing as an average African. As I wrote this book, I found myself generalizing and perhaps overgeneralizing about Americans for the sake of calling attention to "our" stereotyping of Africans. We need to remember, however, that in every era there have been those Americans who did not accept the general view and who spoke out on behalf of Africans.

One of the biggest difficulties with generalizing about American views of Africa concerns the inclusion of African-American views. The problem is complex because American culture is complex. Until at least the 1960s, for example, it was quite common for African Americans to think of Africans as having primitive cultures. This should not be too surprising, considering the dominance of European culture and the fact that most information about Africa was filtered through European-American eyes. Thus when I say that "we Americans" believed Africa to be primitive, it can be taken as somewhat accurate for black as well as white Americans.

On the other hand, since before the American Revolution, African Americans have resisted white efforts to define black reality, and therefore they cannot be said to have invented the idea of African primitiveness, even if they believed in portions of it. They were victims in much the same way that Africans have been victims. Moreover, African Americans largely rejected white American interpretations of race. Furthermore, there have always been African Americans who attempted to teach America about African achievements. Until the mid–twentieth century they were largely ignored, but their efforts make it more difficult to generalize about "Americans."

In this book, I have usually focused on white American myths about Africa—because they have been the most dominant, the most negative, and the most in need of change. Although I have included a brief summary of African-American perspectives in Chapter 5, I have not done the subject justice. Unfortunately, as far as I know, there have been no studies since the mid-1970s that have attempted to investigate the whole spectrum of contemporary African-American attitudes toward Africa. Without such studies, preferably ones undertaken by African Americans, I would not want to write much more than I have already.

What seems most striking and most similar about white and black American perspectives on Africa is that all of us have *generally* "used Africa to think with." Whether Africa has been constructed in a negative or positive manner, we have used the continent to reflect upon who *we* are in relation to each other and in relation to Africa. Much of this thinking, negative and positive, has stereotyped Africa in ways that are explained in this book.

2

How We Learn

In the 1970s, scholars of Africa realized that American high school textbooks were filled with stereotypes about Africa. The most glaring myths had disappeared with the independence of African countries in the 1960s and the American civil rights movement, but less obvious myths persisted. In a 1978 study, *Africa in Social Studies Textbooks,* Astair Zekiros and Marylee Wiley detailed the extent to which our public schools were perpetuating myths and inaccuracies about Africa. They noted that most textbooks were written by "'armchair' authors who rely on weak sources for their own information." Thus, no matter what the textbook authors were discussing, they tended to make Africans look like the Africa they imagined rather than the one that existed.[1] Fortunately, two decades later our textbooks are better. In fact, one of the coauthors of the 1978 study, Wiley, became the Africa specialist for the social studies textbook used by my local high school's ninth grade.[2]

On the other hand, schools have only a modest influence on how we think about Africa. Despite improved texts, by the time students get to college, most still have outdated ideas about Africa. Even college graduates may not have corrected their misconceptions of Africa. In a recent study of preservice social studies teachers, 82 percent thought there were tigers in Africa, 94 percent believed wild animals were common everywhere on the continent, 74 percent understood that most Africans are illiterate, and 93 percent were convinced that there are more kinds of diseases in Africa than in Asia and South America. Respondents commonly used stereotypical "African words" such as tribe (90 percent), primitive (69 percent), cannibals (60 percent), and savages (60 percent). Modern Africa was largely misunderstood.[3]

If our high school social studies teachers do not understand Africa, surely improved texts will have only a minimal impact on students; students are far more likely to pick up their attitudes from teachers than from textbooks. But even more importantly, both teachers and students are bombarded with mistaken images of Africa in our everyday culture. It is not a losing battle, but it *is* an uphill one. If readers of textbooks and teachers of classes are wearing tinted glasses, even the most accurate texts will appear to be the same color as the glasses. What is the tint of these glasses? "Americana," the hue of our cultural heritage. Thus, if we want to know how Americans learn about Africa, we must look at the more general culture in which our glasses get manufactured.

Television Culture

One way to study how we learn about Africa is to look at *popular culture,* the ordinary information we get from television, magazines, movies, novels, and other common sources. This approach leads us first to television because it is our most pervasive everyday source of ideas about practically everything. In about 1990, I began to wonder what programs my cable company offered on Africa. At first I supposed there would be very few, but I found that Africa was better represented than many other areas of the world, sometimes with ten or twenty shows a week.

The shows did not provide a very accurate view of Africa, however, because they were almost all cartoons or wild animal shows. But if we learn our basic ideas about Africa from television, this is where it all begins. Africa appears prominently in *George of the Jungle* and *Johnny Quest,* and regularly in the frequent reruns of cartoons made in the 1940s and 1950s such as *Mickey Mouse* and *Popeye*. Even the newer action cartoons use Africa as a setting in some episodes. Which Africa? Most of the images are stereotyped presentations of ferocious large animals, lost treasure protected by evil genies, and hungry cannibals.

Television nature shows tend to portray Africa as a place filled with wild animals, park rangers, and naturalists who battle against poachers and encroaching agriculture. They also use Africa to emphasize "survival of the fittest" motifs by featuring a great many programs on carnivores. This misrepresents what most of Africa is like. Most Africans never see wild animals because they live in towns or in parts of the continent where the human population is dense. Furthermore, the relationships in nature are vastly more complex than those symbolized by the few large animals that are the favorites of animal shows.

Cartoons and shows about animals have not improved much in the 1990s, but there are a few more programs on African *people* now that the Learning Channel, the Discovery Channel, the History Channel, Black Entertainment Television, and other independent stations are available. From time to time I can watch ethnographies, documentaries, and reruns of Ali Mazrui's *The Africans*. Because I sometimes teach with these same videos, I'm happy they are available to the public.

What is still lacking, however, is a serious understanding of how people live currently in Africa. Today, 30 to 40 percent of Africans live in cities, and most rural Africans are deeply connected to cities in one way or another. Why, then, do the shows we see on television rarely ever show a city scene, a paved road, or a farmer producing a crop that will be sold in a town or eventually reach us? This is partly because rural ethnography is less difficult to film than documentaries about the problems of modern life. Most African governments don't like reporters prying into their public affairs, and they are especially sensitive about urban affairs because that is where they live and operate. Moreover, many American viewers would not appreciate critiques of what Americans and other Westerners are doing in Africa. The American controversy surrounding the production of *The Africans* is a case in point. The video series was partly funded by the National Endowment for the Humanities during the conservative Ronald Reagan years. There were protests in Congress when the Kenyan-American producer, Ali Mazrui, even mildly criticized the West for its imperialist and neoimperialist policies in Africa.

Perhaps a more significant reason for television's preference of ethnographic Africa over modern Africa is that we have a romance with the exotic. We consider rural ethnography and nature more interesting and more enlightening than studies of urban life. Thus, despite the so-called cable revolution and its improved access to Africa, the television image of Africa as full of large animals and tribal natives persists.

If we can't find a whole picture of Africa on most television shows, we should be able to turn to television news to find out about contemporary Africa. Unfortunately, there the picture is even more bleak. During the infrequent times that Africa does appear in the news, it is because of a war, coup, drought, famine, flood, epidemic, accident, or American diplomatic mission. Such events certainly occur, but they are not the essence of Africa or of any other part of the world. To be fair, despite the problems, our reporters are treating such news events more fairly than ever before. Cable News Network (CNN), for example, occasionally runs stories produced by African reporters. In 1994, television coverage of the transition to majority rule in South Africa included a great deal about the history and life of South Africans. Unfortunately, since that time, South Africa has almost disappeared from the news except for occasional reports of trouble.

Of course, charges that our news reportage is biased are common for all areas of the world including American cities. Defenders of television news say that reporters have too little time to provide background and that Americans don't want to watch it anyway. Increasingly, network news programs border on entertainment. We want our emotions to be aroused, but not so much that we actually might feel compelled to think deeply or take some kind of action. Moreover, we could add that news from Africa is expensive. If all this is true, then the point here should be that we learn what we want to learn and that we like our picture of Africans the way it is now.

The Print Media

Newspapers give about the same coverage of Africa as television news and for the same reasons. Unless you subscribe to a world-class paper such as the *New York Times*, the *Christian Science Monitor*, or the *Washington Post*, you are not likely to find more than a couple of column inches of space devoted to Africa *per week*. And the stories tend to be of two kinds, "trouble in Africa" and "curiosities from Africa." The "trouble in Africa" reporting usually follows a pattern. At any given time, there is usually only a handful of American reporters in Africa south of the Sahara, a region that has a population larger than the United States. These reporters are either based in one of the big cities, such as Johannesburg (South Africa), Nairobi (Kenya), or perhaps Abidjan (Côte d'Ivoire), or they are visiting these cities. They report on local events, and, if there is trouble in a neighboring country, they fly in, get the story, and fly out, or they collect what information they can from where they are. News about Congo or Nigeria might be broadcast from Abidjan. It sounds authentic because it comes from Africa, but it might as well be from the United States, which has equally good communications with most African cities. When there is a big story, reporters flock to it, stay for a while, then leave. And because reporters rarely speak local languages or have well-developed local contacts, the result is shallow reporting. In many cases, we hear nothing from a country for months or years, and then it appears in the news once or even every day for a couple of weeks before disappearing until trouble occurs again.

If we try to put a positive spin on reporting about "trouble in Africa," we might concede that our reporting is about the best we can hope for considering the conditions under which reporters must work. We are badly served, however, because our news is superficial, sensationalist, and infrequent. In some cases, it is also clearly biased. In a study of media coverage of the civil war in Angola, for example, Elaine Windrich notes that reporters tended to accept uncritically the U.S. government position concerning our ally Jonas Savimbi. In the context of the 1980s and the Cold War, this was considered acceptable, but the American public was clearly duped. Savimbi was actually a tyrant and a liar, and we eventually had to drop him in favor of his enemies, whom we now support. Everyone, especially Angolans, would have been better served had reporting been more thorough and fair.[4]

Items that can be characterized as "curiosities from Africa" also appear regularly in newspapers. Weeks go by in my local paper without substantial news from Africa, and then the paper (not a bad paper, actually) includes a two-inch story about a man accused of being a witch doctor who was beaten to death in South Africa. Or, there is a brief mention of a hippo that upset a safari canoe at Victoria Falls in Zimbabwe. The white tourists were uninjured, but a black Zimbabwean guide drowned and a white Zimbabwean guide lost his arm.[5] Is this news about Africa? Yes. Is it interesting? Yes. Does it give us perspective on what is happening in Africa? Not much. Is it useful? Helpful? You judge. Once again, however, we should remind ourselves that there has been progress. In the hippo story, an ordinary African was identified by name, was not called a "native guide," and was portrayed as a hero.

After television and newspapers, we can examine popular magazines. We should do better here, because in our magazines there is more space to devote to thinking deeply about what is going on in the world. Indeed, journals such as the *New Yorker,* the *Atlantic Monthly, Current History, Discover,* and the *World and I* have published good articles about Africa in the last few years. Once again, progress. Yet the number of "trouble in Africa" articles outweighs the number of articles that help us to see Africans as real people who are attempting to solve their problems in rational ways, even if the solutions might be different from the ones we would choose. A recent article by Robert D. Kaplan in the *Atlantic Monthly* has been severely criticized for being a classic example of American mythmaking about Africa. Writing in the *Utne Reader,* Carole Collins and Steven Askin take Kaplan to task for perpetuating the popular media image that Africa suffers because of its primitiveness rather than because of how it has been treated by the world.[6]

The above magazines are not scholarly, but they do tend to be highbrow. Most Americans read less sophisticated fare as a daily diet. In the more popular magazines, most articles about Africa typically are of the "African safari" genre. A few wild animals, a few natives, a camp, a curio market, a little art, a gourmet meal, and you're home. For example, *SmartMoney* advertises that "South Africa has it all: gorgeous scenery, fascinating cultures, rhino-filled game reserves—and, best of all, a weak [currency]."[7] In *Outside,* a promotional blurb for an article quotes a safari brochure as promising "unfiltered Africa, an extremely rare, hard-core, expeditionary safari in the oldest style." It also notes that when the author of the article arrived in Zimbabwe, he experienced "fabled wildlife, and mutiny on the veld."[8] There are also the "celebrity goes to Africa," "curious customs," and "African agony" themes, of course. These views of Africa not only evoke stereotypes we already hold, they reinforce them.

National Geographic

One very popular magazine, *National Geographic*—with an astounding global circulation of nearly 9 million—is quite literally America's picture window on the world. What are we likely to see through this window? The editorial policy of the magazine since its early days has been to avoid controversy and print "only what is of a kindly nature . . . about any country or people."[9] That policy, still followed a century later, directs the organization toward wild animals and ethnography and away from the social, political, and economic conditions in which Africans live. In fact, as conditions worsened in Africa in the 1980s, it was increasingly difficult to be kind to modern Africa, at least from our perspective, and there was a corresponding decline in the frequency of *National Geographic* articles dealing with African countries.

Countries like Congo (Kinshasa) and Malawi were featured in the 1970s and 1980s, but now these are widely recognized as repressive and have become unsuitable for *National Geographic*. There are 1990s articles set in these countries, but they treat Congo River travel and Lake Malawi water life, much safer topics than the countries themselves.[10] A 1996 article about Eritrea demonstrates the point: Eritrea could be featured because, as a brand-new country, it was considered full of hope, unlike most other African countries.[11] Likewise, the magazine's 1993 treatment of the life of blacks in South Africa came long after the world had chosen sides on the issue, which made the subject safe and, to my eye, exploited the situation by printing gripping photographs.[12]

A 1993 article on the Horn of Africa also exploited African misery. To me, beautiful photographs of starving children in a magazine that has no pretensions of activism are exploitative. This is an example of what has been termed "development pornography." We are only asked to *look* at others' misery, not do anything about it or even understand it. The author writes that he "found problems common to much of a continent whose people have leaped from small traditional societies to late-twentieth-century nationhood in only a few generations: ancient tribal rivalries, illogical borders imposed by colonial powers, and the legacy of repressive and corrupt regimes supported by the Cold War superpowers."[13] Here, in a bland nutshell, the reader gets a weak analysis of Africa's problems: precolonial ("tribal rivalries"), colonial ("illogical borders"), and postcolonial ("repression and superpower intervention"). But this is a caricature of reality, distorting any genuine understanding of the continent. In the end, you are left with the vague impression that Africa is only a "place of troubles."[14]

Most Africa articles in *National Geographic* treat less controversial subjects or more specifically scientific ones such as rain forests, elephants, gorillas, and the evolution of humans. An article on the slave trade describes how the trade affected Africa.[15] A piece on "fantasy coffins" in Ghana is beautifully illustrated but exotic because it takes a small part of African life and focuses on difference without providing the context for a holistic understanding of African culture.[16]

National Geographic, our window on the world, is rarely a place to get a balanced picture of Africa. This magazine calls itself scientific, yet avoids controversy, thriving on beautiful photography and safe topics. It would have to take such an approach in order to be so widely accepted in the United States and indeed in the world. Is this publication then useless? No; beauty and safety have their places, and, like our other media, *National Geographic* is improving. Thirty years ago *National Geographic* would not have even published on topics such as pollution or environmental degradation, as it does today. Certainly it responded favorably to charges in the 1960s that it exploited Africans by publishing pictures of bare-breasted women. But even if today the magazine doesn't actively exploit, it does reinforce our stereotypes and confuse us by asserting that beauty, safety, and bland analysis (and stereotypes) are somehow equal to science and geography.

Amusement Parks

Busch Gardens in Tampa, a park that uses Africa as its theme, is a good example of how we learn about Africa and also of how this learning process is changing. In the 1970s, the park was called "Busch Gardens: The Dark Continent." At that time, a poster advertising the park depicted a white family in an African environment, the husband in a safari suit and pith helmet holding a chimpanzee and pointing to some off-poster sight with his wife looking on passively. His children are also following his gaze, from the back of an elephant. An Arab or Swahili guide in flowing robes looks on, while three barely visible black African men dressed in loincloths carry the family's luggage.

Fortunately, twenty years later, this racist and sexist poster is no longer used because Busch Gardens has changed its "Dark Continent" image as a result of protests. The 1996 press packet focuses instead on neutral images: the large animal park, replicas of African houses, African-made tourist art, and rides that have mildly African themes. A new section based on ancient Egypt opened in 1996. Now a brochure forestalls criticisms with "a Pledge and a Promise" to provide entertainment plus "education, conservation and research" (cultural presentations, award-winning programs, captive breeding, over 3,000 animals, and so on). There are endless inconsistencies, however. The idea of Ubanga-Banga Bumper Cars (a stereotypical "African" name) in the section called The Congo would be hilarious except for the underlying message it sends about

Africa. It is strange to think of the Dolphin Theater and German Festhaus restaurant being in Timbuktu. The park's Stanleyville area is named after the violent white conqueror of the Congo River, Henry Morton Stanley, and the colonial town that bore his name. Modern Congolese found the name odious enough to change it to Kisangani. And the real Kisangani doesn't have warthogs, orangutans, or a barbecue smokehouse. The conflicts with reality go on and on, but if you knew little about Africa, these inconsistencies wouldn't be apparent. Perhaps in twenty more years we will look back at this version of Busch Gardens as a somewhat silly and misinformed (if not racist) approach to both Africa and entertainment.

Another amusement park, Disney World in Orlando, has become a global pilgrimage destination. On a visit, I was reminded of Africa at several turns (literally) as we took the Jungle River Cruise in boats named after rivers and places where I have lived in the Congo rainforest: Bomokandi, Wamba, and so on. It was all fun and a bit hokey, of course, and the site's designers included elephants and a pygmy war camp. But pygmies don't have war camps—they are more like conservationists than soldiers—and Africa is certainly more than elephants, jungles, and riverboats.

Now Disney has expanded its treatment of Africa with Animal Kingdom, an animal theme park located near Disney World. The African Savannah section of the park is set up to give visitors the sense that they are in a genuinely natural environment. Most importantly, there are no fences between the visitors and the animals. The illusion of real wilderness is made possible by hidden moats around the predators that give the impression that carnivores and herbivores are living in the same space. They are not, of course, because it would be too costly to allow lions to eat gazelles. Besides, viewing real predatory activity would upset most tourists.

But to merely experience nature is not considered entertaining enough. As one brochure puts it, "The imagination of Disney is going to take you on a journey into the mysteries, marvels and thrills of the ever-unfolding story of animals." Indeed, Disney advertises that the park tells the story of *all* animals, "real, imaginary and extinct." Participants in the Kilimanjaro Safari, which visits a recreated African savanna, buy tickets from a window in a building that looks like a decayed colonial-era outpost. Conquest nostalgia is being sold here. (The building is not likely a comment on the maintenance of modern African game parks.) And visitors are escorted in buses outfitted to give the feeling of a "real" safari. Further, as visitors pass certain points, underground sensors trigger appropriate events in the fashion of similar tours in Disney World and Disneyland. This is wild nature on demand. And there is a story line: You are hot on the trail of a group of poachers.

In Disney's topsy-turvy world, fictional animals compete with real ones, entertainment competes with understanding, and corporate profits compete with what is termed scientific research. Captivity promotes wildness, while African complexity is further reduced to stereotypes. And the hunt for poachers models Disney's other enterprises, which from their founding in the 1950s have epitomized the Western dream of the conquest and management of nature through science and technology.

Other Sources

Movies, too, can be examples of stereotyping, whether oldies such as *The African Queen, Mogambo,* and *Tarzan the Ape Man,* or newer pictures such as *Out of Africa, Congo,* and *The Lion King.* There are dozens of such "African" feature films, and each tells a story that seems to be about Africa but in which Africa only provides an exotic background. *Gorillas in the Mist,* perhaps the best of the lot because it deals with a truly African problem, is only a partial exception because the story is mostly about whites and about the personality of Dian Fossey. One funny movie, *The Gods Must Be Crazy,* a South African shoestring product that has become popular as a video release, is another exception because it has many scenes in which Africans are actors. However, it is full of South African white stereotypes of hunter-gatherers, Bantu villagers, Cuban revolutionaries, African dictators, and white damsels in distress—pure entertainment. There is nothing wrong with entertainment, of course, except that this is where we pick up our ideas about Africa. One of my students informed me that in high school he was tested on the content of *The Gods Must Be Crazy,* which his teacher had considered an authoritative source on African life.

Other places we get our ideas about Africa are too numerous to discuss here. How about children's books, place mats in restaurants, and computer games? I've seen Africa used in exotic, inaccurate, and sometimes offensive ways in each of these examples. Yulisa Amadu Maddy, a Sierra Leonean theater artist, director, and novelist, has taken an interest in American children's literature related to Africa. He notes that although children's books today intend to capture the positive spirit of Africa, they still contain mistakes that confuse readers and insult Africans. In *The Market Lady and the Mango Tree,* for example, a greedy market lady claims a mango tree in the market as her personal property and refuses to give mangoes to children unless they pay. She is able to buy a Mercedes Benz with her profits and then begins to sell her mangoes to a jelly factory at such a high price that the villagers cannot afford them. In the end, however, the market lady's guilty conscience makes her sell the car and give the mangoes to children free of charge. It is a good story, meant to be favorable to community values and children, except that it portrays the market lady as a stereotypical, rich, power-hungry African elite and the village as responding in helpless, un-African ways. There is no doubt that there are greedy people in Africa, but this short book—despite its positive effort and excellent illustrations—gives a distorted picture of reality. Says Maddy, "No one in his or her right mind, no matter how greedy, would claim a mango tree in the marketplace as private property."[17]

Maddy also notes that in Ann Grifalconi's *Flyaway Girl,* east and west are confused: a mask and a food item from West Africa are associated with the Maasai of East Africa. In Paul Geraughty's *The Hunter,* African ivory poachers are blamed for killing elephants when, in fact, Western demand for ivory should also be blamed. Frequently, adds Maddy, stories that are based on African folktales rely on colonial sources that are particularly biased. In such sources, the folktales have been modified to make Western moral points, not African ones.

Churches and missionaries also play a role in reinforcing the idea of Africans as primitives. Missionaries returning from Africa often communicate to churches in the West that non-Christian Africans need fundamental change because they are culturally, if not biologically, primitive. Ironically, missionaries themselves are often more respectful of African cultures than parishioners in the United States. Those parishioners who give money for African causes frequently want to feel that they are converting poor, unenlightened savages in the old-fashioned missionary mode.

And museums? It's remarkable that we continue the nineteenth-century practice of putting animals and "native" peoples in the same "natural" history museums such as the American Museum of Natural History in New York, the Field Museum in Chicago, and the Smithsonian Institution in Washington. The implication is that Africans belong to the history of nature, but not the history of civilization. Moreover, such treatment implies that animals and Africans can be considered separately from ourselves in our understanding of the world. Natural history museum curators know of these problems and do what they can to overcome them.

Art museums pose a somewhat different problem. Curators must help us understand that what we consider *art* is not a universal category appreciated in the same way by all humans. When we see African art—in which masks are usually overrepresented—we see something entirely different than what Africans themselves do. I might add that curators in both art and natural history museums are frequently ahead of their advertising departments in teaching us about Africa. Curators are frequently trained as specialists in African studies. Publicists, by contrast, are trained to attract an audience, so they often play on exotic and stereotypical aspects that reflect public interest in Africa. They are correct in assuming that the public is interested in the exotic; but museums are also committed to accuracy, so recently exhibits and their advertising have displayed much less stereotyping.

Corporate advertising also uses Africa to sell products. IBM, AT&T, Visa, and American Express, for example, have run adds depicting Africa to show that their products are used worldwide. They may well be, but very few Africans have the access that the commercials imply. For example, in an IBM commercial filmed in what may be South Africa or Zimbabwe, an African chorus gets its pitch from a child's computer. But such commercials falsely imply that technology equals development and that African villagers are on the verge of a technological revolution. Not only is Africa being misrepresented, its image of backwardness is being exploited to sell *us* technology.

Range Rover, Toyota, Nissan, and other automobile manufacturers sell the idea of durability using African landscapes. If you want to show how strong your product is, have it take on the rigors of Africa. And Samsonite uses an African village to demonstrate that its luggage is "world proof." Advertisers easily pick up on our stereotypes and use them to convince us to buy. Moreover, they educate us about what our culture already "knows" about Africa.

Despite our efforts to treat Africa more fairly, it is difficult for us to do so. Two final examples illustrate this point. In the mid-1990s, AT&T published an internal newsletter with a map of the world depicting its global telephone network. On each continent there was a person in local dress talking on a telephone connected to other continents via wires and telephone poles. In Africa, however, there was a chimpanzee talking on the phone. After objections, the artists apologized, stating that they meant no harm and were just trying to add interest to their drawing. One might consider this racism, but it is more likely ignorance and the unwitting persistence of racist stereotypes. Likewise, in a recent book of essays by non-Americans about their experiences in America, the compilers introduce each author with a short paragraph. The sole African contributor is described as being "native to Zaire," while every other author was "born" or "raised" in their country.[18] This is not meant to be pejorative, and the construction "native to" is not necessarily wrong. But one wonders about the stereotypical association of Africa with "natives" and about how our minds work.

Once you are aware of the ways we commonly treat Africa, you will soon (and perhaps frequently) see Africa treated stereotypically in everyday life. You will also begin to think about why our stereotypes persist. Few such treatments are conscious attempts to make Africa look bad. Far from it. Despite American racism, or perhaps because of it, we are probably more sensitive to this question than most other people in the world.

At least in the public sphere, we make explicit efforts to avoid derogatory allusions to Africa or Africans. Therefore, such stereotypes are all the more indicative of how we see the world. They must indicate that our shorthand references to Africa as full of animals, "the bush," and primitives are so acceptable to Americans that we do not even see these as derogatory. The problem, of course, is that such views become self-perpetuating. Even if we do not want to portray Africa in stereotypical terms, we are bound to do so because we have few other models of Africa to which we can compare these terms.

Part Two

Evolutionism

3

The Origins of "Darkest Africa"

Across the grasslands of West Africa, the epic of Sundiata continues to be told almost eight hundred years after this hero united the kingdoms of the upper Niger River and founded the massive Mali empire. In the best-known prose translation of the epic, the singer-storyteller Mamoudou Kouyaté begins by relating his qualifications as speaker: "My word is pure and free of all untruth." For him, "the art of eloquence has no secrets." Then he commands his audience to pay attention: "Listen then, sons of Mali, children of the black people, listen to my word, for I am going to tell you of Sundiata, the father of the Bright Country, of the savanna land, the ancestor of those who draw the bow, the master of a hundred vanquished kings."[1] In any of its many versions, the ensuing story is full of confidence, adventure, and wisdom. It is the story of "the Bright Country."

How different the Sundiata epic is from the stereotypical Western view of Africa as the "Dark Continent." In the Western view, Africa has been a land of primitives who practice the "darkest" of customs. These include cannibalism, ritual murder, incest, witchcraft, and incessant warfare. Everywhere Westerners looked in Africa they found depravity. Or, they found peoples who had never advanced beyond the stage achieved by European children. They had only a rudimentary ability to speak language, form governments, create art, and, indeed, think.

This dark view of Africa has been so predominant that we must ask where it came from. Scholars have investigated this question by going back to the origins of Western civilization to see whether Africans have always fared so badly. Their conclusion is that the image of the Dark Continent is a recent fabrication, developed in the nineteenth century at a time when Europeans became increasingly interested in both science and African conquest.

Africans in Antiquity

In ancient Greece and Rome, race does not seem to have been a significant issue. Frank Snowden, who has prepared what is perhaps the most complete study of race in the ancient Mediterranean, states that these civilizations regarded "yellow hair or blue eyes a mere geographical accident, and developed no special racial theory about the inferiority of darker peoples."[2] Indeed, Mediterranean peoples referred to exceptional physical traits to assert the fundamental unity of humanity. Thus, the extraordinary fairness of the Scythians and the darkness of the Ethiopians became lessons in how physical difference should make no difference in judging a person's worth.[3] There were cultural conflicts in these times, of course. The various city-states and empires frequently displayed ethnocentrism toward other cultures, and they certainly engaged in war. Nonetheless, at most times there was a certain cultural equality that allowed interaction and relatively free traffic in goods and ideas. It was not considered strange to find Ethiopians living in and succeeding in Greece, Rome, and elsewhere in the ancient Mediterranean.

We also know that Africa contributed to the other cultures of the Mediterranean. Pre-Arab Egypt and even the Upper Nile kingdoms such as Meroe were relatively well known to Greeks by the fifth century B.C.[4] What we do not know is how much the Greeks and others borrowed from Africa. Some historians claim that Greek civilization actually emerged from African ideas and that nineteenth-century European scholarship tried to hide the debt for racist reasons. It will take some time to sort out the evidence, but this debate is largely a modern one over race bias. In the ancient world, the debate would not have made much sense because the people of that time didn't think in such racial terms.

The question of race has also been raised with respect to ancient Hebrews and Christians because they are the progenitors of modern Western religions. There is no indication, however, of Jewish or Christian racism toward Africans or anyone else. One does find an effort in Judaism to exclude those who were not Jews, but this was exclusion based on religion and culture, not race. In modern times, Christian racists have insisted that the Hebrew Bible supports the view that God believes blacks to be inferior. Their primary evidence comes from their understanding of Genesis 9:18–29, where Noah curses his youngest son Ham and Ham's descendants, the Canaanites: "Cursed be Canaan; a slave of slaves shall he be to his brothers." Ham is supposed by some to have been black, and the curse is believed to indicate God's approval of slavery, American segregation, the colonization of Africa, and apartheid. But there is no evidence that the Hebrews saw it this way or that they were anti-African or racist. Today's mainstream biblical scholars are unanimous in agreeing that the passage in Genesis was not a condemnation of the black race but an attempt to explain the rift between Israel and Canaan and to denounce Canaan for its immoral culture. And there is no indication in the Bible that the inhabitants of Canaan were black.[5]

The most frequently studied case where race might be a factor in the Christian testament comes from the story of Philip, a Christian who baptized the black eunuch treasurer of the queen of Nubia. Superficially, this tale from the Acts of the Apostles might be understood as a comment on race and used as an endorsement of either missions to Africa or racial equality. But modern scholars say that it was neither and that the issues of Africa and race were not important in the story. Rather, the point was that Christians should accept even eunuchs, whom Jews had refused to receive as converts.[6] Moreover, Snowden writes, the early Christians adopted the Greek view of the unity of humanity and used both Ethiopians and Scythians to illustrate how Christianity was for all. For example, both Origen and Augustine, early Christian commentators, employed the metaphor of blackness to describe the souls of sinners. But in a play on words and ideas, they contrasted the blackness of the Ethiopian's skin, which was natural, with the blackness of a sinner's soul, which was acquired by neglect. All sinners were black, whereas Ethiopians who followed Christ were white. Although blackness was employed as a metaphor for sin, it was specifically dissociated from the blackness of the Ethiopian's skin.[7]

The Arab conquest of North Africa after A.D. 639 made direct contact between Europeans and black Africans difficult. Thus, black Africa was of minor concern to Europeans for the next eight hundred years. Black Africans did appear in Europe, however, in various roles. One of their most interesting occupations was as "black knights," important characters in some medieval epics. In these epics, African difference was treated in several ways and served as a device to construct medieval ideas about chivalry. In light of modern European racism, it is striking that in the medieval epics black knights were considered fully human and often exceptionally competent.[8] We also know that Europeans traded regularly with Africans south of the Sahara through Arab intermediaries. There is even evidence that the Renaissance in Europe was fueled by the importation of large quantities of West African gold. In addition, the works of a few Arab geographers who traveled to sub-Saharan Africa became available in medieval Europe. Indeed, Arab sources provided the best knowledge on the interior of sub-Saharan Africa until the late 1700s.

Western Views of Africans, c. 1400–1830

Not until the mid-1400s and the opening of Europe's Age of Exploration did Africa again enter European consciousness. This time, the relationship between Europe and Africa and, indeed, between Europe and the rest of the world was quite different. The Portuguese, Spanish, British, Dutch, and French explorers, and others who followed them, were a pugnacious lot who were out to profit from non-Europeans. And yet, although they eventually conquered most of the world, the Europeans were not mere predators. They felt a need to justify their actions in moral terms, and they frequently wondered about the meaning of their relations with other peoples.

Historian Michael Adas argues that until the mid–eighteenth century, Europeans' perspectives on their relationships with non-Europeans tended to be formulated by and confined to missionaries and philosophers. Less educated Europeans who traveled would have found it difficult to originate such broader views, because they were largely ignorant of the nature of the achievements of their *own* civilization. They could not have made comparisons, for example, between Europe and Africa, or between Europe and China. This was fortunate for Africa in the sense that ordinary travelers who wrote accounts of African societies did not filter what they observed through any strong ideological biases.[9]

In his book *The Image of Africa: British Ideas and Action, 1780–1850,* Philip Curtin makes the point more forcefully. Curtin says that in the eighteenth century, when at least 6 million slaves were taken from Africa, Europeans in general "knew more and cared more about Africa than they did at any later period up to the 1950s."[10] This remarkable statement is based on the facts that Europeans could obtain information about Africa from relatively unbiased traders and travelers, and that Europeans *had not yet connected race and culture* in ways that prevented them from seeing Africa fairly.

This information leads to the realization that most of our modern stereotypes about Africa are a result of the nineteenth- and twentieth-century associations of African race with African culture. We know that eighteenth-century Westerners preferred their own culture to all others and were not without racist ideas, but, unlike nineteenth-century Europeans, they did not presume that everything Africans did was inferior simply because of their race. Eighteenth-century links between race and culture were unconscious and imprecise. Curtin calls this a form of "moderate racism," which "condemned individual Africans as bad men—or all Africans as savage men—but . . . left the clear impression that Africans *were* men."[11]

One way to illustrate this attitude is to point out the efforts that Europeans made to help Africans who had been forcibly removed from Africa to return to the continent. In Britain, the example of Sierra Leone is foremost. This colony on the west coast of Africa was conceived in the 1780s by philanthropists who wanted to give free blacks residing in Britain and non-African parts of the British Empire the opportunity to repatriate, and it was organized on utopian principles that were supposedly applicable to all human societies.

This effort was clearly racist in the sense that it rid European territories of many blacks. However, such plans show that in the eighteenth and early nineteenth centuries, Britons still believed that blacks could not only rule themselves in Africa but establish utopian communities if they were provided the proper tools and legal framework. Unfortunately, planners of such resettlement experiments rarely took into account the actual physical conditions in Africa, the training and skills of the settlers, or previous failed attempts to establish utopian communities. In 1808, the British government took over Sierra Leone as a naval base and as a colony in which to resettle the thousands of slaves freed during the effort to end the slave trade.[12]

An American example also illustrates the ambiguous Western attitudes toward race. Beginning in the 1820s, the American Colonization Society supported a "Back-to-Africa" movement that attempted to colonize Liberia, on the coast of West Africa, with groups of freed American slaves. As in Sierra Leone, the organizers had mixed motives. Aiding African Americans to live in Africa was in one sense a vote of confidence for the ability of blacks to rule themselves. However, most society members were northern Whites who were troubled by the growing number of freed slaves in northern cities, and many saw the enterprise as an opportunity to establish Christian missions in Africa. The U.S. government contributed some funds for colonization, and one settlement was named Monrovia after President James Monroe, a member of the society.[13] Unfortunately, like Sierra Leone, Liberia was never prosperous.[14]

The antislavery movement provides another illustration of the "moderate racism" that existed in the minds of Europeans and Americans at the beginning of the nineteenth century. From our perspective it would seem logical that abolitionists were attempting to eliminate racism in their efforts to end slavery. But the abolitionists' arguments were primarily about the immorality of slavery and the slave trade rather than the immorality of racism. Proslavery and antislavery activists alike were racist, but both assumed that cultural factors were at the heart of the slavery question. For proslavery proponents, the Africans' inferior culture justified the institution. Antislavery activists argued that Christian charity required abolition and that Africans had the *potential* to acquire civilized culture.[15]

And there was an economic issue for both sides: Slavery tended to be supported by those who benefited from it and abolition by those who would benefit from its end.

The Birth of the Dark Continent

Sometime in the mid-eighteenth century a new trend in how Europeans viewed the rest of the world began to develop. It did not reach its peak for a century or more, but in hindsight it is clear that the old models were being challenged. The reason for this transition was the series of revolutions that were underway in Europe: the Enlightenment, the revolution in science, the Industrial Revolution, and the resulting global revolution in trading and conquest. These new conditions gave increased prestige and power to those who were concerned with the material world and with domination of other cultures. The revolutions also undermined views of the world that promoted the essential equality of humanity. Europeans had a growing sense that theirs was a superior and powerful civilization.

Michael Adas argues that, as the modern global revolutions got under way, the missionaries and philosophers who had once been the interpreters of the non-West became less important. They were increasingly replaced by traders, scientists, technicians, soldiers, and bureaucrats, who subsequently determined what Europeans thought of the world. These new interpreters had more pragmatic interests—domination rather than conversion or understanding—and they aggressively shaped European thinking to serve their goals.[16]

We can see this shift in perspective in Western attitudes and actions toward China, which had been celebrated in the late seventeenth and early eighteenth centuries as an example of a gifted civilization. A popular artistic style, chinoiserie, imitated Chinese motifs in furniture, architecture, art, fabrics, porcelain, gardens, and the like. Likewise, Chinese laws, administration, commercial practices, and ethics were considered solid, if not perfect. By the late eighteenth century, however, China's image in Europe was in severe decline. European traders complained about excessive bureaucracy, corruption, and trade restrictions. Protestant missionaries complained about superstitions. And many observers derided the Chinese for not achieving more in science and technology. By the time of the first Opium War (1839–1842), when Europe demonstrated its brutality as well as its new technological superiority, Western assessments of China had turned overwhelmingly negative.[17] In the United States, of course, the use and abuse of Chinese laborers in the American West contributed to this image.

For Africa, the shift was equally significant but less noticeable, because Africans had never been held in high esteem among Europeans. In the first half of the nineteenth century, however, Europeans and Americans began associating African race and African culture, linking the two ever more closely. Philosophers and missionaries tended to follow the lead of traders, soldiers, and scientists in the move toward finding justifications for domination. This growing race consciousness was frequently expressed in the new language of science. For America, one of the questions early in the century was whether science supported the biblical account of the origin of the different races. Until the scientific revolution, the most common explanation of human diversity was provided by the Hebrew Bible: God created humans and they were dispersed after the fall of the Tower of Babel. Those who thought more deeply about the question, however, realized that there were problems with the biblical stories. How, for example, was it possible for Adam and Eve's sons to find wives (Gen. 4)? And how could humans who all descended from Adam have achieved such physical diversity?

At the beginning of the nineteenth century, the principal contending explanations for human diversity were either that all humans descended from Adam—the monogenist position—or that there were separate creations for separate races—the polygenist position. Slavers and slaveholders tended to be polygenists because the belief in separate races implied that God could approve of different treatment for blacks. Reformers tended to be monogenists, for the opposite reason. If the Bible could not settle the debate, scientists in America believed they might. They began to ask whether nature, by itself, could have produced the immense diversity of plants and animals on earth. They made two basic assumptions: that nature could cause diversity through the influence of climate and that the biblical account of creation was correct in dating the age of the earth at between 4,000 and 5,000 years. The scientists then concluded that nature could *not* have produced the earth's biological diversity in such a short time. Therefore, by the 1840s most American scientists believed that science supported the polygenist, multiple-creations position, a view that was consistent with racism.[18]

Nineteenth-century science was, of course, heading for a collision with the biblical view of creation. The monogenists and polygenists both assumed that the biblical account of creation was fact and that science needed only to fill in the details. Meanwhile, about the turn of the nineteenth century, new archaeological discoveries in Egypt began to cast doubt on biblical chronology by demonstrating that human life on earth was older than the Bible had indicated. And the study of fossils began to show that the earth itself might be vastly older than the Bible allowed. If these findings were accurate, then neither the polygenist nor the monogenist theory could explain human origins or human interrelationships.

As the long chronology of evolution became more apparent, scientists began to work toward understanding the actual biological mechanism by which diversity could occur. Among the theories proposed early in the century were Herbert Spencer's survival of the fittest and Jean-Baptiste Lamarck's inheritability of learned traits. Then in 1859, Charles Darwin described the theory of natural selection in *The Origin of Species* and showed how species could evolve through an interplay between biology and the environment. Darwin's natural selection theory prevailed, of course, but it caught on very slowly. Moreover, it still did not include an adequate explanation of the biological mechanism by which individuals came to vary from each other.

Darwin himself remained a Lamarckian, believing that learned traits were inherited. He thought that biological variation arose because parents learned traits that they passed to their offspring at conception. Interestingly, the Lamarckian understanding of variation seems at least partially responsible for the fear that some European colonists had of "going native" (taking on African customs) while in Africa. Many believed that by dressing up formally for dinner while in the African "bush," they were more likely to give birth to civilized children. It was only in 1902 that Gregor Mendel's work with plant variation was rediscovered after being lost for a century in an obscure journal, and the genetic theory of variation began to spread. Not until the 1920s and 1930s did American scientists commonly accept Darwin and the genetic theory of evolution, and American cultural acceptance took decades longer. In fact, these theories still have not permeated all corners of our society.

Well before Darwin, the new scientific theories of evolution began to add fuel to Western racism. Race logic in America and Europe concluded that if humans had evolved, presumably from apes, some humans had evolved more than others. Such logic naturally kept the creators of the new myths—white, upper-class, northern European males—at the top of the race hierarchy. Below them came other races and classes, and women. Among the inferior races, Asians were most advanced, then Africans, Native Americans, and Australian Aborigines. These scientific theories, unlike the older race theories, inextricably linked race and culture. Curtin notes that "whereas race had been *an* important influence on human culture, the new generation saw race as *the* crucial determinant, not only of culture but of human character and of all history. Hundreds of variant theories were to appear in the mood of this new emphasis."[19] The scientific proof seemed to be everywhere—in the shape and size of heads, in skin color, in differences between males and females, in comportment, in the complexity of societies, and in the nature of art and religion. The greater the perceived physical and cultural difference from European culture, the less developed the race.

While Europeans developed these pseudoscientific ways of linking race and culture, they also became convinced that they had to conquer Africa. What is striking here is that they waited so long to begin. By the time Europeans invaded sub-Saharan Africa in the 1880s and 1890s, Africa had long remained the only continent unsubdued by European power. The reasons for the delay included the difficulty of the environment, the danger of violence, the slave trade, and the lack of easily tapped mineral wealth. But the second half of the nineteenth century brought the end of the slave trade; improvements in guns, boats, and medicine; an intensified search for industrial raw materials and markets; and heightened nationalist competition among the European states. Explorers set out to "discover" the African interior, traders staked out corners, and missionaries founded stations as far inland as they could while still maintaining their supply lines. As the century progressed, interest in Africa grew until it finally became impossible for European governments to *not* colonize the continent.

This shift toward imperial thinking was already apparent by the middle of the century. In theoretical terms, the shift was marked by fewer arguments for the *conversion* of Africans and more for European *trusteeship* over Africans. Conversion had been an attempt to make Africans civilized like Europeans, implying that Africans were just as human as Europeans. Trusteeship, however, implied that Africans were biologically inferior and needed to be taken care of, a perfect justification for conquest. Europeans in Africa naturally began to look for evidence of why Africa should need European help.[20] Educated Africans, who had formerly been trusted with responsibilities, were moved aside and labeled incompetent. African customs were increasingly described as savage. Cannibalism was imagined in practically every corner of the continent. Childhood became the universal metaphor for the African state of mental and cultural development.

A Myth for Conquest

Thus the myth of the Dark Continent was born. It originated in mid-nineteenth-century Europe when scientific race theory was developed without reference to the actual cultures of Africans in Africa. Then it was transferred to Africa by Europeans who had both a theoretical and a practical interest in seeing Africa as primitive. And when scientific race theory combined with imperialist urges to conquer, there was no end to the primitiveness that could be found.

The Dark Continent myth is still with us a century and a half later, at least in a diluted form. It is the legacy that leads us to many of the "African" words I listed in Chapter 1. Anyone who reads the literature of late-eighteenth-century European travelers in Africa—who describe Africans as human—and then reads the late-nineteenth-century travelers—who criticize Africans as depraved—will wonder if this is the same continent. In the eighteenth century, Europeans on the whole were genuinely interested in discovering what Africans were doing, even if they disapproved of what they found. For example, Mungo Park, who is sometimes considered the first modern European explorer of Africa, traveled to the upper Niger River in 1796; although he underwent many difficulties, he evaluated individuals and experiences on their own merits and did not generally condemn whole groups or cultures.[21] By the late nineteenth century, however, Europeans were able to see only a primitive continent full of tribes of savages and barbarians.

Of course, there was a great deal of hypocrisy involved in this attempt to reduce Africans to the lowest forms of humanity. European violence eradicated African violence. Christian love justified missionary control. And the white race, which had only recently stamped out its own slave trading and slaveholding practices, called Arabs and Africans inferior because they traded and held slaves. When European slave trading in Africa came to an end in the 1870s and 1880s, Europeans engaged in an antislavery campaign against Arab slave traders on the Nile and in East Africa, and then against African traders. As discussed above, in the antislavery campaign in Europe in the early part of the century, the arguments made by both sides were more cultural than racial. Now, however, Europeans demanded that racially inferior Arabs and even more racially inferior Africans allow themselves to be saved from their depravity by racially superior Europeans. Patrick Brantlinger writes:

> The myth of the Dark Continent defined slavery as the offspring of tribal savagery and portrayed white explorers and missionaries as the leaders of a Christian crusade that would vanquish the forces of darkness. . . . When the taint of slavery fused with sensational reports about cannibalism, witchcraft, and apparently shameless sexual customs, Victorian Africa emerged draped in that pall of darkness that the Victorians themselves accepted as reality.[22]

There were actually several versions of the Dark Continent myth, depending on whether the source was Christian or secular evolutionist. In the Christian version, God becomes the sponsor of the colonial effort. Christian missionaries, who are mostly whites, are called upon to save God's pagan children in Africa. This version can be seen clearly in the mission movement that grew dramatically during the nineteenth century. More secular versions of the myth ranged from a crass "survival of the fittest" conquest to a more sophisticated "trusteeship on behalf of civilization." Official government policies tended toward the latter definition, and twentieth-century colonial bureaucrats spoke in terms of the care they were providing: Colonialism was supposedly a generous gift to Africans.

At the popular level, Rudyard Kipling's famous poem "The White Man's Burden" illustrates the secular trend. Although not specifically about Africa, Kipling's poem summarized the secular justification for domination of Africa and other parts of the world at the turn of the century. "White man's burden" is now a common phrase used to capture the essence of the colonial mentality. Kipling's poem was sent to President Theodore Roosevelt just after the American annexation of the Philippines in 1898. It urged Americans to embrace colonialism as the Britons had done:

> *Take up the White Man's burden—*
> *Send forth the best ye breed—*
> *Go bind your sons to exile*
> *To serve your captives' need;*
> *To wait in heavy harness,*
> *On fluttered folk and wild—*
> *Your new-caught, sullen peoples,*
> *Half-devil and half-child.*
>
> *Take up the White Man's burden—*
> *Ye dare not stoop to less—*
> *Nor call too loud on Freedom*
> *To cloak your weariness;*
> *By all ye cry or whisper,*
> *By all ye leave or do,*
> *The silent, sullen peoples*
> *Shall weigh your Gods and you.*[23]

For Kipling, race itself is the sponsor of the colonial enterprise. The colonial burden is not a call from God, but from whiteness. Americans are urged to send "the best ye breed"—presumably upper-class white males—to serve people at the bottom of the racial hierarchy who are "half-devil and half-child." One might presume that the "half-devil" reference is a plea to Christians, but the poem's audience has "Gods"—plural—who are surely secular as well as Christian. Kipling is considered a defender of secular colonialism, not of religious missions. And the reference to "half-child" is pure scientific racism: The more racially different, the more childlike other peoples were thought to be. Furthermore, Americans were to serve their captives forever, in "weariness," because the captives were biologically incapable of learning the ways of civilized peoples.

The most public examples of Dark Continent thinking among Americans come from Henry Morton Stanley and Theodore Roosevelt. Stanley, an orphan who left England as a young man and was adopted by an American, served on both sides during the Civil War and was a newspaper reporter on the American western frontier. He went to Africa in the late 1860s as a reporter for the *New York Herald*. His goal was to find the famous missionary David Livingstone, who had not been heard from in several years, and create one of the biggest news stories of the century. Stanley found Livingstone, of course, but more importantly he became attached to Africa and spent the rest of his life involved with the continent.

From 1875 to 1877, he crossed the continent from east to west, and he described the harrowing journey down the Congo River in his book *Through the Dark Continent*.[24] In the late 1870s and throughout the 1880s, Stanley participated in the conquest of the Congo by Leopold, King of the Belgians.

In both Britain and America, Stanley was easily the most influential explorer of nineteenth-century Africa. Stanley's reputation was made as a bold adventurer who conquered every obstacle, both natural and human. Although some believe that he was not a racist because he did not use the racist jargon of the day, he was nonetheless quick to judge Africans as inferior and quick to turn to violence against those Africans who stood in his way. Throughout the white world, red-blooded men and boys read and talked about Stanley well into the twentieth century. Anyone interested in Africa certainly read Stanley, and there is a direct line of influence from his books to nearly every one of the white adventurers who followed him to Africa. Stanley also inspired the stories of Edgar Rice Burroughs (who created Tarzan) and H. Rider Haggard, authors who were read widely by Americans.

Theodore Roosevelt also read Stanley and developed a remarkably similar outlook on colonialism. Although Roosevelt belonged to the American upper-middle class and was not known as a violent man, he was nonetheless a conqueror. He was an enthusiastic proponent of American colonies, including Puerto Rico and the Philippines, and as president he supervised the construction of the Panama Canal. Like Stanley, Roosevelt saw a similarity between the "wild" American West and Africa. After his presidency, Roosevelt spent a year on safari in Africa (see Chapter 9). In a 1909 dispatch from Africa to American newspapers, he commented that "like all savages and most children, [Africans] have their limitations, and in dealing with them firmness is even more necessary than kindness; but the man is a poor creature who does not treat them with kindness also, and I am rather sorry for him if he does not grow to feel for them, and to make them in return feel for him, a real and friendly liking."[25] This is, of course, a restatement of the sentiment of "The White Man's Burden." Roosevelt's paternalistic and racist views, encapsulated in the adventure of his safari, were widely read and appreciated in the United States.

For most Americans—whether missionary, scientist, or ordinary citizen—Roosevelt's Dark Continent perspective was unquestioned in the first part of the twentieth century. Indeed, this view has been so widely and firmly held that it still persists in various forms and will likely survive well into the twenty-first century.

4

"Our Living Ancestors": Twentieth-Century Evolutionism

Heart of Darkness, by Joseph Conrad, is widely considered to be one of the finest works of prose fiction in the English language. In the story, the character Marlow describes his 1891 trip up the newly explored Congo River in a small, wheezing steamboat. His mission is to find the ivory of Kurtz, a white trader who has "gone native" in the deep interior of the vast Congo rain forest. Conrad's story is gripping because it uses entry into Africa as a metaphor for entry into the dark heart of the human subconscious. As Marlow ascends the river, he experiences ever deeper human depravity until he finally reaches Kurtz, who lives among his own tribe of shouting cannibals with his sensuous African mistress. "Going up that river," says Marlow, "was like travelling back to the earliest beginnings of the world, when vegetation rioted on the earth and the big trees were kings." He recalls that "we were wanderers on a prehistoric earth."[1]

It is a superbly written story, but many consider it racist. Indeed, the Nigerian novelist Chinua Achebe argues that *Heart of Darkness* cannot be considered great literature, no matter what its aesthetic merits, because it rests on racist premises.[2] One might hope that in a future era the story will not make sense without an extensive introduction explaining how people in the nineteenth century connected Africa with the primitive. For the present, however, the story is quite comprehensible because we are still not sure that Africa is not the Dark Continent or that Africans are not primitives. We can see similar thinking, for example, in a 1990 *National Geographic* article about a trip up the Congo River. The author specifically compares the Congo today with the river as portrayed by Conrad: "As the days passed, the river appeared just as it had to Conrad a hundred years ago: Going up that river was like traveling back to the earliest beginnings of the world."[3]

Knowing little of African languages or African thought, the *National Geographic* author jumps from the fact that in the Lingala language the concepts for *yesterday* and *tomorrow* are expressed by the same word, to the stereotypical conclusion that for Congolese "time seemed to stand still. . . . There is now, and there is all other time in both directions."[4] Although this makes for intriguing reading, it is bad science, bad linguistics, and bad anthropology. *National Geographic* can do better.

Biological Evolutionism

The key to our thinking about Africa as primitive is our idea of evolution. Primitive *means* less evolved. Therefore, if we are going to untangle ourselves from Dark Continent myths, we need to deal with evolutionary theory. The problem is not the modern scientific understanding of evolution but an old-fashioned view that still has some currency in American popular culture. This view features three articles of faith relevant to this discussion: the ideas that evolution takes place along a single line that leads to progress, that some species and subspecies are more evolved than others, and that species claw their way to the top.

In this older version of evolutionary theory, change occurs along a line that stretches from the simplest living forms to the most complex, from microbes to mammals. As each successive species evolves, a new and higher rung is added to the evolutionary ladder. Humans, who have climbed to the top, are the most advanced of the species. But all humans are not equal. White human males of the upper socioeconomic classes are at the very top of the human segment of the ladder. Others trail in a biological hierarchy constructed according to class, sex, and race.

The mechanism by which evolution worked in this nineteenth-century theory was "survival of the fittest." Those species and subspecies that could dominate others would rise to the top. The *exact* way this would happen was not clear because scientists did not have a firm grasp of genetics until well into the twentieth century. What did appear clear was that species were in competition with each other for survival. The "law of the jungle" was "eat or be eaten."

When Conrad wrote in *Heart of Darkness* that he was going back in time as he went into Africa, he did not just mean that he was going back in historical time. He meant that he was going back in evolutionary time. Africans were literal biological specimens of what whites had once been. Whites had left these living ancestors in the evolutionary dust. In America, as in Europe, this "truth" was held almost universally. President Theodore Roosevelt, writing to Americans from East Africa in 1909, shortly after his retirement, echoed this view: "[In Africa,] nature, both as regards wild man and wild beast, did not and does not differ materially from what it was in Europe in the late Pleistocene."[5]

Evolutionism

In the second half of the nineteenth century, evolution became one of the primary ideologies by which Westerners organized and perpetuated their world. They applied theories of biological evolution to societies and devised a system that became known as Social Darwinism. Since Darwin's version of evolutionary theory was more accurate than the versions used in Social Darwinism, the association of his name with this social theory is somewhat unfair. Many scholars, therefore, now refer to it as Social Evolutionism, or simply *evolutionism.*

Evolutionism is composed of a variety of nineteenth-century theories about how societies advance from the simple to the more complex and how the degree of advancement in one's society is related to the degree of advancement of one's race. In America, a widely used model was developed by Lewis Henry Morgan (1818–1881), an upstate New York lawyer turned anthropologist. He described three categories of peoples: *savage, barbarian,* and *civilized.*[6] Savages were hunters and gatherers, barbarians were agriculturists, and the civilized lived in cities, used writing, and had organized states. For Morgan, progressive human inventions allowed early humans to evolve psychologically, and, as a result, societies advanced toward civilization.

William Graham Sumner (1840–1910) proposed a more overtly racist theory, arguing that all men were not created equal and that competition within and among the races would result in the elimination of the ill-adapted and encourage racial and cultural progress. Sumner, a Yale professor, was widely known in America as an ardent advocate of laissez-faire capitalism, individual liberties, and evolutionism. Culture, he believed, originates in instincts such as the sex drive and hunger. He was against providing any societal help to the lower classes because of their biological inferiority and because it would drain resources from the superior middle class.

Evolutionism eventually filtered into the popular imagination in Europe and America. For example, Gaetano Casati, an Italian explorer, expressed the "survival of the fittest" model quite graphically as he described what he observed in Central Africa in the mid-1880s:

> The life of primitive nations is an incessant agitation for the attainment of progressive comfort, which leads to higher civilization. Ignorant of the future and careless of the present, the savage tribes instinctively attack and destroy one another. Sooner or later the weaker are reduced to impotence, the stronger fortifies itself, rules, and assimilates with the conquered, and in the end makes the weaker submit to its caprices.[7]

President Roosevelt described Africans in evolutionist terms that are both unilinear and racist. In the foreword to his collection of dispatches from East Africa, he noted that "the dark-skinned races that live in the land vary widely. Some are warlike, cattle-owning nomads; some till the soil . . .; some are fisherfolk; some are ape-like naked savages, who dwell in the woods and prey on creatures not much wilder or lower than themselves."[8] Roosevelt also included several pages describing the low state of African culture, such as the following: "Most of the tribes were of pure savages; but here and there were intrusive races of higher type; and in Uganda . . . lived a people which had advanced to the upper stages of barbarism."[9]

According to the logic of evolutionism, race and culture were one; superior races produced superior cultures, and, naturally, the white race and white culture were superior. Who would devise such a theory and put themselves anywhere except at the pinnacle? Evolutionist theories also had a self-justifying aspect to them. Other cultures were defined not just in terms of how they *differed* from Western culture but in terms of what they *lacked* that Western culture had. With this kind of logic, other cultures and races were always bound to lose out when compared to the West, because Western culture and race were the only standards that counted. Africans as well as others with very different cultures were inferior *by definition*.

The Primitive African

The logic of evolutionism assumed that Africans were mentally equivalent to children and therefore could not produce art, religion, language, writing, literature, or political structures that were as advanced as those of the West. Perhaps in the distant future, in hundreds or even thousands of years, Africans would evolve to become capable of higher forms of culture.

Let me illustrate by describing the Western evaluation of the Mangbetu of northeastern Congo, the African culture with which I am best acquainted.[10] In the eighteenth century the Mangbetu consisted of many small and separate clans who spoke closely related dialects. Interspersed among them also lived clan groups of peoples speaking several unrelated languages. Toward the end of the century, one particular Mangbetu clan, the Mabiti, began to dominate the others through force and clever marriage alliances. By the mid–nineteenth century the Mabiti leader had carved out a small kingdom, which he organized into chiefdoms ruled by family members. Over time, the king could not maintain the unity of his lands, and some of the subordinate chiefs broke away to found new kingdoms. In 1873, the original kingdom itself was conquered by non-Mangbetu neighbors, leaving the purely Mangbetu kingdoms arrayed in a ring around the usurpers. The usurpers largely adopted the Mangbetu culture of their subjects.

This centralization of the Mangbetu kingdoms led to a courtly lifestyle for the rulers. Georg Schweinfurth, the first European to visit the region (in 1870), was greatly impressed as he described the capital of the central kingdom in his travel account. The large village included a broad central plaza surrounded by the houses of King Mbunza's favorite wives, a meeting hall that measured 150 feet long and 50 feet high, and a large royal enclosure where the king had storehouses of weapons, food, and regalia. Thousands of people were present for public gatherings. Schweinfurth employed words such as "elegant," "artistic," and "masterpiece" for the wide range of Mangbetu artistic culture that he observed—music, dance, dress, architecture, metallurgy, woodworking, basketry, and pottery.[11]

Although all of the Europeans who visited the Mangbetu were impressed, they did not consider the Mangbetu their biological or cultural equals. Instead, they fit them into the evolutionist hierarchy, proclaiming the Mangbetu to be more evolved than their neighbors, who had not yet developed kingdoms. The Europeans perceived that the Mangbetu rulers had slightly more European physical features such as lighter skin and longer noses, and deemed this to be the reason for the higher level of Mangbetu culture. But they still considered the Mangbetu less evolved than the lighter-skinned Arabs who came to the region in the 1880s to trade in slaves and ivory.

Schweinfurth qualified his positive evaluation of the Mangbetu so they could fit into the racial hierarchy. He portrayed the Mangbetu as *advanced savages,* noting, for example, that in Africa it was possible to speak of "culture, art, and industry in but a very limited sense."[12] He also depicted Mbunza as "a truly savage monarch" in whose eyes "gleamed the wild light of animal sensuality."[13] Most importantly, Schweinfurth created the myth that the Mangbetu were the world's greatest cannibals, with Mbunza dining daily at cannibal feasts (see Chapter 7).

It is astounding today to realize that Schweinfurth evaluated the Mangbetu after spending only three weeks in the area and without speaking a local language or even mixing with the Mangbetu more than a few times. He excused his lack of language skills by declaring that the Mangbetu language was rudimentary and that direct observation was a superior way to understand others. Even more astounding, Schweinfurth's 1870 evaluation went unchallenged until after the 1960s. Those who followed him as explorers, conquerors, colonizers, and missionaries largely accepted his perspective. Regarding cannibalism, for example, when others found that the Mangbetu were not as hungry for human flesh as Schweinfurth had reported, they attributed this to the fact that Europeans had outlawed the practice.

The Western evaluation of the Mangbetu and their neighbors is duplicated for African groups everywhere south of the Sahara. The more an

African culture resembled a Western culture, the more evolved its creators were supposed to be. The lighter an African people's skin, the more Europeans found advanced features in their culture. In all cases, however, Africans were still deemed primitives.

Virtually every Western academic discipline worked out classifications that connected African culture to biological inferiority. In religious studies, for example, the use of magic and witchcraft, the worship of multiple gods, and reverence for ancestors were considered not only backward but irrational. Missionaries who labored to convert Africans therefore believed that although many Africans outwardly complied with the forms of Christianity, they would always need missionaries because, like children, they could not understand the religion's deeper meanings and were always in danger of backsliding.

Psychologists, led by such notables as Sigmund Freud and Carl Jung, believed that Africans and other "primitive" peoples could provide clues to the human subconscious because Africans were thought to operate at a more basic mental level than Westerners. Freud wrote: "We can . . . judge the so-called savage and semi-savage races; their psychic life assumes a peculiar interest for us, for we can recognize in their psychic life a well-preserved, early state of our own development."[14] He adds that "a comparison of the psychology of the primitive races . . . with the psychology of the neurotic . . . will reveal numerous points of correspondence."[15] Other theorists proposed that Africans actually desired a dependent, colonial relationship with superior Europeans.[16] In popular culture, Africans who began to think and act like Europeans were frequently said to "ape" the Europeans because their actions were considered imitative rather than fully intelligent and conscious.

Likewise, African artists were considered only basic and imitative. Westerners came from an artistic tradition of realism, so the abstractness of much of African art was thought to be an indication of African inability to produce realistic depictions of natural forms such as the human body. Because Westerners value overt displays of creativity in art, they did not recognize that in Africa forms tended to endure, while artists played with variations on form. Assuming that Africans did not know how to create, Western observers missed the significance of abstraction, the subtle creativity within similar forms, the importance of individual artists, and the wide variety of African creative arts that were not linked to religion or leadership.

One of the major ways that Westerners evaluated Africans was in terms of science and technology. European culture was strong, of course, in its understanding of the elements of nature and in its ability to combine those elements into practical tools. Whether it was firearms, clocks, trains, boats, medicines, matches, cloth, or axes, Westerners could produce more, higher quality, and less expensive goods than Africans. We might even say that in the late nineteenth century, Europeans were so far ahead of Africans in the technology of domination (guns, boats, trains, medicines, and so forth) that the gap between the two has never been larger, before or since, thus making conquest easier and cheaper than it would have been at any other moment in history.

This technology impressed Europeans as much as Africans. Indeed, many scholars believe that the whole evolutionist idea of progress became primarily associated in the late nineteenth century with the conquest of nature and the acquisition of wealth. For Westerners, the symbol of progress was machinery, with each new invention symbolizing ever greater progress—the clock, steam engine, locomotive, light bulb, telephone, automobile, airplane, radio, rocket, television, and computer. Africans in the nineteenth century did not have trains or steamboats. They did not even have wheelbarrows or plows.[17]

What Africans did have was knowledge of overall human dependence on nature and the technology necessary to survive in many different African environments. Dependence on nature was frequently expressed through elaborate rituals that evoked natural powers, spirits, and ancestors. However, Africans also utilized their extensive and accurate knowledge of nature in hunting, gathering, farming, herding, fishing, house building, pottery making, woodworking, and other technologies. Westerners frequently mistook African ritual for African science and therefore made erroneous comparisons with Western science and technology. Yet, despite its degradation of African knowledge, colonialism always depended heavily in practice on African understanding of both society and nature.

Changing Paradigms

Most of us no longer talk or even think about Africa in the stark evolutionist terms discussed above, because our civilization made significant changes in this regard during the twentieth century. It is important to reflect on how we have changed and how our own views of Africans are still in the process of changing. For simplification, we can divide the ways our views have changed into three broad categories: views of ourselves, views of others, and views of nature.

Changing Views of Ourselves

The Dark Continent portrayals of Africa developed at a time when Westerners envisioned themselves to be potential masters of both society and nature. Indeed, there was much to encourage them. The peoples of Africa were subdued and organized into colonies that produced raw materials for the West's growing industries, while the Asian colonies continued to increase their output as well. Scientists made regular and important discoveries, and technological advances poured forth in medicine, transportation, communication, weaponry, electricity, and many other fields.

But even while the West was making such progress, Westerners began to discover that colonialism, science, and technology had limits and drawbacks. World War I serves as an example of certain ambiguities in terms of progress. The allies confidently heralded the conflict as the "war to end all wars," yet it became the most destructive war in history to date. White-on-white violence escalated as Europeans killed each other with airplanes, tanks, machine guns, chemical weapons, and other inventions of modern genius.

The rest of the twentieth century produced similar ambiguous "successes." Despite their progress, Westerners continued to experience massive setbacks: a global economic depression, a second world war more destructive than the first, the Holocaust, the dropping of the atomic bomb, the Cold War, the decline of colonialism, and threats to the environment. Achieving global empire proved impossible, and science and technology became problematic. America experienced the difficulties of a pluralistic, urban, consumer-oriented society where racial, ethnic, gender, and class relationships were in constant turmoil. Westerners had to take second and third looks at the optimistic assumptions they had made about themselves at the beginning of the century. They could no longer be sure that they had all the answers.

Changing Views of Others

A second major way in which twentieth-century thinking has changed concerns Western views of other cultures. Two primary influences forced a reinterpretation of non-Western cultures: anthropology and the collapse of colonialism. Anthropologists were the first to take the so-called primitive cultures seriously. From about 1900 onward, a growing number of them assumed that Africans were humans equal to whites, with complex cultures, significant histories, meaningful philosophies, high art, and so forth. This transformation took a century to complete, and in a sense it is still in progress; however by midcentury it was well under way and spreading quickly to other disciplines.

There is no one moment or place where this transformation began, but the work of Franz Boas, an American anthropologist, is illustrative. Boas, a German-born and -educated natural scientist, became interested in the 1880s in the cultures of the Native Americans of western Canada and the U.S. Pacific Northwest. Originally convinced that natural laws governed human conduct and social evolution, Boas changed his mind after he had lived with and studied Native American peoples. Once Boas began to accept these peoples on their own terms, he found them to be his equals. He concluded that the differences among human societies were solely due to the various ways that societies learn to adapt to their circumstances. In addition, Boas came to understand that all societies had "evolved," but in a multilineal fashion. To Boas, there were no primitive peoples and no primitive cultures. He became a proponent of what is widely known as *cultural relativism,* the idea that each culture should be understood on its own terms rather than in comparison to others.

Boas proposed that, to discover how a particular society came to be the way it was, one had to take into account many different factors including environment, history, cultural practices, nutrition and disease, invention and discovery, and borrowing and trade. The anthropologist therefore had to adopt a holistic perspective on culture, studying practically everything a society did. Boas insisted that professional anthropology had to include *fieldwork,* in which scholars actually lived with the peoples they studied and participated in their daily lives.

In the evolutionist climate of the day, Boas' work was not immediately accepted by scholars or by Americans in general. Over time, however, his influence on anthropology and on the American view of other cultures has become enormous. He taught at Columbia University for forty-three years (until 1942) and trained many of the most famous American anthropologists of the first half of the twentieth century, including Margaret Mead, Ruth Benedict, and Melville Herskovits. Boas is considered the founder of modern anthropology in America. Not surprisingly, the race supremacists of Nazi Germany rescinded his Ph.D. and banned his books in the 1930s.

When anthropologists began to adopt relativist perspectives and undertake serious fieldwork among Africans, they found that they agreed with Boas. The customs that the West had considered primitive were found to be both rational and creative efforts to cope with environment and history. Indeed, after about 1960, anthropologists began to look at European and American societies in the same way they looked at nonmodern societies, and they discovered that the West was no more rational or creative than African societies.

Building on the work of Boas and many others, anthropologists of today are reticent to make generalizations about cultures or to trust systems that purport to explain the evolution of societies. For example, although many anthropologists categorize the world's societies according to different types, virtually none link categories to race or consider one type of society to be superior to another. Many anthropologists have abandoned classification entirely because they see that all labeling does injustice to the enormous variety of societies and situations.

Modern anthropologists are even less likely than Boas to suppose that ultimately they can understand what is going on in societies. They believe passionately that they can *improve* our understanding, but now see cultures as infinitely complex. They are similarly cautious about the idea of progress, believing that we need to understand progress in the same way we understand societies, that is, holistically. An activity that appears to represent cultural progress may, in the long run, cause a disaster because of some unforeseen flaw. If we can identify progress at all, it must include the well-being of global society and the global environment. Many anthropologists are also coming to believe that the idea of cultural relativism and the practice of fieldwork, useful as they have been in changing our racist perceptions of other cultures, can themselves be ways to distance and exploit others. There is more discussion of this topic in Chapter 12.

The discoveries of twentieth-century anthropology spread slowly to other disciplines and then began to filter into American popular consciousness. Scholarship was not, however, the only force pushing us toward new views of other cultures. The West's colonial empires began to crumble after World War II; Europe was simply too exhausted and too preoccupied with rebuilding to hold on. India and Pakistan gained their independence from Britain in 1947, and other European colonies in Asia followed, by consent or by revolution. The Philippines, Hawaii, and Puerto Rico moved away from U.S. colonial control, either by gaining outright independence or by modifying their relationship with the central government in Washington. In the United States, African Americans made headway against racism. And in Africa, Western-educated Africans led the push for independence in the 1940s and 1950s. By the mid-1960s, only a few African territories, including the five white settler colonies of southern Africa, remained under white rule.

The newly independent countries of Asia and Africa were fragile, frequently in need of aid, and vulnerable to pressure both from their former European colonizers and from the two global superpowers—the United States and the Soviet Union. But global realities were nonetheless changing. In the mid-1970s, a news commentator observed that a recent global summit had been the first occasion when world leaders had all sat at one table, and each had considered everyone else to be fully human. Essentially, the commentator's observation was correct. The independence of Africa had finally forced the West to consider Africans as real people, even if they were poor or powerless.

Changing Views of Nature

The third major twentieth-century change that modified our view of Africa is the transformation in the way we view nature. The old evolutionist model of unilineality, human racial diversity, and survival of the fittest has been deeply undermined by the biological sciences. In fact, we now know that many of the evolutionists' ideas about nature were completely backward. Instead of life evolving along only one pathway, it evolves along many. Instead of humans belonging to many races, they belong to only one (see Chapter 11). And instead of survival of the strongest, there are multiple survival strategies including the ability to cooperate and fit in.[18]

At first, evolutionists and racists attempted to take the new biological knowledge and turn it to old purposes. They were, for instance, deeply interested in linking discoveries in genetics with human behavior. An example is the idea of eugenics, advocated by the English scientist Francis Galton in the second half of the nineteenth century. Galton suggested that marriage partners ought to be selected so that superior men and women would breed and produce a superior race. The American Eugenics Society, founded in 1926, argued that immigration from the "inferior" nations of southern Europe ought to be limited; that insane, retarded, and epileptic persons ought to be sterilized; and that the upper classes attained their positions because of their superior genes. Indeed, Congress did limit immigration, and many states passed sterilization laws. Eugenics began to lose followers, however, after the atrocities of Nazi Germany, which called for the elimination of Jews, Gypsies, blacks, homosexuals, and others based on such reasoning.

One of the most important biological lessons of the twentieth century is the realization that we *must* cooperate and fit in if we are to survive. The relatively new biological science of ecology is founded on the model of life as a web, not a race or a ladder. The late Lewis Thomas, a physician, scientist, and author of thoughtful essays, reminds us of the dangers of one-path evolutionism and the belief that only our path represents progress:

> A century ago there was a consensus that evolution was a record of open warfare among competing species, the fittest were the strongest aggressors, and so forth. Now it begins to look different. The great successes in evolution, the mutants who have made it, have done so by fitting in with and sustaining the rest of life.
>
> Up to now we might be counted among the brilliant successes, but classy and perhaps unstable. We should go warily into the future, looking for ways to be more useful, listening more carefully for signals, watching our step and having an eye out for partners.[19]

Lingering Evolutionism

Evolutionism is an attractive theory for many Americans because it puts whites at the top of nature's ladder. A theory like this will certainly die a slow death in the minds of those who most benefit from its comfort. Indeed, deep pockets of evolutionism remain despite the twentieth-century lessons of history, anthropology, and biology. The most apparent Dark Continent images of the first half of the twentieth century are thankfully behind us, but more subtle versions remain.

One place where we can still identify lingering traces of evolutionism is in contemporary racist thought. It is very difficult, however, to find specific examples of how racism affects our current attitudes toward Africa because, since the mid-1900s, most Americans have learned to hide their race prejudices from public view. Perhaps the clearest cases we find are in off-the-record comments made by national leaders. We know, for example, that President Richard Nixon and many prominent members of his staff routinely used racist slurs when talking in private about African affairs.[20] We cannot, unfortunately, accurately estimate the effect of such racism in sustaining Africa's current marginal position in international affairs.

Some segments of our society, however, do not hesitate to express openly their race prejudice toward Africans. As just one example, Stanley Burnham, in *America's Bimodal Crisis: Black Intelligence in White Society,* includes a chapter entitled "Primitive Society in Africa."[21] Repeating practically every Darkest Africa myth in his discussion of precolonial Africa, Burnham concludes that "cognitive deficiency" was the cause of Africa's perceived backwardness. Likewise, his chapter on modern Africa is filled with horror stories; Burnham quotes psychologists of the 1930s and 1950s to document a "real-life personality profile" characterizing Africans as having "a short attention span, an impatience with abstractions, and a relative inability to empathize with others."[22] In light of what we know today about culture and psychology, it might seem that Burnham himself fits the profile better than an African. But to see such untruths in print serves as a painful reminder that the harshest of American race evaluations of Africa have not completely ended.

Even if Americans could rid themselves of racism, they could still maintain substantial portions of the evolutionist myth. For example, I frequently hear people state, "Africans are living as we did seventy-five years ago!" or ask, "How far behind us are Africans?" Such statements and questions imply a kind of cultural evolutionism, the idea that African cultures will someday evolve to look like our culture. Cultural evolutionism seems plausible because we know that a hundred years ago we, too, lived in a mostly rural society and that Africans are currently moving into cities and working to build modern societies. Thus many assume that Africans will inevitably pass through certain historical stages—"like we were in the 1920s"; "like we were in the 1950s"—and then eventually "catch up" to us. But history doesn't work this way. There is a more complete discussion of the problems with "catching-up thinking" in Chapter 6.

The idea that there are no backward peoples, no primitives, is difficult to grasp. It is not the same as saying that there are no ideas, individuals, or societies that are dysfunctional. And it does not mean that there are no irrational or incompetent individuals. It merely means that, on the whole, other people are about as rational *and* irrational as we ourselves are. If they are different, it is because they have lived in different circumstances, with different understandings of reality and different problems to solve.

The Paleolithic era is long past, and we find ourselves living together on the planet in the twenty-first century. Those who are most *unlike* us are just as much a part of the present as we are. They should not make a headlong rush to "catch up" to what Lewis Thomas called our "classy and perhaps unstable" Western culture. We have many lessons to teach the world, and we also have much to learn in order to build a society that is able to sustain all of us, as well as the planet itself. Our best partners may be those who are *not* going in exactly the same direction as we are.

5

Real Africa, Wise Africa

As Dark Continent images lose their relevance in America, there are opportunities for more positive images of Africa to emerge. To give a mundane example, First Lady Hillary Rodham Clinton used an African proverb, "It takes a whole village to raise a single child," in the title of a book that urges Americans to work together to nurture their children.[1] Likewise, a store in the town where I live that sold African artifacts called itself "Tribal Gatherings," an effort to emphasize a positive, communal aspect of African life. Such views of Africa are much-needed correctives to our Dark Continent stereotypes.

There are pitfalls, however, even in our positive approaches to Africa, because they tend to ignore modern Africa life. Some people even make conscious efforts to exclude modern and foreign aspects so as to portray a mythical *Real Africa*. And, as Dark Continent images recede, the Real Africa is increasingly interpreted as a *Wise Africa*. Ironically, this new Africa seems to be almost the opposite of a dark continent as it symbolizes the attitudes and feelings that we would like to incorporate into our own lives: community, lack of stress, harmony with nature, natural healing, and healthy personality. However, the Dark Continent and Wise Africa constructions are not really opposites. Their common source is the presumption that Africans represent *difference*. In the negative Dark Continent, Africans are savages or children, and their differences are emphasized so we can convince ourselves that we have evolved. In the positive Wise Africa, Africans are naturally good, and their differences help us to criticize our own society and consider how we can live as we were originally created, as we were "meant to be."

A few examples will reveal how we look for the Real Africa, often to portray a Wise Africa. These fall into six categories: ethnography, art, tourism, African sexuality, Africans in America, and African Americans.

Ethnography

Anthropologists have produced many ethnographic studies of African cultures that are based on fieldwork in Africa and on the assumption that Africans are the human equals of Westerners. Unfortunately, most of these studies are written for other scholars and are difficult for ordinary Americans to access. Our popular versions of African ethnography tend to be found in magazines like *National Geographic* and in television documentaries. Such popular presentations of Africa are relatively infrequent, but they usually attempt to treat Africa with care, avoiding any blatant Dark Continent depictions.

Popular ethnography is not immune, however, from Wise Africa stereotypes. A 1990 article in *National Geographic,* for example, portrays the cliff-dwelling Dogon of Mali in a favorable light but depicts their culture as a static relic. The author informs us that "the Dogon's ways have changed little over the centuries. They are like the wild grass whose name they share."[2] His intent may be positive, but he romanticizes the Dogon and makes them seem distant and incomprehensible. Moreover, the author contradicts himself when he informs us that a good proportion of the Dogon have converted to Islam and Christianity, and that most of the Dogon cliffside dwellings have been "abandoned for more prosaic settlements on the flats below." The culture is hardly unchanging.

The same author is "wild with excitement" when some Dogon show him a secret cliff-cave tomb of the Tellem, an extinct people who left the Dogon area in the sixteenth century.[3] Why? We can assume that it is because he believes he is discovering the unchanged and untainted Real Africa that he seems to be searching for throughout the article. And he assumes that his readers will be equally interested in this Africa. He is probably right.

Anthropologists themselves can fall into the same trap. One recent example is Katherine Dettwyler's *Dancing Skeletons,* in which the author describes her first medical anthropological fieldwork in Mali. Her task was to investigate the diets of children who lived in some of the poorer suburbs surrounding the capital, Bamako. Several months into her research, Dettwyler was asked if she could undertake a study of infant nutrition in a rural part of Mali. The goal was to help an international development organization prepare teaching materials for rural Malians that would enable them to feed their children better. She jumped at the opportunity both because of the data that she could use for her own research and because of the opportunity to visit rural villages. She explains, "The 'real Africa,' the one I'd read about and studied in countless ethnographies, lay out there, beyond the influence of the capital city, beyond the influence of the West. Here it was, being offered on a platter. I tried to control my emotions and sound casual."[4]

Dettwyler is not alone among anthropologists. Dennis Hickey and Kenneth Wylie, in a study of twentieth-century American writing about Africa, comment:

> All too often Africa's siren call proved too much for the field investigator, bent on his or her personal adventure into the unknown. Here, seen in hindsight, is one of the more evident "failures" of anthropological practice, if not of theory. How could any young American, of whatever sex, religion, or race, avoid that inevitable rush of adrenaline when he or she heard the first drum across the river on his or her first night in the "bush"? It was true that Africa possessed "tribal" (i.e., pre-industrial) peoples, many of whom lived in romantically round thatched dwellings, amid circling forests or hills. . . . But of course, even in the 1920s, an urban Africa existed and was rapidly expanding, not to mention an Africa of dynamic social and cultural transformation where, if anything, little of the old was preserved if anything of the new could be acquired. . . . This Africa . . . was rarely considered by anthropologists until the decade of the 1970s.[5]

Dettwyler, in *Dancing Skeletons,* is refreshingly honest about her eagerness to visit "the real Africa," and she talks openly about her ambivalent feelings toward Africa as a sympathetic, urban Westerner. More frequently, anthropologists have described rural Africa as though it had no significant connection to the modern world that has been impinging on it since at least the beginning of the twentieth century. There is a propensity to "factor out" these influences, even in locations where towns are only twenty or thirty miles away, where people go to jobs or schools in town, and where they sell their crops through towns to the world market. The anthropologists themselves are invisible in most of the classic ethnographies. They don't have typewriters, cars, radios, refrigerators, girlfriends or boyfriends or spouses, or, for that matter, opinions. It all looks very scientific and pristine.[6]

Professional anthropologists have now begun to recognize these problems in their work and have searched for ways to overcome them. They are now more likely, for example, to openly include information about themselves, their living arrangements, their personality clashes, and their biases. They also take more care to present a broad view of African culture and to acknowledge that change and foreign influences are also a part of Africa. Furthermore, anthropologists today recognize that African cultures, like our own, contain ambiguities and contradictions. They increasingly attempt to include many different points of view, including those that are critical of the anthropologists' own findings. Although the new ethnographies *look* less objective and scientific, because they include personal information and leave loose ends, they more accurately reflect both African culture and the ethnographic enterprise because they do not hide their weaknesses behind facades of pseudoscientific scholarly authority.

Art and Artifact

In the twentieth century, African art made a remarkable transformation from symbolizing African savagery to representing African genius. At the beginning of the century, African art appeared in natural history museums not as art but as artifacts, ordinary material objects produced by Africans. By the 1980s, African art occupied its own wing in New York's famed Metropolitan Museum of Art and its own museum in Washington—the National Museum of African Art, a branch of the Smithsonian Institution. Both museums treat African art as they do the art of other civilizations. Across the United States, museums of art and natural history have recently created or hosted major exhibitions of African objects as art.

Museum professionals have been at the forefront of efforts to educate the American public about African cultures. Yet even those with Africanist expertise and sufficient funds struggle to interest the American public in wider African culture. Casual museum-goers enjoy looking at stereotypical masks and statues, and they remember "the fetish with all the nails in it." However, they are less impressed with everyday objects such as baskets and pots, and museums have a difficult task in situating African art in its modern context. After all, we expect museums to preserve and feature difference, not similarity. To a great extent, museums must provide what the public believes is the Real Africa, if they are to attract patrons.

A 1996 exhibition in Philadelphia serves as an illustration. The Franklin Institute (primarily a technology museum with many interactive exhibits) presented a special exhibition on Africa created by Chicago's Field Museum (a large natural history museum). The Franklin Institute also prepared special programs on African innovations in technology, the astronomy of African skies, and African wildlife. All of this was done well, and it certainly intended to depict Africa in a positive light. Yet a look at the museum's "School Field Trip Planner," a guide for teachers, portrays Africa largely as rural and natural. The guide's cover features a zebra, an artistic crocodile, a mask, baskets, men with spears, and a woman adorned with traditional jewelry. Only a faint background map of countries and capitals gives a hint of modern Africa (see Chapter 10). The exhibition celebrated Africa, but this publication emphasized rural and historical stereotypes rather than Africa's modern context.[7]

An interesting way to think about how we view African art in American museums is suggested by Wyatt MacGaffey, an anthropologist whose work has focused on the Bakongo people of Central Africa. He explains, "In order to allow art works their full artness, we believe we should behave toward them in a particular way—should enter, in fact, into a sort of social relationship with them. We speak of encountering art, of being in its presence, of allowing it to speak to us."[8] He notes that Bakongo *minkisi*, objects that the Bakongo considered to have magic power, are analogous to objects we call *art*. The Bakongo would not call their *minkisi* "art" and we would not call our art "*minkisi*," but in both there is a mystical power attributed to objects. We have appropriated African objects and turned them into African "art," and now we expect that the Real Africa will speak to us, as art. Indeed, we prefer certain kinds of African art—masks, statues, and power objects such as *minkisi*—because they hold more magic for us than baskets and pots.

Private collectors and dealers have generally done much less than museums to help Americans understand Africa in a contemporary context. The reason is that the supposedly primitive qualities of African art have acquired status among collectors. The prestige enjoyed from owning a well-made "traditional" statue or mask can be likened to that gained from owning a Western painting or statue by a well-known artist. Just *any* African art won't suffice. It must be old and in decent condition, and it must have been used, preferably in an important ritual. For most collectors, masks, statues, and objects in the form of people or animals are better than objects that are only decorated with geometric designs. In other words, the best art for a collector tends to feed on and reinforce stereotypes about Africa.

Art collectors and dealers have so highly commercialized African art that damage has been done to Africa. Dealers and their agents scour the continent looking for the most desirable pieces. Many African countries have laws that prohibit or restrict the export of such national treasures, but certain types of art have acquired so much value in the United States (and in Europe, Japan, and elsewhere) that sellers and customs officials can rarely resist the money they are offered. Thieves, smugglers, and forgers also find the high prices an encouragement to enter the market.[9] Consider an experience I had recently while leaving Nairobi, Kenya. Waiting for my plane, I struck up a conversation with an American who turned out to be a collector of African art. He confided that he was joyful because he had just bought a precious mask. African traders had smuggled the mask out of a distant West African country where laws prohibit the export of authentic art pieces. The American had landed in Kenya that afternoon on a through flight from Madagascar to New York. He had taken a taxi to his dealer in town and picked up the mask, and was now flying out to Frankfurt. Because he was a transit passenger, he was not likely to be searched, and even if he was, the Kenyan customs agents would not know the mask's value since it was from another part of the continent. The man was ecstatic. Sadly, he was also a professor of African art who was profiting from his knowledge and presumably his love of Africa.

Many of those who smuggle great works of art out of Africa argue that the pieces are better off in America than in Africa. In Africa, they will be destroyed by use or by environmental conditions or be sold anyway by corrupt officials. Besides, say collectors, more people will enjoy them in America. Whatever the merits of these arguments, theft is theft. Museums in Africa need help in finding the resources to keep and preserve African art in Africa. With prices as high as tens of thousands of dollars, often neither African nor American museums can afford to purchase even legitimately acquired pieces.

African arts are also available to Americans in the form of crafts and inexpensive copies of original pieces. With increasing frequency I see African baskets, textiles, jewelry, masks, statues, designs, and other forms of art as clothing and as decorations in homes and public places. This is beneficial because it trains the American eye to consider African forms as beautiful and approachable. Such Americanization of Africa has its problems, too, however. If we merely adorn our lives with Africa's objects and designs, we are missing opportunities to build relationships that will sustain both Africa and ourselves. At the very least, when we buy a basket we could learn where it came from and how it is used. We might also explore how it came to us. Who actually made it? Does the maker ever use such an object, or was it created to please Westerners who think this is how an African object ought to look? How much was the maker paid? How do such objects come to our stores? In this way our image of Africa can be connected to contemporary Africans.[10]

Touring Africa

There is an episode in the first *Star Trek* series in which Captain Kirk and a few members of the *Enterprise* crew find themselves on a planet created as an ultimate vacation spot by an exceedingly clever culture. On this planet it is possible to live out one's deepest fantasies in complete safety because everything is an illusion. For example, one can fight heroic battles and die, but then be made whole again in a special hospital. Captain Kirk and his companions do not understand what is happening; some of the crew members are killed, and the survivors are terrified. When an alien arrives and explains the circumstances, however, Kirk decides to stay a few more days and have a romantic fling with a woman from his past. He also decides to beam down the whole *Enterprise* crew "for the best shore leave they have ever experienced."[11]

Such a planet would be a tour operator's dream: a safe opportunity for tourists to create their own desired reality. Lacking such a destination, however, the tourist industry works to create safe, satisfying illusions here on Earth. In general, most tourists desire physical comfort and an environment that is different from home but still pleasant. Physical comfort is easy to quantify: good hotels, clean food and water, safe roads, air-conditioned buses, and an absence of thievery and violence. Pleasant difference is more difficult to achieve. Tourists' expectations of both familiarity and difference must be met. The Las Vegas casino industry and Disney World have found successful formulas for combining the comfort of familiarity with the illusion of difference. Western Europe is also successful as a tourist destination because it offers Americans similar cultures that are still mildly different from home. Of course, most tourists in Europe do not see it as it really is. Rather, they see a tourist-oriented Europe that is set up to cater to their illusions of what the Real Europe is like: museums, restaurants, cathedrals, monuments, shopping arcades, boat rides, and bus tours.

Africa can provide some of what tourists seem to want. Egypt, for example, affords Western-style amenities plus spectacular antiquities, although it is having some trouble providing safety due to political unrest. East and southern Africa deliver well-managed animal safaris. West Africa offers a number of heritage tours that are increasingly popular with African Americans. Most capital cities in Africa support a museum, a crafts market, and souvenir shops. Some provide urban re-creations of traditional life and tours to rural villages. For example, in Nairobi, the Bomas of Kenya is a theme park with an amphitheater for cultural programs, a cluster of houses in architectural styles from different parts of Kenya, and a crafts market. If tourists in Kenya want to visit rural Africa, they can purchase a bus tour of a Maasai homestead, complete with dancing and singing. South Africa is even better organized for tourists. Perhaps it offers less wildness in its game parks than other countries, but it is a good choice for those who want to do more than watch animals. Many features of daily life in South Africa resemble life in the United States, and, therefore, the country provides numerous opportunities for experiences that feel comfortable to Americans, such as Western-style restaurants, museums, zoos, mall-type shopping, and easy car rental and driving. In addition, South Africa has its own local tourism trade that supports experiences such as Shakaland, a Zulu culture resort and theme park.[12]

Tourist Africa isn't the real Africa, just like tourist Europe isn't the real Europe. It is carefully managed, commercialized, and exoticized. The dancing and drumming of cultural performances are pitched to tourists' illusions of what they would like Africa to be, with seams covered up and a bit of quaint wildness added. The villages visited by tour buses put on a show and collect their pay. This Africa is satisfying to most tourists, but one quickly reaches the geographical limits of the tourist cocoon. Whereas in western Europe an American can spend weeks traveling alone, in Africa, a wandering American will soon encounter real differences and many raw edges. Beyond a few tourist havens, Africa is frequently neither comfortable nor pleasantly different to the inexperienced traveler. If you want to go beyond the safe confinement of the well-managed tour, find a friend or a special tour guide.

A few tour operators offer more variety in African experiences. When the political situation permits, for example, one can pay to ride in an open truck and camp along the Trans-African Highway. This "highway" is mostly a dirt road that transits the Sahara Desert from Tunisia to Niger and then winds through Nigeria, Cameroon, the Central African Republic, Congo, Uganda, and Kenya. I have seen trans-Africa tourists arriving bedraggled in northeastern Congo and would recommend this adventure only for the young and hardy. Besides, how much of Africa can you see while riding all day in a truck and setting up camp every evening? You will see more if you tour Africa on a bicycle or with a backpack.[13] For an interesting account of Americans backpacking through Africa, read Pam Ascanio's *White Men Don't Have Juju*. Ascanio and her husband sold their belongings and experienced Africa by public transport and without prior African travel experience. She relates her adventures with a healthy amount of skepticism and a clear love of humanity.[14]

College and university study tours are further ways to see a more ordinary Africa. Two of my favorite people, a professor I had in college (now retired) and his wife, have conducted study tours to Africa for at least twenty-five years. Participants stay in ordinary hotels and even homes, eat in ordinary restaurants, walk on the streets, shop in street markets, ride in local buses and trains, listen to Africans tell about their lives, visit villages, and engage in a host of other quite common activities. The resulting tour is much more interesting and much less expensive than the commercial tours, and the extra effort is manageable even for senior citizens. More importantly, these "intentional tourists" do not just consume Africa and leave. When they return home, they are in a much better position to understand Africa than tourists who have paid thousands of dollars more.[15]

Even on study tours, however, one can mistake Africa. Study-tour guides report, for example, that participants often have an urge to find the Real Africa in rural areas. They like to imagine that they are explorers who are discovering Africans who have never seen whites before. They frequently see rural Africans in idyllic terms, as rustics who have captured the basic meanings of life and are unencumbered by the modern world. Study-tour participants also tend to despise more conventional tourists, saying "we're not like them"; nonetheless, they enjoy the tourist experiences at major attractions, souvenir shops, and game parks, which they frequently regard as the Real Africa, unspoiled by humans. By contrast, some study-tour participants only focus on negative aspects of everyday Africa and reconfirm the Darkest Africa myths. Interestingly, college and university professors who are on their first trips to Africa can also be reluctant learners. Social scientists, especially political scientists and economists, frequently have such preconceived notions about how the world operates that they spend their time looking for evidence of those theories rather than experiencing Africa as it comes to them. Scholars in literature, art, and music tend to be better listeners and observers.[16]

An incident related by a friend who led a study tour to Zimbabwe can illustrate the tourist search for the Real Africa. The American university students on the tour first spent a few days in the capital, Harare, where they studied culture, politics, and language while living with urban families. Then they spent a couple of nights in a village living with rural families. The village had brick houses with concrete floors and corrugated iron roofs. Village kids went to school, listened to the radio, followed Zimbabwean soccer and politics, and knew about international and American music. One of the university students was assigned to the house of the village chief where, on the first night, there was a funerary celebration of some sort. The next morning the wide-eyed student told the group that he had finally seen "the real Africa." Of course, what he meant was that he had isolated something that corresponded to his stereotypes and had identified it as the Real Africa.

Selling Sex

In the West, Dark Continent myths portray Africans as lascivious. This is not the place to explore African sexual attitudes, but we can note that there are many factors that are responsible for African attitudes and that attitudes differ considerably from one place to another. In this complex context, it is curious to see African sexuality reduced to lust, however positively it is portrayed. In an episode of the TV sitcom *Home Improvement*, a joke about Africa refers to sexuality. Tim's neighbor Wilson is robbed and becomes very upset because his African "mucus cup" (whatever that is) has been taken. The police officer asks what it's worth and Wilson says, "Not much in Detroit, but in Africa it'll get you six goats and a virgin."[17] This feeble joke objectifies African women and makes fun of African men.

In a health food catalog, an advertisement for *yohimbe,* an aphrodisiac sometimes used in West Africa, notes that "anthropologists tell us Yohimbe has been used for thousands of years. Yohimbe is derived from the reddish bark of a West African tropical tree. In its native land, it is enjoyed as a ceremonial herb in the mating rituals of African tribes."[18] This is rubbish, even if positive, entertaining rubbish.

The 1998 *Sports Illustrated* swimsuit edition includes an article on the Maasai of Kenya that shows swimsuit-clad white women in semierotic poses with blanket-clad Maasai herders. The photographer prefaces his photographs with a paragraph that explains: "The idea was to capture the raw, unspoiled beauty of this place and this people." He wants the Real Africa. Who is he kidding? His white guide arranged with the Maasai "chief" to pay $1,000 for a day of photography: "We won't bother anyone, and besides, it'll be fun! [The Maasai headman] had obviously had plenty of experience with what Westerners consider 'fun.'" So much for unspoiled. (Kenyan middle-class society is in fact very modest about sexuality, and the country has strict laws against pornography.) The photos themselves show the Maasai men with passive faces, while the women display a variety of typically sexy poses.[19]

The juxtaposition of Western models and rural African men is oddly consistent in this article. *Sports Illustrated* might argue that the goal is to show both groups of subjects in a positive light, as "unspoiled beauty." But in each instance there is an artificial construction of an illusory *object* meant to be taken as real. Neither the Western women nor the African men are portrayed as whole, complex people. To add insult, the swimsuit article is preceded by a page of "facts" about Kenya, such as: "Youngsters run through the rain with butterfly nets to catch flying ants, which they bake in a mud oven and eat"; "A tattoo on the right shoulder of a Turkana warrior means he's killed a man; on the left, a woman"; and, "In the Luo tribe, the ritual circumcision has been replaced by the practice of extracting four to six teeth from the lower jaw."[20] These bits of information represent pure exoticism because fragments of culture are extracted from their context and allowed to stand for the whole. *Sports Illustrated* paints Africans as primitives and ignores almost completely the modern context in which they live. The excessively cute comments that accompany these "facts" (e.g., "They wash [the flying ants] down with a nice merlot") demonstrate that Africa is being made fun of.[21]

Africans in the States

Quite a few Africans have come to the United States as immigrants, permanent residents, and visitors. They arrive as athletes, professionals, students, refugees, and in many other capacities, and their stories are always interesting and frequently courageous. Some accounts are available in print; for example, the story of a young Nigerian woman's childhood and arrival in America,[22] or the experience of an East African man.[23] Western-educated Africans can help us understand our own perceptions of Africans. Many of them sense that Dark Continent images of Africa are still very much alive in the United States. Here, for example, are excerpts from an interview with an African economics professor who teaches in the United States (and happens to like Americans):

> *Q: How do you think that Americans perceive Africa?*
> A: The Dark Continent.
> *Q: Do people really say that?*
> A: Oh yes. They ask me if I live in trees.
> *Q: Do they really say things like that, or do they mean it as a joke?*
> A: No, they really ask. They don't know. They ask, "Do you live with animals?" "Do you eat snakes?" Things like that. I've had colleagues say to me, "Oh, you must not be typical." One person asked, "Is one of your parents white? The stuff you're telling me is not my idea of Africans."
> *Q: Did you grow up with white kids at all?*
> A: No. Once in a while we'd see an expatriate, a British or American person, coming to our little town. We would go out of our way to welcome them. But we would just say Hi to them and then leave.
>
> They think of Africa as a big safari. They say, "Oh, I want to go and watch animals." One person told me his fantasy is to put on his walkman and listen to Diva while watching elephants passing by. That would be like me saying I want to put on a walkman and sit in Tiananmen Square and watch all those Chinese riding their bikes.[24]

Another African I interviewed said that Americans often ask her whether she lived around elephants when in Africa. She also related that recently she went to a slide show given by an American who had just returned from a mission station in Congo (Kinshasa), her home country. The show was filled with stereotypical photographs of poor people, "like *National Geographic* photographs." She became so upset that she was unable to talk to people after the show.[25]

In contrast, Americans can also pay great respect to Africans in the United States. For example, Malidoma Somé has become something of a celebrity in several American subcultures including the men's movement. Somé, a Burkinabe (a person from Burkina Faso) with doctorates in both political science and literature, became involved in the American men's movement when he was a student and perceived the movement's potential relevance to a wider audience. In his book *Of Water and the Spirit*, he describes how he was taken from his home as a very young child and raised by dictatorial French Jesuit priests. Fleeing back home at age twenty, Somé could no longer understand his Dagara traditions or even his language. The elders struggled to reunite him with his people and culture through a dangerous initiation ritual. Eventually, Somé became a Dagara shaman and he now teaches Dagara wisdom to Western audiences. One of his messages is that all males can learn from African initiation ceremonies how to mark the passage from boyhood to manhood, overcoming the crises of adolescence and becoming comfortable with adulthood.[26]

I find Somé an exceptionally interesting writer. Yet the book is still problematic as a window on Africa, because it is written specifically in response to American (and African?) longing for a place where life is wise, prime, basic, and good. It might be an antidote for overdoses of Dark Continent myths and Western civilization, but it also falsifies and obscures contemporary Africa. An advertisement for an audiotaped lecture produced by Somé announces that "Somé addresses the desire to recover our 'inner indigenousness'—being at home in our bodies, the natural world, and our communities. He describes the right use of ritual, importance of expressing grief, and working in same-gender groups."[27]

Another African who has become a popular cultural interpreter to Americans is Mpeti Ole Surum, a Kenyan. When studying in the United States, Surum discovered how ignorant most Americans are about Africa, so he started to visit schools and churches to offer stories about his Maasai homeland, as well as songs and dances in which audiences were invited to participate. Soon he had developed such a thriving business that he engaged three booking agencies.[28] The major Kenyan newspaper, the *Daily Nation,* reported the story and also published a critique by Mutahi Mureithi. Mureithi noted that Surum was quoted in American newspapers as having said that the Maasai lived "as they have for 2000 years" and that they "still leave the earth the way they found it."[29] The African critic complained that Surum's positive ecological message was confounded by a perpetuation of the myth that Africans live and have always lived static lives. Moreover, one might add, the ecological point could also be challenged.

Mureithi quotes Surum as telling Americans the following story about his father. Surum once gave a portable radio to his father, a cattle herder. The old man enjoyed the "small people" inside who were talking, but when he tired of listening and did not know how to turn it off, he smashed the radio with a stick. Evidently, the story was widely believed and enjoyed in America. Mureithi was shocked, however, and concluded that "your guess is as good as mine what the audience were left thinking about the intellect of the African."[30] The critic asked whether, if respect from foreigners is so hard to come by, Africans ought to tell Americans such falsehoods. Kenyans, even very old Kenyans, have lived with some form of modern technology for decades and are not stupid.

Surum made a videotape, *Wandering Warrior,* describing his life because he could not keep up with the American demand for personal appearances. An advertisement for the videotape gives further insight into what he and his publicist see as being important to potential viewers: "Even the most complacent high school students sit up and take notice when Tom bellows tribal incantations across the stage while dressed in full hunting regalia." The choice of words—*tribal, incantations, regalia*—emphasizes the exotic aspects of the experience, while his adopted American name, "Tom," makes the exotic acceptably positive and familiar.[31]

As a final example of ways that Americans perceive Africans in the United States, I'll relate a story told by author George Packer about an African friend, Simon Tamekloe, who had been one of his Peace Corps trainers in Benin. An extraordinarily able teacher, Tamekloe had experienced numerous problems getting a good job or a graduate education. In frustration, he quit teaching in Benin, took a job at a beachfront hotel, and began running part-time cultural tours for English-speaking foreigners. Knowing the European and American tourists' taste for the exotic, he billed himself as a "voodoo tours specialist." Competition was tough, but he enthralled his clients and finally got a break when a wealthy African-American woman from Houston invited him to the United States to give talks. In Houston, his hosts treated him as a celebrity, arranging lectures at colleges and civic organizations and writing glowing reviews in local newspapers. Tamekloe played his role as an authority on the Real Africa in convincing style, wearing traditional Benin robes and giving lectures on traditional Benin customs. But when he returned to Africa, he went back to his Western-style clothing, to the same limited opportunities, and to a series of letters from Americans who made promises of help that they never kept. Tamekloe's comment? "I'm like a puppet dangling on a line, manhandled and manipulated this way and that for the pleasure of onlookers."[32] Perhaps Tamekloe's experience represents the way that African culture is often treated in America.

An African-American Example

During the Dark Continent era, most African Americans more or less accepted the dominant European-American belief in African backwardness.[33] The reasons are multiple. Because the general cultural climate in America promoted evolutionism, it would have been exceedingly difficult to see Africa in any other terms. Most African Americans were Christians and believed that most Africans, as non-Christians, needed salvation. Moreover, because whites gathered and interpreted nearly all the information about Africa, African Americans had little opportunity to imagine or discover a nonprimitive Africa.[34]

Even an unknown and backward Africa, however, could symbolize "home" for African Americans. From the beginning, Africa represented freedom and played an important role in black American discourse about slavery, racism, and oppression in white America.[35] A prominent example of Africa's place in African-American consciousness occurred in the 1920s when black Americans demonstrated widespread enthusiasm for the Back-to-Africa movement led by Marcus Garvey. Although Garvey's movement never sent emigrants to Africa, during its brief period of success it enrolled hundreds of thousands (some say millions) of African Americans in the cause of liberating Africa for the black race. Historian John Hope Franklin calls this "the first mass movement" among black Americans and notes that it indicated their doubts about ever achieving equality in America.[36]

Ethiopia also played an important role in African-American consciousness. In the eighteenth and nineteenth centuries, both whites and blacks frequently employed the word *Ethiopia* as a synonym for Africa, following the biblical and classical traditions. In the early twentieth century, the country of Ethiopia (or Abyssinia) was the only part of Africa that remained independent of Western colonialism, a result of the crushing African defeat of an Italian army in 1896. Moreover, Ethiopians were mostly Coptic Christians, not so-called pagans. Thus, the country could symbolize African-American aspirations for their own, as well as African, freedom.[37] Historian William Scott notes that, although American blacks knew little about Ethiopia itself, Ethiopianism was a "gospel of worldwide African redemption" that had been preached in black communities throughout eighteenth- and nineteenth-century America.[38] In the 1920s, Marcus Garvey's Back-to-Africa movement tapped into widespread Ethiopianism, and when fascist Italy invaded Ethiopia in 1935, American blacks strongly protested.[39]

In the anti-Italian campaign, African Americans projected themselves for the first time into global politics. They campaigned for American support for Ethiopia and offered material aid and soldiers for the Ethiopian army. Yet this interest in the actual Ethiopia—rather than an idealized Ethiopia—caused many problems related to race. For example, Ethiopians, whose skin is relatively light-colored, did not consider themselves to be black, and they often treated American blacks as racial inferiors. Moreover, some American blacks opposed aid to Ethiopia because Ethiopians were not black enough. Many white Americans also had difficulties with the situation because they disliked fascist Italy but didn't want American blacks helping Ethiopians. They also used the Ethiopian claim of whiteness against African Americans.[40]

Until the mid–twentieth century, the few American voices that proclaimed the value of African achievements were usually African-American. Even before the American Revolution, various black intellectuals described precolonial African history in positive terms. In the nineteenth century, such well-known figures as William Wells Brown, Frederick Douglass, and Martin Delany spoke of a civilized Africa. In the first half of the twentieth century, Carter G. Woodson and W. E. B. Du Bois became the preeminent American spokespersons for African accomplishments. Woodson founded the Association for the Study of Negro Life in 1915 and the *Journal of Negro History* in 1916, and his 1922 college text, *The Negro in Our History,* included a chapter on African history.[41] Du Bois championed African-American consciousness of African greatness, and he promoted Pan-Africanism, a movement that linked black leaders in North America, the Caribbean, Europe, and Africa. At the same time, he opposed Garvey's Back-to-Africa movement because he felt that the African-American "home" was America, not Africa. A focus on Africa, he said, would divert blacks from the struggle for equality in America.[42]

As Africans and African Americans gained power in the second half of the twentieth century, an increasing number of Americans, both white and black, came to understand that Africa has always contributed to global history. African-American scholars played important roles in making accurate information available. In 1947, for example, John Hope Franklin published a widely read history of African Americans that opened with a solid discussion of African civilizations. After African independence and the civil rights era of the 1960s, Dark Continent myths largely vanished among black Americans.

Yet for black Americans, Africa continues to be "useful to think with," because American society is still race conscious and evolutionist. Now the temptation is to create countervailing Wise Africa myths.[43] In the extreme, some African Americans believe in a mythical, superior Africa whose only problems are contamination and degradation by the West. In some versions of what is labeled Afrocentrism, for example, the Real Africa is always culturally wise and frequently culturally superior. Not long ago, I attended a workshop on Africa in which Afrocentrist graduate students verbally attacked the Africans who were presenters. The crux of the assault was that, because the Africans had Western educations; because they were Christians, Muslims, or secularists; and because they did not espouse Afrocentrist views, they were not really Africans. The American Afrocentrists claimed to be the real Africans.[44]

Such a Wise Africa is a mirror image of the Dark Continent, but it is still an American image. It is still American because it is about American racism and because it frequently accepts American definitions of progress. Wise Africa is constructed to compete with the equally mythical Wise West, which defines progress primarily in terms of great states, great wealth, great discoveries and inventions, complex technologies, universal religions, and other Western benchmarks.

The Noble African

Westerners have constructed positive images of Africans and other non-Westerners for a very long time. As far back as classical Greece and Rome,

Western authors idealized various peoples on the fringes of the known world. And from the era of European expansion onward, Amerindians, Polynesians, and other non-Westerners sometimes appeared in Western literature in the form of wise characters who critiqued Western civilization. One example comes from the French philosopher Jean-Jacques Rousseau, who, in the eighteenth century, employed a version of the "noble savage" to assert that democracy was the best form of government. The idea of the noble savage, which developed in the late seventeenth century, maintained that so-called primitives lived as God intended all humans to live. Rousseau believed that originally people were neither sinful (as in the Bible) nor in need of kings (as in Thomas Hobbes's defense of monarchy), but were noble, healthy, happy, good, and free. Democracy, said Rousseau, would reestablish the original condition of humankind.

After about 1800, the widely held Dark Continent myths made it difficult to sustain positive images of the primitive African. Increasingly, Africans were seen as savages who needed to be controlled and, if possible, trained to do useful work. Yet both colonial missionaries and secularists preferred to employ Africans who were "uncorrupted" by the West. Government officials frequently found that Western-educated "trousered blacks" and "mission blacks" caused problems because they could challenge the West on its own terms. And missionaries preferred Africans who were "innocent," meaning those who would accept Christianity in a biblically appropriate "childlike manner."[45] When Africans read the Christian scriptures, they sometimes concluded that it was the missionaries themselves who were not following the Bible. Thus, for many colonists, the Real Africa was an illusionary place where Africans were good children.

I can illustrate the last stages of the colonial Wise Africa with a Broadway show that opened in 1947. *Angel in the Wings* included a song entitled "Civilization," which has a line that might be familiar to some readers: "Bongo, bongo, bongo, I don't want to leave the Congo." The character who sings the song is a stereotypical African "native" who describes the problems of civilization. Missionaries, he says, try to convince Africans that life is good in civilized societies, but he has heard that people have to work, pay for things, and endure tremendous noise and violence. There is even an atom bomb. So, "Bongo, bongo, bongo, I don't want to leave the Congo. . . . I'm so happy in the jungle I refuse to go."[46] In this song, Africa is a land of innocent primitives who don't work, but Africa can also offer wisdom to civilization.

In the second half of the twentieth century, Westerners attributed more dimensions to Africans, so that we now view Africans as more complex and more like us than ever before. Nonetheless, our positive stereotypes, like our negative ones, still focus on difference. African people who are *tainted* by experience with the West do not serve well as authentic symbols of difference, because they are too much like ourselves. Thus, in our positive myths, we are generally less interested in Africans who are modern and urban (or even Christian and Muslim), and more interested in Africans whom we can portray as truly different, truly authentic—those who reinforce whatever we believe to be more traditional, more rural, more noble, or more ancient about Africa. As we have seen above, some ethnographers, art collectors, tourists, European Americans, African Americans, and even Africans themselves adhere to this focus on difference. Indeed, we all do it, to some extent.

Such Wise Africa myths are understandable because they are "useful to think with." They help us overcome our Dark Continent images. They allow us to reflect on what our civilization does to us. They serve as critiques of ongoing racism and, for some, as focal points for efforts to build self-respect and community. But although such myths are understandable in the American context, they are problematic for Africa itself. They put "the real Africa" in an idyllic past or an isolated village. The real Africa is *neither* savage nor idyllic, and it is not isolated from urban Africa or from ourselves.

6

We Should Help Them

I sometimes show my classes a short video about a village named Wassetake, which is located in northern Senegal.[1] The purpose of the video is to demonstrate how life in much of rural Africa is orderly and dignified. Viewers follow village families as they go about a typical day and year—keeping house, tending fields, going to Koran and French-language schools, entertaining guests, and making decisions that affect the village. The village is poor, but it is attempting to improve itself. For example, the

---

I have not attempted to document this chapter completely because the various arguments as presented here are more or less commonplace, even if they are much more complex in fuller discussions. The potential sources for this chapter are more extensive than for any other chapter in this book, and new sources appear frequently. For those interested in further reading, a good overview of African economic policies can be found in Virginia DeLancey, "The Economies of Africa," in *Understanding Contemporary Africa,* ed. April A. Gordon and Donald L. Gordon, 2nd. ed. (Boulder: Lynne Rienner, 1996), 91–128. A general discussion of development policies is available in Aguibou Y. Yansané, "The Development of Development Thinking in Africa: The Theory Revisited," in *Development Strategies in Africa: Current Economic, Socio-political, and Institutional Trends and Issues,* ed. Aguibou Y. Yansané (Westport, CT: Greenwood Press, 1996), 3–62. Claude Ake's *Democracy and Development in Africa* (Washington, DC: Brookings Institution, 1996) contributes a thoughtful African political perspective. The modernizing perspectives of the International Monetary Fund and the World Bank are reflected in analyses by the World Bank, which are available on the Internet at <http://www.worldbank.org>. A moderate economic analysis and a proposal for macroeconomic alternatives is provided by James H. Weaver, Michael T. Rock, and Kenneth Kusterer in *Achieving Broad-Based Sustainable Development: Governance, Environment, and Growth with Equity* (West Hartford, CT: Kumarian Press, 1997). Many recent documents on African development policy are available from the Africa Policy Information Center, a nonprofit church-supported organization with an Internet archive at <http://www.africapolicy.org>.

elders discuss the construction of a larger school building and decide to request money for cement from some of the young people who have left the village to look for work in the capital city, Dakar.

When I first began to show this video, a student came up after class and remarked, "We should help them!" Soon I discovered that quite a few students felt a desire to help this and similar villages. I was surprised because the video was not meant to elicit sympathy but to demonstrate that most Africans live satisfying lives and that they are working to solve their own problems. Many students saw poor people who needed help; I saw strong people coping with their lives. This is an interesting contrast in point of view that is worth exploring. Does Wassetake village really need our help? What is wrong with life as they live it? What kind of help would be truly useful to them?

For the last 150 years many Americans and Europeans have gone to Africa to help. Colonialism justified itself with the "White Man's Burden" ideal of taking care of Africans, not exploiting them. The mission movement attempted to spread the "good news." The Cold War included an effort on the part of the United States to save Africa from communism. We have frequently intervened to help people who are refugees from war or victims of famine. And today, we assist in "developing" Africa by providing the tools to reform governments, economies, and lives.

Why then, we might ask, is Africa worse off in many ways than it was just forty years ago? A logical conclusion might be that Africa's problems are so large that our help has been insufficient. Our evolutionist viewpoint on Africa supports this idea, in fact. We generally suppose that African societies are backward and need help so they can evolve to become more like ours. We believe that the West has discovered profound truths about reality that should be diffused to the rest of the world.

Our impulse to help Africa catch up to us is sometimes called our "civilizing mission." During the colonial era, Westerners assumed that helping Africans become civilized could only be partially successful because of Africans' inferior race.[2] As the colonial era ended and racism declined, however, we have come to believe that so-called civilization can be quickly diffused to Africans in a top-down process called "development." For example, in response to the independence of African countries, the United Nations labeled the 1960s and 1970s as "decades of development" and urged the industrialized countries to offer Africans "aid." The key to such development efforts was "modernization," changing African cultures so that they were more modern, more Western.

Thus we continue to help Africa through efforts to make African societies look more like our own. What we need to ask, however, is whether many of Africa's contemporary problems might be a *result* of our efforts to help. Perhaps our assumptions about becoming modern are faulty and our approaches to helping Africa themselves contribute to Africa's problems. Perhaps becoming more like us is not really the goal Africa ought to be striving for. The point is not that our modern civilization has nothing to offer Africa. Rather, by assuming that we know what Africans need and by trying to help Africans from the outside in, from the top down, we may in fact distort the process of change so badly that the result is an African *inability* to develop.

In order to explore these ideas, we can look at five different models of assistance to Africa: authoritarianism, the market economy, gift giving, conversion, and participation. The purpose here is not to be comprehensive but to point out that helping Africa is not as easy as we might at first assume.

Authoritarian Help

All sorts of Africans participated in the independence struggle against Europe, but those who gained control of the newly independent states in the 1960s and after tended to be "modern men." These new elites had Western educations and professed a modern vision for their countries. Finally, they proclaimed, Africa would "catch up" with the West. What they envisioned, for the most part, was economic development defined as industrialization. But since the majority of Africans were uneducated traditionalist farmers, most new leaders assumed that the only hope for rapid industrialization lay with the state. The model of the Soviet Union's apparent success at state-sponsored development was readily available. Moreover, the predominant theorists in the new Western discipline of development studies focused on capital accumulation as the engine of economic growth. The key idea for Africa was that governments should raise capital through taxes, borrowing, and foreign aid and then invest it in education, health care, roads, state-run factories, and other development projects.

This top-down plan turned out to be a recipe for disaster because it funneled development resources through the hands of small groups of African leaders who were neither disciplined nor skilled at implementing such policies. The plan allowed the leaders to divert funds to other purposes such as increasing their own wealth and power, often exacerbating the many social divisions in their countries. In a short time, bureaucracies, police, and military forces grew dramatically; independent voices were squelched; and leaders used divide-and-conquer tactics among their own peoples by appealing to ethnic, religious, regional, and class loyalties. Moreover, the top-down method of industrialization reduced profit incentives and efficiency and concentrated resources in urban areas so that poor rural people streamed into already overcrowded cities. The

West complained but nonetheless cooperated because it needed the support of Africans in the Cold War, because profits still flowed toward the West, and because Westerners assumed that Africans were backward and thus unable to manage any better.

By the 1970s, the continent as a whole was slipping badly. Added to the internal mismanagement by African governments were sharp rises in the price of oil imports, sharp drops in the prices of exports, and global inflation. Underpaid, underserved, and overtaxed farmers decided to grow fewer crops, resulting in even less income for governments. Cash-starved governments borrowed money, hoping that a turnaround in world prices would allow them to repay their loans. This didn't happen. There simply wasn't enough money in Africa to repay the debts, maintain the national economies, and support the by now institutionalized corruption. As a result, communications, water, power, and transportation systems deteriorated and collapsed. Spare parts, fuel, pesticide, and fertilizer grew scarce. Food had to be imported to feed the urban populations. A few elites lived like royalty while most citizens barely survived.

What is important for our discussion is that the failed authoritarian model of development in Africa was deeply conditioned by the West's evolutionist ideas of development and by the West's efforts to help. Colonial systems were schools for demonstrating government centralization of politics and economics. And after independence, we promoted industrialization as the road to development, we supported dictators (or anticommunist rebels) in the Cold War struggle, and we supported the assumption of the new African elites that ordinary Africans were too backward to know how to develop on their own. New studies in the 1960s and after revealed to economists that African farmers make rational market decisions. Thus, it now appears that African governments, not farmers, lacked the skills and attitudes to promote economic growth. Authoritarian development failed because those who were supposed to make it work made evolutionist assumptions, because they could not be held accountable to the ordinary citizens they claimed to serve and because they were dependent on a global economic system that did not support development.

Market Help

The West could not allow Africa to descend into chaos in the 1980s. Our own self-interest and humanitarianism required some kind of new help for African problems. Therefore, Western political and financial leaders decided on a new plan, one that would get the inefficient African governments out of the way. Deeply in debt and unable to repay, Africans were told that if they wanted Western help they would have to abandon the goal of industrialization and return to an emphasis on the production of raw materials. For the most part, African leaders complied because without Western help they could not remain in power.

The new plan was largely implemented through a giant international agency run by wealthy Western countries, the International Monetary Fund (IMF). Country after country had to adopt an IMF "structural adjustment plan" (SAP) that would reduce government and shift economic growth to private hands. This entailed drastic changes that included lower taxes and tariffs, reductions in education and health care, the sale of government-owned businesses, an end to urban food subsidies, higher prices for farmers, and the devaluation of currencies.[3]

The outcomes of structural adjustment in Africa have been uneven and controversial. By some measures, SAPs produced economic growth and more income equity. Shrunken governments, for example, had less ability to fleece the African people, and the programs saved money by shutting down schools and health clinics. Higher prices for raw materials encouraged the production of crops and minerals that could be sold to Westerners. The lifting of government restrictions made space for new small-scale African businesses. The sale of unproductive government-owned businesses allowed rejuvenation by efficient new private owners. Africans began to pay back some of the billions of dollars of debt they owed to the West.

On the other hand, Africa's modest recovery is extremely fragile and vulnerable to external factors such as weather and global economic conditions. Moreover, SAPs produced enormous economic and social disruption. They undertook radical surgery, more extreme than belt-tightening or even shock therapy. In the many countries in which they were applied, SAPs suddenly took away the safety nets of millions of people. Many lost jobs. Steep inflation destroyed the value of local currencies. Educational, health care, and social welfare systems were gutted. Even today, African countries frequently pay more than 20 percent of their meager overseas earnings on their debt. One Nigerian observer, Claude Ake, has protested that "these grim notions of policy reform can be inflicted only by people who do not belong to the adjusting society or by those who are immune to the impact of the reform."[4] Indeed, many African observers who condemn the rapacious behavior of African governments also ask whether the goal of structural adjustment was to help Africans or to help the West. The West reaps the rewards of African raw materials, investments, and interest on bad loans, while Africans struggle to survive. Many Africans argue that the West used the economic crisis to once again impose foreign ideologies and force Africans to produce raw materials for Western powers, as in the colonial period.

Criticisms of the SAPs come not only from those who see them as another form of Western imperialism, however. Many Western economists argue that structural adjustment didn't go far enough toward creating markets in Africa. SAPs move *toward* market structures, but they cannot completely strip away the old bureaucracies or ensure their commitment to market principles. Dwight Perkins, director of the Harvard Institute for International Development, notes that "most developing nations are never going to be willing to turn as much over to the market as, say, Hong Kong. . . . [Therefore] a high-growth economy must learn to make both the market and the bureaucracy perform efficiently."[5] In Africa—where kinship ties, patron-client relationships, and corruption are widespread—it has been extremely difficult to eliminate the influence of government bureaucracies or to convince bureaucrats to embrace market principles and "perform efficiently." The required "market culture," say these Western economists, is a "modern culture" that does not exist among African rulers and bureaucrats.

In trying to implement a market economy in Africa from the top down, the West has run into all sorts of difficulties. Educated, urban, and well-connected Africans, as well as foreign corporations, have benefited most from the forced transition to market economies. They understand what is happening and can, for example, move quickly to buy up bankrupt government factories or claim as their own the collective land of lineages. They are most able to manipulate the government bureaucracy to promote their schemes. In contrast, the top-down market agenda can crush people who are less advantaged and who themselves do not have the cultural knowledge that would allow them to either protect themselves or succeed in the imposed market economy. Thus, although the new market orientation was supposed to help ordinary people, it does enormous violence to them. And without a base in local cultural values, the IMF-sponsored reforms will most likely deteriorate as soon as foreign regulations and support exit the scene.

Conversion Help

Does the conversion model of assistance produce better results? It is certainly less violent because it is based on persuasion rather than state-imposed capital formation or a foreign-imposed market. On the other hand, the conversion model still constructs an evolutionist world in which African cultures are inferior, and their goal should therefore be to become more like the West.

The prototypical conversion experience is, of course, religious conversion, which continues throughout sub-Saharan Africa to this day. There are, however, more secular forms of conversion, such as education and commercial advertising that attempt to convince Africans to adopt new ways. Africa is, in fact, bombarded with messages that suggest lifestyle alternatives. Schools teach Western history, philosophy, and economics. Development workers promote scientific methods of nutrition and hygiene. Billboards advertise Mercedes, Coke, and Marlboro. Television broadcasts *The Cosby Show, Santa Barbara,* and CNN, while radios play Michael Jackson and other Western stars. The Voice of America and the British Broadcasting Corporation proudly teach English and spread Western points of view.

Under the best of circumstances, those who are converted will gain skills and ideas that can provide them with a greater ability to cope with the world. Africa could not defend itself in a global arena without its many Western-educated professionals who are able to speak the same intellectual language as the West. Likewise, one would hope to spread knowledge about safe sexual practices in the face of AIDS and other sexually transmitted diseases. But not all conversion is beneficial. For example, in an infamous example, in the 1970s the Swiss-based Nestlé Corporation advertised that bottle-fed babies are healthier than breast-fed babies, targeting mothers throughout the developing world. As a result, thousands of infants died each year from malnutrition (because families could not afford sufficient formula) and from gastrointestinal disease (because families used unsafe water to dilute the formula). An international boycott of Nestlé products produced an agreement in 1984 in which the company agreed to abide by a World Health Organization (WHO) code.[6] However, the company continues to market its products in Africa and elsewhere by trying to convince mothers that bottle-feeding is good for babies. And, Nestlé is still a target for a boycott led by Baby Milk Action, a British-based group that is supported by a number of churches and child-focused nonprofit organizations.[7]

In any culture, it is painful to see people converted to self-destructive tastes and habits. In Africa it is particularly so because of the limited resources available. To see people drinking Coke or smoking Marlboros when their children have inadequate nutrition is troubling. And while American tobacco companies are increasingly restricted in the United States, they are expanding their advertising campaigns in the developing world. In the late 1980s, Pierre Pradervand, a Swiss development specialist, decided to initiate a counterconversion with regard to cigarette smoking in Africa. Whenever he went into a village, he played a "matches and money" game in which he asked men to burn the amount of money that they would spend on cigarettes (or alcohol, or kola nuts) in a year. No one could bring himself to do this, of course. Pradervand's point was that with the money "burned" on cigarettes the villagers could purchase tools that would promote development.[8]

There is another danger in conversion. Frequently, those who gain special, modern skills dissociate themselves from their villages and countries. The "brain drain" of African professionals who emigrate to Europe and America is legendary. Less noticed, but equally significant, is the drain of talent from African villages to towns and cities. Even more important, in terms of the damage done, are those who become Westernized and then use their knowledge to exploit ordinary Africans. Churches in Africa often sponsor young people in achieving Western educations, so they can later return and serve the church. But once they are trained, the youths often either abuse church positions of trust or leave the church entirely and use their educations to become privately wealthy. This is not surprising, given human nature and the individualist values implicit in Western education, but it is a major pitfall for those who want to help by converting Africans to Western ways. In my own teaching experience in Congo (Kinshasa), I probably trained as many functionaries for the oppressive central government as I did citizens who aspired to promote development in their communities.

With all of the strong conversionist messages bombarding Africa, one wonders on what cultural foundation Africa could best build its future. Ali Mazrui, a Kenyan who now teaches in the United States, has considered the confusion that arises in the clash between African, Western, and Islamic cultures and concludes that "Africa has lost its way."[9] The modern assault of individualism, consumerism, and alternative lifestyles is even more problematic for Africans than it is for ourselves. Presumably, Africans will find creative solutions in the midst of the confusion, but cultural harmony has not been not a hallmark of this era.

Gift-Giving Help

A popular misconception holds that American foreign aid is a huge government expenditure. Actually, all U.S. foreign aid to developing countries amounts to only 0.5 percent of our national budget, the lowest of any industrialized country. In 1997 our development assistance to Africa (as opposed to military aid, disaster relief, and other aid) was only 0.08 percent of GNP, again the lowest among the industrialized countries.[10] Since the fall of the Soviet Union and the end of the Cold War, the United States has tended to consider Africa as marginal to American foreign policy. It is not surprising that from 1990 to 1997, our government's development aid to sub-Saharan Africa fell by 37 percent.[11] Only because we have such a large economy do our small percentages still represent more in absolute terms than what others give. And only because private American citizens are generous do our overall contributions remain substantial.

Whether to give aid is one of the most debated topics in our relations with Africa, and critics point to numerous reasons why aid is too much, too little, misdirected, useless, or harmful. Most of these problems fall outside the scope of this book, but several are relevant. We should note, for example, that most aid packages have an evolutionist basis because they assume the transfer of resources "downward" so as to help inferior Africans "catch up." Moreover, except for disaster relief, aid is rarely a free gift. Most frequently, aid is connected to donors' ideas about what is good for Africa and either explicitly or implicitly requires Africans to change their societies so they can make use of what is given. Ideally, Africans are supposed to receive exactly what they need for development. More frequently, gifts are mixed blessings.

A few examples will illustrate this problem. In the 1970s, development workers began to realize that most aid for relief and development was reaching African men but not women because of Western assumptions that men were the breadwinners and would share with women. In much of Africa, however, men and women keep separate accounts, and property and roles are sharply divided along gender lines. Women do most of the work of growing, storing, and preparing food. This means that aid going only to men has contributed to a long-term decline in the status of women and the condition of children.[12]

Friends from Senegal tell of two recent instances of donors who did not understand the needs of the country as perceived by Africans themselves. A well-known nonprofit development organization was attempting to spread the use of mosquito nets among villagers to prevent malaria. They trained African agents to talk to people about the use of the nets and convince them to buy nets at a nominal price. But the villagers saw the agents as intruders because there was a drought at the time and all their available money had to go for food. Besides, in a dry year mosquitoes are in short supply. In another instance, the World Health Organization provided millions of dollars so that Senegalese children could be immunized from polio. This seems like a good idea, but local health workers were unhappy because Senegal has very few polio cases and was desperately short of medications for more common diseases.

In a further example, a large American televangelist organization decided to build school classrooms in northeastern Congo (Kinshasa). American builders arrived, and schools quickly rose in four or five villages. The villages used the classrooms but did not take care of them because they had not built them. When the buildings fell into disrepair, there was no motivation or organization to fix them. A request to America for more money and another builder went unanswered because the American organization had moved on to other projects.

Aid can also benefit urban elites at the expense of villagers. In war-torn Mozambique, the IMF imposed a structural adjustment program aimed at getting the economy working again. But, according to Joseph Hanlon, the result has been the growth of an "aid industry" that flourishes while many rural problems go unattended.

> Virtually everything is done through aid projects. To turn on the lights, the Ministry of Agriculture needs aid money. Donors buy up the best people—most engineers will not work for the government for $100 a month when they can earn 20 times that much working for a donor. Mozambique now has about 3,000 foreign aid workers employed by the United Nations, World Bank, bilateral donors and non-government organizations. Often they simply fill gaps caused by other donors having hired Mozambican technicians at high salaries.
>
> The enormous aid industry fuels a dollar economy unaffected by rapid devaluations. This new Mozambican and foreign elite—beneficiaries of the enclave dollar economy—expect European lifestyles, and shops and restaurants in Maputo now cater to this. . . .
>
> Meanwhile, donors increasingly channel their aid toward imports rather than support of domestic production. Maputo has 2,116 registered import-export businesses—four times the number of businesses that produce export products. . . .
>
> In rural areas, four years after the war, many roads remain closed because the government roads department is starved of funds and few donors are interested in the glamorless task of building or repairing rural dirt roads.[13]

Clearly, gift giving can foster dependence, weaken local initiative, and empower people who are not legitimate leaders. It can advance ideas and tastes that are not good for Africa. It can promote superior-inferior relationships between the West and Africa. In fact, there are so many aid failures and so few successes that some observers have asked whether *all* of our aid efforts have been misguided and ought to be halted.[14] Most, however, would argue that aid has a potentially important role to play in helping Africa. What we need is a better sense of what kind of aid is really helpful.

Participatory Help

In recent years, one of the buzzwords of development help to Africans has become "participation."[15] Participation implies that development must be a bottom-up rather than a top-down process and that development cannot be done *to* or *for* someone. Those who are developing must therefore take part in deciding what they need, what they are willing to build, and what they can maintain. Most definitions of participatory development also include the idea that successful development is "self-reliant," meaning that it receives only small amounts of outside help. Here, for example, is one definition: "Self-reliant participatory development is an educational and empowering process in which people, in partnership with each other and with those able to assist them, identify problems and needs, mobilize resources, and assume responsibility themselves to plan, manage, control and assess the individual and collective actions that they themselves decide upon."[16]

Participatory development assumes that local people themselves have knowledge and resources and that their greatest needs are for self-reflection, self-confidence, organization, and self-discipline rather than gifts or conversions. If outside funds, equipment, or knowledge are provided, they should come only in small, "appropriate" forms and amounts, and they should go only to local groups that have already had small successes on their own. Thierno H. Kane, secretary-general of the Fouta Federation of Village Associations of Senegal, put it this way: "To understand the dynamism of the grassroots we must correct our false and mystified perceptions, [and] we must move away from our 'development' mentality and stop thinking that external intervention is what is needed."[17]

To some extent participation is now recognized as an important component of every development project in Africa. However, participation comes in many forms and degrees. For example, in the 1990s, after the fall of the Soviet Union, the United States began to require that African governments become more accountable to their citizens as a condition for receiving more aid. Once we no longer feared the Soviet Union, we could drop our support for African dictators and begin to impose democracy on Africa. There have been some advantages for Africa in terms of our causing governments to adopt more democratic practices. But *imposed participation* is a contradiction. We required more democracy but forbade Africans to choose to deviate from their structural adjustment plans. Moreover, imposing democracy is like imposing the market. When either is undertaken unwillingly from the top, there are many opportunities for those already at the top to abuse the system. It is certain that few African leaders have given ordinary Africans' problems any priority in their agendas.

At the local level, real participation is also hard to achieve. The everyday work of development is most often done by development agencies, mostly nonprofits, commonly known as nongovernmental organizations (NGOs). Many of their names are familiar—World Vision International, Save the Children, Care, Bread for the World, Food First—but there are hundreds more, both African and foreign, both nonprofit and for-profit. It is now common for the agents of foreign NGOs to ask for grassroots participation, frequently in the form of surveys or focus groups. But most NGOs have their own agendas (such as mosquito nets, vaccines, clean water, or nutrition) and need fast, concrete, and impressive results, which appeal to contributors. Thus, agents often construct a facade of participation that hides what is essentially top-down development. They ask questions and make suggestions based on the NGOs' preconceived ideas about what the target villages need. Or, participation is elicited, but those who participate are the "important people" in a village, who may have their own agendas. Some development researchers mockingly turn "participate" into a passive verb, stating that Africans "are participated" in such top-down projects.

It is difficult to find NGOs and individual agents who can and will facilitate true bottom-up participation for ordinary village people and the urban poor. Effective work requires actually living in villages and learning African languages. Progress is often slow because true participation necessitates that villagers develop themselves with only minimal input from agents. It is a complex and even dangerous process, since every "community" has its own hierarchies of power that will be upset when real development occurs. When one group (such as women, poor farmers, or wage laborers) gains wealth and power, others (such as men, richer farmers, or government agents) can feel deeply threatened.

In spite of these difficulties, most development experts are now calling for more attempts to facilitate real participation. NGOs are working on ways to increase Africans' participation levels and educate their Western contributors on the benefits of participation and patience. Many NGOs are adopting the slow-but-effective participatory policies that have long been used by such low-profile agencies as the Heifer Project and the Mennonite Central Committee.[18] Even Western governments are channeling more of their development dollars through NGOs rather than through African governments, the U.S. Agency for International Development, or Western corporations. Slowly, African development is coming to be viewed as a bottom-up enterprise.

The Failure of Help

In the 1970s, one of my friends was staying at a mission guest house in Dar es Salaam, Tanzania, where he made the acquaintance of another guest, an elderly white man who was visiting the country to see old friends. Remarkably, before Tanzanian independence this man had been the missionary who ran the guest house. Rather than experiencing a joyful return, however, the old man was distraught because the guest house, now run by Africans, provided dreadful service and was falling apart. All of his years of caring for the place had only resulted in this. "I tried," he said, almost crying.

We might sympathize with this man. After more than a century of our trying to help Africa, the continent's condition is worse than ever in many ways. Indeed, many of the stereotypes we have about today's Africa—war, disease, famine, corruption—have some basis in fact. These are painful years, both for Africans and for those who would help Africa. In the midst of our concern for and even despair about Africa we must be careful, however, not to fall back on our old assumptions about helping Africans. Our cultural myths would have us blame Africans for their failure to become modern. This is another version of evolutionism. But the problem is less about Africans than about the project that we undertook and about the methods we used. Like the missionary, we focused on the guest house while we should have been focusing on something else. Or, to paraphrase Mark Twain, if your tool is a hammer, all your problems will appear to be nails.

The elderly missionary defined development as a well-run and well-maintained guest house, and he tried to teach Africans how to accomplish this. But these were the missionary's goals and methods, imposed on people who had their own cultures and their own ideas about what development meant. The point is not that modernity, technology, and assistance are useless. Nor should Africans be left alone to live however they choose. Abandoning Africa would be cynical (and impossible) after the centuries of mutual involvement that have shaped today's Africa and world. Rather, we need to throw down our hammer and find different tools, different concepts, and different methods of development. The model of development that has been defined as "catching up" has not worked well.

Such thinking is also problematic because it replicates the nineteenth-century error of measuring Africans by what they lack, while measuring ourselves by what we appear to do well. As a result, we focus our gaze away from our own problems. For example, if we portray all of our actions in Africa as "helping Africa develop," it becomes difficult even to imagine that we might be exploiting Africa. Thus, we have been able in good conscience to support dictators who have fought our Cold War, to configure African economies so that raw materials exports continue to flow, to sell Africans products suited to our culture but not theirs, and to employ thousands of experts who provide top-down advice. Instead, we need to remind ourselves that our modern way of life produces problems, such as economic inequality, violence, and overconsumption of resources, that we ourselves have not been able to curb. Our planet simply cannot sustain a world full of people living as we do.

Overall, our four decades of postindependence assistance have produced poor results. Africa has improved its literacy rates, primary school enrollment, and child survival rates, but not as quickly as other developing areas. Foreign investment in Africa is still very low, while the level of development assistance needed, as well as Africa's debt, are extremely high. We do not yet know what really helps, and an astounding number of voices—both African and Western—have suggested often-conflicting versions of how to achieve development. One author characterizes our present situation as a "development impasse."[19]

Rethinking Development

There are numerous ways to help Africa—including the methods described above—but many current practices need to be rethought and reconfigured. One way for us to approach the problem is to explore alternatives to our assumptions about development. We could, for example, begin to reconsider the *metaphors of relationship* implied by development. Our helping interventions in Africa have mostly utilized hierarchical, unilineal evolutionist metaphors such as "parent-child," distinguishing between the "developed" and the "underdeveloped." New metaphors of relationship might imply respect for difference and equality of purpose. I have, for example, recently heard "teacher-student" used to describe our role in Africa. The point in this case was that the failures of Africa's SAPs were due to the fact that we, the teachers, failed to understand the culture of Africans, our students. Perhaps this is an improvement over the parent-child metaphor of colonial days, but it is still paternalistic and hierarchical. And it won't work because it implies that we are taking responsibility for what Africans must figure out and eventually do for themselves.

Health researchers Andrea Cornwall and Rachel Jewkes suggest that we ought to relate to Africa in a "collegial" manner "in a process of mutual learning where local people have control over the process."[20] Likewise, the image of "partnership" is appealing because it suggests that people are working toward a common goal and that each partner has something to contribute. "Friendship" might work because it is a "no strings attached" model where our friend's well-being is the only stated goal. Perhaps "neighbors" might apply as well. Or it may be that there are African models of cooperation that we are not acquainted with. There are, of course, those who abuse collegiality, partnership, friendship, and neighborliness. We must not do so ourselves, and we must choose our partners carefully.[21] And somehow we must also take account of the fact that we have our own interests to watch out for.

In rethinking development, we might also explore new names for our goal. The current term, *development*, is too closely associated with Western concepts of economic development. To broaden the term's meaning, it might be useful to pair it with a modifier, such as "human development," "alternative development," "sustainable development," "ecological development," or "participatory development."[22] A number of development specialists talk about abandoning the word altogether, but as yet no substitute words or phrases carry the full meaning that we need to express. Belgian scholar Thierry Verhelst suggests that what we should be striving for is "a good life," not development, but this term does not seem likely to catch on.[23]

It is more probable that we will have to retain the old word and give it new life. We cannot know exactly what meaning might emerge, but we can explore new definitions. In fact, many development theorists and practitioners have begun this work. Following is a short and incomplete list intended to suggest possibilities for a new meaning for development:

1. All individuals and cultures need development. The criteria of development should afford broad goals that *all* cultures can aspire to rather than only the so-called underdeveloped cultures of today.
2. Development includes material comfort, but economic growth, efficiency, and wealth should not be its primary goals. Adequate definitions of development must also include "human values" such as those associated with learning, self-confidence, aesthetics, spirituality, and community. Development will mean different things for different people.
3. Development empowers communities and ordinary people. This implies that responsibility for the development process lies with participants, not with outsiders or the powerful. Development can include roles for outsiders who provide resources, but these should be minimal so as not to interfere with the process. The development agenda, the primary energy, and most resources must come from those who are developing.
4. Development is equitable. Developed systems will benefit a broad base of people rather than just those who are clever, efficient, or powerful enough to respond to opportunities. In a world in which survival depends on peaceful coexistence, individuals, groups, or societies who exploit others cannot claim to be developed no matter how developed they feel or appear to be. The development of one must sustain the development of others.
5. Development improves the environment. Our physical world is so fragile that we need to go beyond the current term *sustainable development*, to ensure that we are well within the margins of environmental sustainability.

Helping Out

This is a good place to return to the questions posed at the beginning of this chapter: Does Wassetake village really need our help? What is wrong with life as they live it? What kind of help would be truly useful? Although I was surprised at first by my students' comments, I actually came to agree that "we should help them." But the way we should help is not what one might first think.

Surprisingly, we might be of most help to Wassetake if we act here in the United States to ensure that the policies of our government, our corporations, and our NGOs are not exploitative. This would first require study. How, for example, do American policies affect the prices Wassetake farmers receive for their cash crops? In what ways might we be supporting a Senegalese government bureaucracy that is insensitive to villagers? How might the opportunities of "the market" be unavailable to Wassetake? What foreign corporations operate in Senegal and what methods do they use? How do the international organizations that we control affect people in Senegal and Wassetake? How can we define development in ways that are more constructive to both Africans and ourselves?

Pierre Pradervand offers an initial list of partnership issues for the industrialized countries. He notes:

> Real partnership would include a general agreement on a series of key issues, which until now have been negotiated in a haphazard manner, if at all. Key issues include the cancellation of debts or their rescheduling, the pricing of raw materials, technology transfer, the "brain-drain," capital flight, access for African products to markets in the [industrialized countries], immigration policies, food aid, human and political rights, and many others.[24]

Another recent treatment of international development issues suggests that we ought to regulate international corporations, create a World Environment Organization, and reform international economic organizations—including the Group of 7 (G-7, the major industrialized countries), the IMF, the World Bank, and the World Trade Organization—to include more representation by Third World countries.[25]

If we want to help Wassetake village more directly, we should begin, once again, with study. Ideally, we might learn their languages and quietly live in the village. Over time, we would certainly discover that Wassetakeans have their own valid ideas about what "the good life" means. We would also discover that they are intelligent and creative actors, not just backward victims. We might learn how to help without getting in the way.

Few of us, of course, will choose to go to Wassetake or even to Africa. Instead, we can help by working through one of the many NGOs that are already in Africa and already sensitive to the issues of development. This brings up the question of which NGOs to support. Disaster relief is of first priority, but beyond emergency help we can seek out those NGOs that have a philosophy of participatory development and that actually practice it. Again, this requires study on our part. We must get to know the agencies we support. What are their philosophies of development? Do they actually do what they say they do? How much of their budget actually goes to work in Africa as opposed to paying for fund-raising and administration here in America?[26]

Helping Africa requires more than gifts of money. It requires knowledge of oneself, of others, and of the environments in which others operate. It also requires will, effort, organization, knowledge, participation, and community. We might even say that helping others develop requires the same skills as development itself. Helping Africans is an opportunity for developing ourselves.

Part Three

Further Misperceptions

7

Cannibalism: No Accounting for Taste

Many Americans believe that cannibalism existed in Africa in the not-too-distant past, and some believe it exists today. Sixty percent of preservice social studies teachers who were surveyed about their knowledge of Africa associated the word *cannibalism* with that continent.[1] In spite of general belief, however, we do not know whether Africans ever practiced cannibalism, because we have no reliable evidence. Nineteenth-century explorers, especially those in Central Africa, were certain that cannibalism existed, and many reported that they had witnessed it. But, as we will see below, modern scholars are not sure that such reports can be trusted.

Most references to African cannibalism in our own time occur in humor. On the Internet, for example, there are many cannibal joke sites. Most cannibal jokes fall into the same category as Polish jokes and other forms of ethnic humor; although we may laugh at such jokes, few of us really believe that Poles are stupid or that today's Africans are cannibals. In fact, it seems that most (but not all) of today's cannibal jokes have been stripped of any specific identification with Africa, or with any other part of the world for that matter. Our cannibal "tastes" have changed from the 1950s, when cannibals and Africans (and missionaries) appeared regularly in the same jokes. It is now more likely that a cannibal joke will be obscene than that it will be about Africa.

Here are four examples that are not specifically African, not copyrighted, and—in the interest of decency—not obscene:

> Cannibal: "Shall I boil the new missionary?" Chief: "No, he's a friar."
> When do cannibals leave the table? When everyone's eaten.
> Did you hear about the cannibal who loved children? He just adored the platter of little feet.

Why did the cannibal refuse to eat the accountant? There is no taste for accounting.

Computer programmers and mathematicians also seem to find cannibal situations amusing. Here is a version of a problem used in a math class at my institution: "Three missionaries and three cannibals are on one side of a river. Their boat can take one or two people at a time. If the number of cannibals on either side ever outnumbers the missionaries, the cannibals will eat the missionaries. Get all of the missionaries and cannibals across the river without any snacks in the process." A cannibal situation is admittedly more interesting than, say, a similar problem with foxes and rabbits.

A number of recent books assert that cannibalism was prevalent in precolonial Africa, especially Central Africa. For example, Stanley Burnham writes that some "African river tribes" owned slaves so they could eat them. "At least one of these tribes, the so-called Fang, depended on cannibalism to such an extent that it supplemented its captured slaves by purchasing slaves from other tribes for the same culinary purpose."[2] In his study of the Congo River, Peter Forbath says that Africans commonly submerged their victims chin-deep in streams before cooking them, "since suffering was believed to tenderize the meat for the cooking."[3] And David Lewis's history of the European conquest of Central Africa explains that "Cannibalism had always been a predilection among some of these [Congo basin] peoples: enemies captured in war were often eaten, and the flesh of slaves was sometimes consumed to give strength to ailing persons. But until the Swahili infestation, it had been held in check by traditions of warfare and ritual."[4] With the chaos of Swahili slave and ivory raiding in the 1880s, says Lewis, there was a "wave of flesh-eating that spread from inveterate cannibals like Bakusa to Batetela, the Mangbetu, and much of Zande."[5]

These recent accounts of historical African cannibalism do not rely on careful fieldwork in Africa but on nineteenth-century European accounts that were deeply prejudiced by Dark Continent myths. They are unreliable. One anthropologist who has taken an interest in this subject, William Arens, claims that despite frequent reports from explorers, missionaries, and travelers, there has never been a substantiated case anywhere in the world of cannibalism as a regular cultural practice. Except in extreme and isolated cases such as the Donner Pass incident,[6] says Arens, cannibalism never existed.[7] Arens is supported by Philip Boucher, who argues in *Cannibal Encounters: Europeans and Island Caribs, 1492–1763* that although Columbus's description of Caribbean island peoples as cannibals has seemed plausible to Europeans from 1492 to the present day, it has no basis in fact. Columbus's cannibals influenced the work of Shakespeare, Hobbes, Locke, and Rousseau, but they were mythical cannibals.[8]

Some scholars support the idea of cannibalism as an established human practice. For example, anthropologist Marvin Harris believes that cannibalism did exist in our ancient past, either as a source of protein or as a threat to neighbors. He writes that, for a small-scale society concerned about self-defense, the warning "We will eat you!" is a powerful deterrent to enemies. But, he says, when societies become larger and more powerful, they want to incorporate their enemies, not frighten them, so they adopt a more welcoming message: "Join us and you will benefit!"[9] Personally, I believe that human culture is flexible enough that under the right circumstances whole societies might condone and engage in cannibalism.

Like Arens, however, I am skeptical about whether cannibalism ever existed in Africa as a *regular* practice. I have spent most of my time in Africa with the Mangbetu, a people living in Central Africa and identified by historian David Lewis as "inveterate cannibals." Georg Schweinfurth, a German who in 1870 became the first Westerner to visit the Mangbetu, reported:

> The cannibalism of the Monbuttoo is the most pronounced of all the known nations of Africa. . . . The carcasses of all who fall in battle are distributed upon the battle-field, and are prepared by drying for transport to the homes of the conquerors. They drive their prisoners before them without remorse, as butchers would drive sheep to the shambles, and these are only reserved to fall victims on a later day to their horrible and sickening greediness. During our residence at the court of Mbunza the general rumour was quite current that nearly every day some little child was sacrificed to supply his meal.[10]

Such information was accepted as truth by subsequent visitors to the Mangbetu and by many others, so that the Mangbetu soon became the most infamous of African cannibals.[11]

I am convinced that Schweinfurth and other Westerners never saw a cannibal feast or even a roasted human leg or hand. Such persistent and widespread events would likely show up in African oral histories, and they do not. *If* cannibalism existed in the nineteenth century among the Mangbetu or any other Africans, I suspect that it was limited to ritual cannibalism intended to frighten enemies, honor the dead, or assist in acquiring attributes of the dead. For Europeans, however, the idea of African cannibalism alone seemed to justify the conquest of Central Africa. They believed that they had come upon a truly depraved practice that demanded their intervention. Reports of African cannibalism increased in the 1870s and 1880s, when Europeans were on the verge of conquest, and declined precipitously in the late 1890s after conquest had ended. By 1900, Europeans were claiming that there was much less cannibalism in Africa because they had stamped it out. In fact, whatever cannibalism had existed was largely in the conquerors' own minds. When they felt in control, they no longer needed to imagine Africans as cannibals.

It is entirely possible that in the late nineteenth century, Westerners in Central Africa actually thought they had seen cannibal meals because they were predisposed to believe that such events occurred and might have mistaken another kind of meat for human meat. But even if late-nineteenth-century Westerners in Africa did not witness cannibal feasts, they nonetheless would have had good reasons to say they had. People back home were convinced that cannibalism pervaded the Dark Continent and an explorer, soldier, or missionary who had no experience with it would have been suspect. Their books would not have been as interesting or have sold as well without descriptions, discussions, and condemnations of cannibalism.

Africans themselves often added to Western suspicions because many Africans used metaphors of cannibalism. In Cameroon, for example, some people I spoke with believe that sorcerers dig up the dead and eat them. It is also common in many places to say that someone "ate" something, meaning that that person stole or used it up carelessly—as in "He ate the money." But even if people took such metaphors literally, cannibalism didn't necessarily exist in reality.

The conviction that others are cannibals has not been a one-way street. Indeed, many Africans came to see Europeans as cannibals. The idea that slaves were taken from Africa for use as European food was apparently common for centuries. Schweinfurth himself mentioned that the Mangbetu were suspicious of him when he wanted to buy skulls for scientific experiments.[12] Today, old Mangbetu men note that in the past they thought that the pictures of people on containers of baby food, corned beef, or oatmeal sold by whites might be indications of the contents. An informant among the neighboring Budu told me that during the colonial period the Belgians caught African children on the roads and put them in their cellars in town to fatten and eat. As with most tales, he said that he hadn't seen it himself but that he knew someone who had.

Here, I think we come to the crux of the issue. Cannibalism is one of the strangest practices *any*one can think of, and therefore it is potentially one of the most powerful of symbols. Adding the practice of cannibalism to a ritual makes that ritual seem sacred in a way that nothing else can. If a new king eats human flesh as part of his inaugural ceremony, he becomes godlike, different from his ordinary human subjects. Indeed, the Christian act of communion is so powerful because it is metaphorical cannibalism: "This is Christ's body, broken for you." Literally! Here, cannibalism is a symbol of incorporation. In baser circumstances, cannibalism can come to symbolize the barbarism of others, or our fear of others. The more different others are, the more likely they are to be accused of cannibalism.

Because of the mutual accusations by both Westerners and Africans and the lack of evidence on either side, it becomes more or less irrelevant whether cannibalism ever existed in Africa. What is important is that *accusations* of cannibalism existed. Cannibalism, as an extreme metaphor for otherness, became "useful to think with" for both ourselves and Africans.

It is especially interesting to note that Africans, too, make jokes about cannibalism. In fact, Mangbetu elders today are quite aware of their notorious reputation and, rather than fight it—deserved or not—they often derive enjoyment from it. A researcher friend told me he was present when a group of Swedes traveling across Africa camped overnight at a Mangbetu chief's compound. Around an evening fire, the tourists asked about local customs including cannibalism, and the elders present began to poke fun at the tourists' misperceptions. They were having fun with standard Mangbetu gags such as how monkey meat tastes "almost as good as human," and the tourists ate it up (oops!) in all seriousness.

I've heard a number of such humorous stories in conversations with Mangbetu elders. Once, I was asking some Meje men (the Meje and the Mangbetu speak the same language) about the first white man to visit them, an American soldier named Thornton who worked for the Belgians in the conquest period of the early 1890s. I had read official colonial documents from the era reporting that Thornton had been killed and eaten, and I was curious about the incident. Here I was, interviewing the sons of the supposed cannibals, now old men. So I asked whether the reports were true. After a small private conference, a spokesman said that they had killed Thornton because they feared the Belgian invasion. They were going to eat him and first boiled his boots, thinking them to be a part of his body. But the boots turned out to be so tough that they didn't bother with the rest of him!

This is a great joke because it deflects the question and shows that the Mangbetu recognize the powerful emotions connected with cannibalism. It also reflects parallels with our own cannibal jokes. Yet it is also a sad comment, because it represents an unequal balance between African and American myths about cannibalism. This Mangbetu humor is largely defensive, intended to defuse accusations that are probably false to begin with. Western humor is offensive in two senses of the word, because it also accuses Africans of savagery.

American cannibal humor has changed as we have become increasingly aware of its negative ramifications. In the late 1970s, two "Frank and Ernest" cartoons showed the pair in African cannibal pots. In one cartoon, Frank says to Ernest, "One way to look at it—it's a *very* fitting end for a consumer advocate."[13] In the other, a father with a young child says to Frank, "Don't be such a grouch—say 'Snap, Crackle, Pop' for the kid."[14] In the late 1980s, however, those "The Far Side" cartoons that featured generic "natives" included no cannibals and invariably made fun of us, not of others. Today's cannibal jokes contain fewer specific references to Africa and more self-critical references.

The following poem by Roger Lell uses cannibalism in a humorous and self-critical way:

Missionary Cannibal

COME, he said
HEAR THE TRUTH I SPEAK.
CANNIBALISM IS FREEDOM FOR ALL.
CANNIBALISM IS LIFE FOR SOME.
KILL YOUR ENEMIES & EAT THEM.
THEN THEY WILL NO LONGER BOTHER YOU.
THERE IS NO GREATER PLEASURE IN
LIFE THAN TO EAT THE ONES YOU HATE.
EAT BEFORE YOU ARE EATEN.

They listened & they came in droves,
thousands of them, to hear
the words of the great Cannibal Missionary
from Africa.

COME, he told them, FOLLOW ME.

So they left their homes, their families,
& their possessions & followed him
to the Great Cannibal Feast.

They were the best meal his people had
eaten in years.[15]

Here Lell turns the "missionary and native" themes of earlier cannibal jokes upside down. For him, cannibalism is a metaphor for whatever negative influences Christian missionaries had on African culture. The missionaries "ate" the Africans' cultures.

As with other accusations of savagery directed toward Africa in the past, accusations of cannibalism have diminished in recent years because of increasing awareness and protest. Indeed, as in the Lell poem, the joke is more and more on us. But the use of cannibalism as a veiled symbol for African otherness still appears on Internet sites and in television cartoons, computer games, novels, and movies. It will likely remain so, if we continue to mistake Africa for something it is not.

8

Africans Live in Tribes, Don't They?

When African students come to the college where I teach, one of the first questions they are asked is, "What tribe do you belong to?" The African students usually respond happily until they discover that the American idea of *tribe* is much different from theirs. Then they become amused or angry at American ignorance and stereotyping. For us, to be part of a tribe sounds exotic and somewhat savage. The label *tribal* can imply an unthinking, primal attachment to kin. As we will see below, however, Africans understand tribe in a different way. Modern Africans have attachments to their kin, but they also have professional, religious, regional, national, and other loyalties. Moreover, modern African "tribes" are just that, modern. They bear only superficial resemblance to the organizations that existed fifty years ago or to those that Europeans found a century ago when they conquered the continent.

Most scholars of Africa have, in fact, abandoned the term *tribe* because it is too confusing and inaccurate. They fear that if they were to use the word in the African sense, they would be understood in the American sense. Indeed, many scholars see the almost knee-jerk American association of Africa with *tribe* as our most salient stereotype about Africa. The myth of Africa as tribal confuses us because it relies on outmoded concepts that were formed during a more racist and imperialist era. If Americans are to understand Africa today, they need to abandon their old ideas about tribes.

For this reason, it would be helpful to investigate what *tribe* means and why it came to be associated in the American mind with Africa. We can also examine other words that scholars now prefer.[1]

A Textbook Definition

The word *tribe* is used today by some anthropologists, so first we ought to be clear about what it refers to in a technical sense. A popular anthropology textbook designed for college students defines *tribe* as one of four major types of social organization: band, tribe, chiefdom, and state. A tribe, says the author, is "a group of nominally independent communities occupying a specific region, which speak a common language, share a common culture, and are integrated by some unifying factor."[2] Tribes consist of one or more subgroups with integrating factors that are not centralized around a single individual, as they are in a chiefdom. Frequently, kinship (vertical unity) as well as associations and age-grades (horizontal unity) are the organizational factors of such groups. Some tribes are integrated by a "Big Man" who holds the group together loosely by the force of his personality and whose position is constantly contested and not hereditary.

By this somewhat technical definition, Africa is not full of tribes; historically, about half of African societies would be excluded because they were organized in bands, chiefdoms, or states. And many of the remaining societies do not fit the definition of *tribe* for other reasons. For example, the Amba of Uganda and the Dorobo of Kenya are sometimes called tribes, but the Amba have two languages, while the Dorobo live among the Nandi and Maasai and do not have their own territory. Moreover, strictly speaking, tribes cannot exist at all in modern Africa because all African peoples live in modern states, which hold ultimate sovereignty over their populations.

Classifying types of societies is an extraordinarily difficult task that requires scholars to understand how each society operates and then to select a few characteristics that are equally representative of several societies so as to make up a category. But reality is vastly more complex than classification schemes, so *any* scheme will be partly inaccurate. In a sense, we *impose* our classifications on reality, and some categories fit better than others. In Africa, *tribe* barely fits at all.

A Word with a History

The word *tribe* has a very long history. It comes from a Latin root, *tribus* (pl. *tribi*), used to describe a unit of the Roman state. Originally, Roman tribes were based on territory—at first there were four urban and sixteen rural tribes—and each territory/tribe was considered to have its own culture. The tribes performed administrative functions such as taxation, conscription, and census taking. By 241 B.C. there were thirty-five rural tribes, and more were added as the Romans conquered new territories. Later, people could also formally *enroll* in a tribe, indicating that they had lost their primarily territorial and cultural bases. Increasingly, different tribes lived among each other. The lower classes and freed slaves tended to join urban tribes.

The Latin derivative *tribe* entered the English language through Old French in the thirteenth and fourteenth centuries. It was often used to translate Hebrew and Greek words that signified the organizational units of ancient Israel and Greece, as in "the tribes of Israel." It appeared in translations of the Bible and occasionally in Shakespeare. *Tribe* was a useful word, because it could summarize the very different political organizations of Israel, Greece, Rome, and other ancient societies.[3] Similar developments occurred in other European languages.

The word was also useful for describing many of the peoples whom the British encountered as they began to establish their global empire after about 1600. Thus, distinct groups of Native Americans, Africans, South Asians, and others were referred to as "tribes." At this time, however, the word still had a neutral meaning and was interchangeable with the words *nation* and *people*. The terms all meant a generalized group of people who shared a culture, and they were applied to Europeans as well as non-Europeans.

These words began to diverge in meaning in the late eighteenth century. Europeans, who increasingly thought of themselves as more advanced than other peoples, needed words to distinguish themselves from others. The word *people* retained its general usage, but *nations* came to be thought of as larger groupings with more complex social structures and technologies. The word *tribe* was reserved for groups that were smaller and, supposedly, simpler and less evolved. Our modern ideas about primitives and the Dark Continent emerged in the same era. By the mid–nineteenth century, the word *tribe* had assumed a negative meaning that implied political organizations that were primordial, backward, irrational, and static. A person didn't join a tribe; one was born into it. People in civilized societies could actively select from among different, creative courses of action, but tribal people followed tribal customs without thinking. It was indeed fortunate for tribes that they had such customs to guide their actions, because members were so limited intellectually. Of course, "tribalism" was expected of such people. In other words, to be tribal was to be genetically incapable of more advanced thought or political organization.

In the twentieth century, the meaning of the word *tribe,* as it applied to Africa, developed in two directions. The first, favored by white politicians and colonial administrators, was a variation of the nineteenth-century definition of tribes as having closed boundaries and unchanging customs. This was administratively useful because it allowed colonialists to make sense of and create order out of the bewildering variety of African political organizations. Administrators needed a way to get a handle on Africa, and if they could do so organizationally rather than by force, the task would be easier. Therefore, administrators rearranged African reality to fit the tribal model.

Writing of colonial rule in British Tanganyika (today's Tanzania), historian John Iliffe notes that in the 1920s administrators believed that all African social organization was ordered by the kinship principle. To them, "Africa's history was a vast family tree of tribes. Small tribes were offshoots of big ones and might therefore be reunited."[4] And all tribes needed to have chiefs, theoretically because chiefs were more advanced than village councils, and practically because white administrators could rule Africans more easily when they could work through a clear chain of command. When the British were done, Tanganyika had been fully tribalized. British administrators in the 1920s did not consider themselves to be doing violence to African political organizations. Rather, they intended to help Africa by putting it *back in order*.

Because the reordering was based on history that didn't exist, however, history had to be extensively reinvented to fit it. For this task, the British had the cooperation of many Africans. Indeed, Africans—like all peoples—had long been adept at reinventing their histories in order to suit current political needs. Since the major integrating principle was kinship, groups that were combined or split creatively manipulated their genealogies to make sense of the new arrangements. In the same manner, Africans who sought power as chiefs could be quite sure of finding historical "proof" for their claims. Likewise, because colonial rule disrupted African cultures, many Africans were looking for new identities for themselves and found them in invented historical roots.[5] We now speak of the invention of tribes in Africa. There have been many studies in the past several decades that have described how tribal self-consciousness developed during the nineteenth century and the first half of the twentieth century.

As an administrative tool, the ideology of *tribe* caused a great deal of difficulty for both Europeans and Africans. This was because it had two contradictory purposes, to change and to remain the same. Administrators wanted docile Africans who would produce cash crops, and they expected to get this by transforming Africans into orderly "tribesmen." But *tribe* implied a childlike people, something that Africans were not. Whenever Africans resisted, the British could apply the ideology of African childishness to justify the use of force: Those who didn't cooperate needed firm parental discipline. Yet the need to use force revealed the fundamental contradictions in the idea of colonialism as a progressive institution.[6]

The second direction in the development of the word *tribe* was favored by anthropologists. In the 1920s, anthropologists began to live with Africans and to take their day-to-day lives more seriously. Their experiences revealed that the nineteenth-century definition of *tribe* was deeply flawed. They found that tribal peoples were neither unthinking nor less evolved than Westerners. And they learned that tribes were constantly changing and adapting, just as were their own societies. Anthropologists have sometimes been called servants of colonialism, because they provided the information and categories necessary to organize African peoples. Although this negative label has some validity, it is also true that anthropologists were among the first to recognize that African complexity was creative rather than irrational and chaotic.

The End of the Tribe

In the 1960s, studies on African tribes took on a new urgency as most African countries became independent and colonial definitions became clearly irrelevant.[7] Anthropologists focused on the flexibility of various African tribal organizations, which linked or separated small groups as needed. The evidence was already there, in administrative reports and ethnographic studies, and only needed reinterpretation to support the new model. Colonial administrators had used African flexibility in this area to form and re-form administrative units. And the field anthropologists of the colonial era had recognized that Africans frequently used invented traditions to reconstitute their political organizations.

Morton Fried argued in the same decade that *tribes* did not evolve by themselves out of simpler forms, as had been thought. Most tribes, he said, form in reaction to *external* pressures, not internal ones. The only way tribes become as cohesive as those described by our traditional definition is when groups of people are forced to unite for self-defense. And, Fried asserted, major external pressures are applied by larger political units. He concluded that colonialism *caused* tribes to form.[8]

Also, beginning in the 1960s, some scholars began to argue for the abandonment of the word *tribe* in reference to *urban* Africa, where Africans live more modern lives. The major contender to replace *tribe* was *ethnic group*. Surprisingly, the terms *ethnicity* and *ethnic group* are not very old, having been initiated by North American sociologists after World War II. The terms were invented to describe the kind of cultural consciousness that a group might develop in a modern city. Urban *ethnicity* was seen as more fluid and diffuse than the group consciousness of people in rural areas. The word *tribe* was then reserved mainly for rural peoples.[9] By 1970, *ethnic group* had been solidly accepted by many Africanists. In that year, two Northwestern University professors published an extensive proposed syllabus for university-level African studies courses that made the distinction between *ethnic group* for towns and *tribe* for rural areas.[10]

This distinction did not last. *Tribe* was so widely recognized as imprecise and tainted with primitivism that it largely ceased to be employed by Africanists. By the late 1970s, anthropologists, sociologists, historians, art historians, ethnomusicologists, political scientists, and other scholars had switched to the term *ethnic group*.

This new usage was also supported by many African intellectuals. Usually educated in Europe or America, these Africans knew of the popular Western association of *tribe* with savage, and they also knew about the complexity of the situation in Africa. Moreover, they wanted to help defeat so-called tribalism in Africa. For such Africans, the concept of the clearly definable tribe—developed as a tool of colonial domination—was a primary obstacle in postcolonial domestic and international politics. What Africa needed was to break down the rigid "tribes" that were not, in fact, African. A new image of Africa in Europe and America that downplayed tribes would help, because foreigners would see Africa more accurately and because they would not continue to dominate Africa by playing one so-called tribe against another.[11]

Contemporary African Uses of *Tribe*

For Americans, one of the confusing aspects of modern Africa is that ordinary Africans continue to use the word *tribe*. This would seem to suggest that Africans themselves recognize that they live in tribes. To some extent they do, because contemporary political and social systems are derivatives of earlier systems. We should be careful, however, not to assume that Africa's idea of *tribe* is the same as ours. Most Africans do not equate *tribe* with the savage or the primitive. Their use of the word seems more like the meaning of our phrase *ethnic group*. Moreover, Africans are aware that they have *various* identities and loyalties including kinship, language, region, religion, country, town, continent, school, profession, and class. *Tribe* takes its place among these other factors to form complex and changing patterns.

As pointed out at the beginning of this chapter, one of the first things an American usually asks an African is what tribe he or she is from. This is because we assume that one of the most important subjects to Africans is their tribe and that this topic will help us connect. The question can reveal our ignorance, and it can be insulting. Most Africans in fact do not think of themselves as part of a tribe so much as part of a lineage. The tribe is large and diffuse, whereas the lineage is small, cohesive, and immediate. In addition, because most Africans have layers of identity, asking about their tribe may be puzzling to them. Why would you want to know immediately about tribe and not, say, about family, region, religion, or profession?

The question can also be insulting because many Western-educated Africans know that the word *tribe* is frequently American code for primitive. Moreover, in the African political context, the bold question "What is your tribe?" can create tension. It would be like asking a new acquaintance in the United States, "What is your socioeconomic class?" instead of "What do you do for a living?" Likewise, if we saw someone whose race was not clearly evident, we would not immediately ask, "What is your race?" At least for public purposes, we strive to act out our belief that "all persons are created equal" because we know it is essential for public order.

Of course some Africans, like some Americans, broadcast their ethnic identity. It is still possible to find Africans who are *creating* tribes for many of the same reasons they were created during the colonial period. This brings up a thorny problem. To see Africans demand to be identified first by their tribe tends to confirm the American cultural suspicion that, in Africa, we are facing a primal force that is uncivilized, undemocratic, and unmodern. We react similarly to anyone who demands to be identified first by their race, or sex, or class. But, once again, there is more to consider.

Mainstream Western white culture has long used the concept of the primitive, in reference to tribe, race, sex, disability, abnormality, and so forth, as a way to maintain power over others. Those who strike back by wearing their difference as a weapon seem threatening. On college and university campuses in the United States, for example, white students sometimes complain about African Americans or Hispanics who have their own organizations or who sit together at lunch. Yet if whites have similar, whites-only organizations, they are labeled racist. It may be regrettable that we live in a society that fosters such self-segregation, but the fact is that this behavior is thoroughly modern and not a throwback to so-called tribal times. In the United States, being self-consciously ethnic has provided many minorities with psychic and even physical protection against the frequently hostile larger society.

Some modern Africans have also felt it useful to be self-consciously ethnic. The writer Ken Saro-Wiwa, for instance, had long identified himself as a Nigerian and had participated in the wider Nigerian culture. But in the 1990s, he felt it necessary to publicly declare himself Ogoni in order to defend his Ogoni people against exploitation by the Nigerian government and Shell Oil. He protested the loss without compensation of Ogoni oil and the pollution of Ogoni land. The government responded that it was acting on behalf of all Nigerians, who should share the oil. It branded Saro-Wiwa a tribalist, a traitor, and an instigator of violence, and, to the horror of the world, he was executed in 1995. It is clear now that the oppressive military government in Abuja framed Saro-Wiwa so they could be rid of him.

A question we might ask in the context of Saro-Wiwa's execution is whether his version of tribalism bears any resemblance to what Americans currently conceive of as African tribalism. The answer is, very little. The Western definitions of *tribe* recall precolonial African political structures and do that badly. But our inaccuracies in describing the past are mild compared to our inability to describe the present. Today's worst "tribal" conflicts have taken radically new, modern forms. Saro-Wiwa acted in a modern arena defined by cities; by state bureaucracies and armies; by newspapers, books, radio, and television; by automobiles, airplanes, telephones, video cameras, fax machines, and computers; by foreign corporations and foreign governments; and by Western-educated Nigerians.

Africa's contemporary *tribes* and *tribal conflicts* are simply not captured by the American understanding of these words.

Other Tribes

You may note that we continue to use the word *tribe* for Native Americans and that there is little protest. There is a difference, however, because our concept of a Native American tribe is not the same as our concept of an African tribe. In the nineteenth century, Native Americans were considered just as primitive as Africans, and they were herded into reservations or killed. But in modern times, Native Americans have become more mainstream in American culture, or they have become almost "sacred" to many Americans as shamans, ecologists, artisans, and artists.

Interestingly, under different circumstances most Native Americans would probably not use the word *tribe*. United States history has made the term politically useful, however, so Native Americans have embraced it publicly. A U.S. Supreme Court decision of 1946 obligates the federal government to compensate those Native Americans who could claim exclusive occupation and use of their land since time immemorial. Such compensation is legally due only to bureaucratically defined "tribes." "Under these circumstances," says Morton Fried, Native Americans "have vested interests in the concept of tribe and are obliged to provide the deepest history for it."[12] Providing such deep history is easier if people consider themselves tribal today. Thus, the terms *tribe, tribal council,* and *tribal elder* are common in public discourse even though other terms might be more accurate or preferred.[13]

Tribe is also used to designate minority groups in Latin America and across Asia. In some cases it is applied technically, as a description of a type of social organization, and is not meant to connote primitiveness. This is how anthropologists might apply it. But, more frequently, *tribe* is employed by a majority to imply that a minority is primitive. In the latter case, the term seems similar to our application of it in Africa.

The continued use of the word *tribe* around the world, varied as its meanings are, may help us explain why we find the word acceptable for Africa. Because most so-called tribes do not complain, why should we change? We have to remember, however, that the people who are labeled as tribes usually cannot complain, because they lack the tools and opportunities to make their voices heard.

African Tribes in America

In the 1970s, American use of the word *tribe* in reference to Africa dropped dramatically. Apparently, the media were listening to Africanist scholars and Africans themselves. Yet the word still appears here and there in such prestigious publications as the *New York Times*. Likewise, when television news comments on events such as those in Rwanda, Liberia, or South Africa, the word is often considered an appropriate tool of both description and analysis.[14] It also tends to appear in other places where the public is the intended audience and the author is not a scholar of Africa, such as labels for museum exhibits, documentaries, movies, and music recordings. Judging from freshman students at college, I would guess that it is in frequent use in high school social studies classes.

The persistence of the word *tribe* has at least two roots. One is our lack of awareness that the word does not fit African reality. Many Americans are well meaning but ignorant. And even if they are not well meaning, Americans have shown themselves willing to drop derogatory terms for the sake of "political correctness." We no longer find it acceptable to use certain racial, ethnic, or gender labels in public even though prejudice is still very much a part of our society. If we knew that so-called tribal peoples around the world objected to being referred to as such, many of us would change our words in order not to be publicly offensive.

But there is a second, deeper reason for our failure to change: Americans still equate *tribe* with *savage* and believe that modern African problems can be explained by African primitiveness. In this sense, the word we use is irrelevant. If, for example, we substitute *ethnic group* for *tribe* but continue to apply it in the same way, there is no gain. In fact, some reporters who have abandoned the word *tribe* out of political correctness continue to analyze African situations from a nineteenth-century point of view.

For example, early press reports on the 1994–1995 civil war in Rwanda frequently called it a tribal war or, if the journalist was more aware, an ethnic conflict. Much was made of the fact that Tutsi and Hutu slaughtered each other in brutal ways that were incomprehensible to civilized Westerners. The conflict was portrayed as having origins in ancient tribal animosities. In reality, the war was vastly more complex. This is not the place to fully analyze the situation in Rwanda, but such "tribal analysis" grossly distorts Rwandan facts. Reporters should have situated it within the contexts of European colonialism, the Cold War, neoimperialism, class structure, personal power struggles, global markets for raw materials, arms merchants, and a number of other factors. Most importantly, (1) Belgian colonialism created Rwandan "tribal" problems and dependence on foreigners, (2) the manner of the Belgian exit provoked a 1960s civil war and massacre, (3) Cold War support for military dictators deepened these problems, (4) poverty due to dependence on the global coffee market pushed local farmers to the economic edge, (5) competition between the United States and France led France to secretly arm and encourage Hutu extremists in the 1990s, and (6) international pressure to hold multiparty elections terrified urban Hutu politicians, who were likely to lose their grip on the privileges of power.

Ethnic consciousness played a large role, but not "age-old" ethnicity. This ethnicity was created and maintained in modern times. And it was not the kind of ethnicity that Americans think of when they use the terms *tribal war* or *ethnic war*. Not only do Hutus and Tutsis share the same language and culture but their relationships are mediated by modern institutions such as states with armies, identity cards, state-run newspapers and radio, cash-crop markets, and, for the Hutus, a secret hate-radio station. Moreover, there has been considerable regional and urban-rural tension *among* the Hutus.

To mistake the Rwandan civil war for a stereotypical "tribal" war is very dangerous because it causes us to misperceive what really happened. The United Nations, and the United States and other governments, now admit that they did not act quickly or decisively enough to stop the slide toward genocide. Last-minute efforts were too little and too late. But considering that Western governments did not really understand the problems in Rwanda to begin with, this is not surprising.

Perhaps a major reason that "tribalism" colors our first analysis of an African political problem is that we do not adequately prepare our news reporters. Reporters who do not know much about Africa, let alone individual nations like Rwanda, are likely to fall back on stereotypes and other simple ways to convey complex events. Surely they are not unsympathetic to Rwandans as people. They are just unprepared and in a hurry, and so is their audience. In Rwanda, it was as though the news teams had just arrived on the scene of an accident and were trying to make quick sense of what had happened.

In a deeper sense, however, we quickly resorted to portraying the Rwandan conflict as primordial because such a response provides support for our American view of the world. Specifically, by portraying African conflicts as age-old conflicts, we Westerners do not have to take responsibility for our share of the *causes* of modern African history. Moreover, if the causes of a conflict are so basic as to be tribal, meaning savage, then we can imagine that *solutions* will be almost impossible to find. Thus we can congratulate ourselves for relief efforts for victims, but not feel responsible for addressing even the African causes, let alone the Western ones. Some problems are just too deep to resolve, we can rationalize. "Tribal analysis" walls off Rwanda from modern history, making it appear as if Rwanda does not participate in the same world in which all the rest of us participate.

During the Rwandan crisis I was asked by a congressman to brief him on what was going on. I prepared to give a ten-minute presentation on background causes and alternative analyses of current events. My presentation was basic because he obviously knew little about the situation in Rwanda. When I arrived, I found that he did not really *want* to know what was going on. His only concern was whether the brewing "tribal" trouble between the Hutus and Tutsis in neighboring Burundi might in some way spill over into his world and necessitate involving U.S. troops.

I can sympathize with Anthony Appiah, a Ghanaian scholar living in the United States, who suggests that the way we use the word *tribe* facilitates exploitation of Africans. He writes that "race in Europe and tribe in Africa are central to the way in which the objective interests of the worst-off are distorted."[15] What he means is that we have an interest in actually promoting tribalism and the myths of the tribe in Africa. This effort may be conscious or unconscious, but by keeping ourselves thinking that tribe matters, Africans will be easier to ignore or exploit.

Wole Soyinka, a Nigerian and winner of the Nobel Prize for literature, has applied the same logic to Western considerations of African governments. He criticizes scholars who say that Africa's ethnic divisions *require* dictators in order to keep the peace. The supposed African tribal mind becomes an excuse for the West not to hold African leaders to international standards.

Alternatives to Tribe

Soyinka recognizes that our word *tribe* is a problem for Africa, but rather than criticize us, he throws the word back at us. He has started calling white and black Americans the white tribe and the black tribe. Soyinka knows that we will immediately recognize that identifying Americans as living in tribes, at least the kind we think of, is threatening to our social order. It oversimplifies, promotes division, and hinders our ability to solve our *many* kinds of problems. Africans respond in the same way to our use of the term for them.

Soyinka's counterattack will not make the word disappear, however. It is too ingrained in our consciousness and too widely used around the world. What we can hope for is that Americans become aware of *various* meanings of the word. Yet we should not use the word in reference to Africa because African reality, both past and present, is not accurately described by *any* meaning of the word. *Tribe* distorts African reality and therefore makes it impossible to understand the continent.

As mentioned above, the principal contender to replace *tribe* is *ethnic group*. But if we elect to substitute *ethnic group,* will this new term serve us well? Its primary benefits are that it is less negative than *tribe,* that it is applied to groups all over the world (making Africans seem more like people elsewhere), and that the concept was invented to describe people's group consciousness in modern societies.

The main drawback to *ethnic group* is that the term is just as ambiguous as *tribe*. How can a single phrase apply both to a European American's mild sense of attachment to the "old country" and to the intense feelings of hatred that have arisen between warring factions in the former Yugoslavia? The only real connection among the many different uses of *ethnicity* is that the term describes a feeling of closeness to one's own group that arises in the face of contacts with other groups. It does not, however, describe the intensity of the feeling or even its precise nature. And it does not adequately describe the nature of the group itself. Moreover, if we use *ethnic group* in Africa in the same ways that we used *tribe,* we have not accomplished much. *Ethnic group* may just hide the fact that we still think that African groups, whatever their name, are composed of primitives.

Are there other options? A genuinely useful word would help us distinguish different kinds of situations and different kinds of groups. It would help us understand the negotiations and conflicts between groups and also the negotiations and conflicts between individuals and their groups. Unfortunately, there is no such word yet. It is for this reason that we must be especially careful. To pick one word and let it stand for many different situations is to mistake Africa.

A variety of words are now being used by those who are aware of the problems with *tribe*. *Ethnic group* is just one. Other possibilities include *people* (the Zulu are an African *people* who live in southern Africa); *group* (the Ogoni are a *group* in Nigeria); or simply the name of the group (the *Tiv* of Nigeria live near the confluence of the Niger and Benue Rivers).

With any of these alternatives, you still must be careful. *People* and *group* are emotionally neutral words with sufficiently vague definitions that they can serve in most contexts, but they are not precise enough for careful analysis. If you identify a person by the name of a specific group, that person might be offended that you picked out this characteristic as important rather than some other. A Tiv might prefer to be called a Nigerian first, or an author, or a mother, or by the name of a clan. Moreover, by using *Tiv* you might be implying that the Tiv are all uniform, with one set of customs, one attitude, and so forth. The Tiv, like other African peoples, are quite diverse.

Sometimes you might not want as inclusive a word as you first might think. For example, consider using some of these words and phrases: community, society, village, farmer, herdsman, rural people, rural dweller, urbanite, citizen, local people, kin group, clan, lineage, and family. These words have more specific meanings. And when discussing precolonial Africa, words like band, chiefdom, kingdom, empire, state, ministate, city-state, and others might convey a more exact meaning.

You might be tempted to use the word *nation,* because in the United States and Canada, *First Nations* is employed by some to dignify Native American groups. In the modern African context this would not be a good idea, however. Throughout the world, most people think that nations ought to have their own sovereign countries and that countries ought to be composed of only one nation. By this logic, if you identified the Tiv as a nation, you would be implying that the Tiv should form their own country with their own state government. If you were Tiv and held such beliefs, you would be considered treasonous by the Nigerian government, which is trying to foster a feeling of Nigerian nationality.

The basic problem is that we need labels, but almost all labels are inaccurate and easily contested. There really is no satisfactory way to solve the labeling problem. We can, however, make a reasonable attempt to be fair to Africa if we remind ourselves of two principles. First, beware of analyses that emphasize only one or two factors. Tribalism is much too general a category with which to explain modern Africa. As we learn more about specific situations in Africa, we will see that many factors are likely to be relevant. Second, strive for precision. Learn the meanings of words and try to use them appropriately. There are many terms that are more accurate than *tribe,* even if they are not themselves entirely satisfactory.

One final note: You might be curious about how Africans you meet orient themselves to the world they live in. Do they consider themselves part of a tribe? Should you ever ask? That would depend on the context. You probably should not go directly to the T-word. You can ask about country, region of the country, and hometown first. Since most Africans you meet in America will be city or town dwellers, you might ask what part of their country their family comes from originally. This is a relatively neutral question, and they can answer by revealing as much as they want about themselves. Such answers can help you discover a great deal about ways that people conceive of themselves. If you feel you must ask about tribe, you might get a small lecture on why ethnicity should not be important, why *some* people think it is important but *they* do not, or why

Americans ought to stop thinking of Africans as primitives. On the other hand, most Africans will take your question kindly. For them, ethnic diversity is a fact of life and tribe does not have the same adverse connotation as it does for us. Many people will be thankful that you have simply taken the time to show interest.

9

Safari: Beyond Our Wildest Dreams

One of the major ways we connect with Africa is through its wild animals. Most Americans easily associate Africa with images of lions and elephants and words such as *safari* and *simba*. In fact, brief reflection will reveal a surprisingly large number of ways that Americans "interact" with African animals. We are sometimes hunters and photo-tourists in Africa, of course, but here at home we are also visitors to zoos and animal parks; viewers of nature programs on television; purchasers of products that use elephants, lions, and other African animals as "salesbeasts"; and patrons of movies like *The Lion King*. Even *Sesame Street*, a television show that is comparable to mother's milk for American children, has a segment featuring an outline map of Africa that morphs into a lion, a hippo, and an ostrich while a voice repeats, "Africa, Africa, Africa."[1] Images and experiences of African animals deeply shape our understanding of the continent.

My purpose in this chapter is to investigate the ways we interact with African animals. I am particularly interested in exploring whether there are common meanings to our interactions or whether each kind of experience—safari, zoo, movies, and so forth—stands on its own. This problem was first posed to me by a student who told me that he was a hunter and was interested in going to southern Africa to kill big game. In hunter culture, southern Africa is one of the most attractive destinations because of the availability of large animals such as lions, elephants, and Cape buffalo. My student—I'll call him Richard—had dreams of hunting Cape buffalo somewhere in South Africa, Zimbabwe, Botswana, or Namibia.

I was interested in knowing how Richard would describe what hunting in Africa meant to him. His major point was that facing down a Cape buffalo would be the most "real" experience he could ever have. This animal, particularly known for its vengeful ferocity, will literally stomp you to a pulp if you don't succeed in killing it. Richard shared the thoughts of hunter guru Jeff Cooper, who argues that, for humans, "danger—not variety—is the spice of life. Only when one has glimpsed the imminence of death can one fully appreciate the joy of living."[2] Richard also directed me to *Meditations on Hunting* by Spanish philosopher José Ortega y Gasset, which, in brief, asserts that hunting is the only real way by which humans can become their "natural selves." Modern humans are condemned to live in society, says Ortega y Gasset, but by hunting they become animals again and thus momentarily rejoin nature.[3]

Richard added that hunting has nothing whatever to do with the more popular photographic safaris or, for that matter, with American zoos, nature TV, or *The Lion King*. Hunters criticize those who view nature in cages or through a camera's eye because they are mere observers rather than actual participants in nature. From Richard's perspective, hunting is a unique experience that focuses only on the hunter's union with nature.

Richard opened the American hunter's world to me, and I began to read further. My response to him then and now, however, is that whatever uniquely "real" experience hunting might provide, how we hunt and what it means are deeply cultural. The African hunters I have hunted with or read about seem to approach nature differently from Westerners. No doubt, both have to know nature well to succeed, but the Africans' motivations, means, and results are not the same as those of American hunters. The "African safari" is a Western invention undertaken by Westerners with Western motivations and Western means. It is therefore bound to be different from an African hunt undertaken by Africans. Moreover, there is a common Western theme that links the hunting safari, the photographic safari, natural history museums, nature TV, zoos, and *The Lion King*.

Where the Wild Things Aren't

Our quick association of Africa with wild animals is not an invention; Africa does indeed harbor the greatest number and variety of large, wild mammals on earth. There are vast savannas teeming with elephants, zebras, wildebeests, rhinoceroses, antelope of many sorts, lions, cheetahs, and a variety of other animals. Likewise, there are rivers and lakes harboring crocodiles and hippos, and rain forests where leopards stalk. By contrast, the Americas and Australia are poor in large mammal species because of large-scale extinction during the late Pleistocene era (about 11,000 years ago). Perhaps 80 percent of the big animal species in the Americas died out, for reasons that are unclear but that may be related to human activity. In the past 5,000 years, populations of megafauna in Europe and Asia have mostly disappeared as a result of human agency.

We should, however, dispose of the stereotype that animals are plentiful all over Africa. This myth was brought home to me when I helped lead a student group to West Africa. The student tourists felt it imperative to see animals so they could match their experiences to their myths. Unfortunately, we leaders had neglected to warn students that West Africa is full of people, but not wild animals.[4] The pressure for a safari was strong enough that we added a brief side trip to the tiny Abuko Nature Reserve in the Gambia where we saw crocodiles, lions, and a few other animals that had once been plentiful in the region; we did not see them in their natural habitat, but in cages and pens. Abuko's meager offerings comprised more animals than most West Africans ever see, but far fewer than we could view in any moderate-sized American zoo.

The animals of Africa live either at the margins of human habitation or where they have been protected from humans by modern wildlife management techniques. This means that most African animals are found in Central Africa or in the north-south corridor along the east coast from Kenya south and across to Namibia. Even in these regions the natural habitat is shrinking rapidly. Environments that are especially fragile, such as those of the mountain gorilla or those adjacent to dense human populations, are under extreme threat.

"The Good Old Days"

I asserted above that the African hunting safari is a thoroughly Western experience. A good example of this is the life of Theodore Roosevelt, our twenty-sixth president. Roosevelt was both a hunter and conservationist, avocations that are not as antithetical as they might at first seem. Roosevelt's intense interest in nature showed itself early. As a boy he created his own natural history museum, which eventually included over 2,000 specimens. The adult Roosevelt undertook trips to the American West, where he killed large mammals such as bison; here he came to understand the importance of preserving our lands for future generations. Roosevelt became our first conservation president, adding five national parks, sixteen national monuments, and fifty-one wildlife refuges to federal management.

When Roosevelt left the presidency at the age of fifty, he turned first to Africa. He decided to organize and lead an enormous hunting safari to East Africa so he could visit "these greatest of the world's great hunting-grounds."[5] He also wanted to introduce African wildlife to the American people through the preservation of specimens for the Smithsonian Institution. Thus, for a full year from 1909 to 1910, he shot and collected wild animals in East and northeast Africa.

Up to this point, Roosevelt's safari seems almost heroic: the exploit of an ex-president who could do anything he wanted, but who nonetheless desired to do good for humanity and so provisioned a national museum with scientific data. There are, however, deep contradictions in Roosevelt's story. His colorful dispatches from Africa, sent regularly to American newspapers to help pay for the expedition, give the impression that the safari was about more than a love of nature and hunting. Roosevelt was certainly interested in science and conservation, but he was also interested in exploitation and conquest. Moreover, by broadcasting his experience of Africa to America, Roosevelt reinforced America's image of Africa as inferior.

Roosevelt's account of his African safari begins with a commentary based on nineteenth-century Dark Continent myths. Like his early-twentieth-century contemporaries, he views Africa as an unevolved world where one could experience a pristine environment and where the backward inhabitants would be favored by colonization by superior whites. He then describes his safari, one of the largest ever undertaken, which comprised nine white men, including Roosevelt's son and one of the most famous professional hunters of all time, Frederick Selous. The safari required hundreds of Africans—amounting to 2,000 over the course of the year—who served as trackers, gun bearers, guides, porters, tent boys, horse boys, cooks, skinners, and soldiers.

Roosevelt lauded the "strong, patient childlike savages" who as porters transported tons of salt for curing hides, hundreds of traps, ammunition, food, tents, beds, books, animal specimens, and a bathtub. Roosevelt insisted that each day "a hot bath, never a cold bath, is almost a tropic necessity."[6] It was not unusual in safaris at that time for each white person to require as many as thirty porters, each of whom carried about sixty pounds of supplies.[7] The safari could therefore not move more than about ten miles a day. At every campsite, the African workers set up a small tent village.

Each morning the white men and those Africans involved in the hunt would leave after breakfast. They sometimes traveled ten or more miles from camp to find the game they were looking for, but usually they hunted much closer. Once an animal had been killed, the skinners would set to work quickly in order to preserve the hide for a museum display. The portly president denied himself his noonday meal because it seemed unmanly to eat while hunting, but he and his party were nonetheless pampered. In the evening, he dined well on the best game available, including a favorite, elephant trunk soup. Naturally, he had water carried and heated for his bath.

Roosevelt was a sensation in East African colonial circles. An American president, even an ex-president in the days before America became a world power, was a major celebrity. Both Roosevelt's rugged, individualist personality and his legendary conversational ability fit well in white Kenyan frontier society. But even in a colony renowned for the excesses of its whites, there was something in the president's behavior that disturbed many. For example, Roosevelt frequently took wild shots from his horse at great distances, without stalking, and he used ammunition too liberally. He also killed many more animals than was necessary for a good collection. In southern Sudan his party shot nine white rhinoceroses, animals Roosevelt knew to be in danger of extinction. He even shot three more than his license allowed, including four cows—so many that local people still know the site as Rhino Camp.[8] Elsewhere, Roosevelt noted that the British East Africa colonial government was trying to protect elephants and that "it would be a veritable and most tragic calamity if the lordly elephant . . . should be permitted to vanish from the face of the earth."[9] But his party killed more elephants than he needed for the collections he was establishing.

Some of Roosevelt's actions can be explained by his physical condition. Rarely ill and an eager and energetic participant, he was nonetheless so obese that he could not easily stalk animals on foot. In addition, he could see with only one eye, so he judged distances badly and fired frequently to be sure he hit his target. Furthermore, one can imagine that his publishers encouraged presidential record setting so they could sell newspapers.[10]

Many white East Africans, however, attributed Roosevelt's demeanor to his Americanness. Americans had long had the reputation of being generally excessive and more interested in good results than in good technique. The British settlers emphasized the sport rather than the kill. Animals needed a "fair chase," which implied that the hunter had to discipline himself to keep on relatively the same level as the animals. This attitude was made law when, after the motorcar was first used for hunting in the 1920s, the colonial government ruled that hunters had to be at least 200 yards from the vehicle before they could shoot. By the 1960s, the rule had been expanded so that the animal had to be at least 500 yards away from the vehicle. Contrast this approach with a hunt in the 1920s in which two infamous Americans killed 323 lions between them and caused the Tanganyika government to limit hunters to 5 lions apiece.[11]

The excesses attributed to Roosevelt's Americanness reveal the contradictions of his safari. Here was a lover of nature who sought to preserve nature because he understood that people like himself would otherwise destroy it. And yet there was really not much difference between the Americans and the British. Big-game hunting in Africa quickly became a sport in which white men directed Africans in the mechanized and commercialized conquest of African nature while hoping that not too many other white men would want to do the same thing. Whether conducted with British sportsmanship or American brute efficiency, the safari was about colonialism and the subjugation of nature more than about conserving or understanding nature.

An illustration of Africans on a hunt is a useful contrast to Western and specifically American attitudes. One day, Roosevelt observed a group of about twenty-five young Nandi men who were hunting lions with spears. The men spread out in a long line and walked forward, beating the bush until they found a lion. Then they circled the beast and closed in. Roosevelt describes the resulting kill:

> At last the tense ring was complete, and the spearmen rose and closed in. The lion looked quickly from side to side, saw where the line was thinnest, and charged at his topmost speed. The crowded moment began. With shields held steady, and quivering spears poised, the men in front braced themselves for the rush and the shock; and from either hand the warriors sprang forward to take their foe in the flank. Bounding ahead of his fellows, the leader reached throwing distance; the long spear flickered and plunged; as the lion felt the wound he half turned, and then flung himself on the man in front. The warrior threw his spear; it drove deep into the life, for entering at one shoulder it came out of the opposite flank, near the thigh, a yard of steel through the great body. Rearing, the lion struck the man, bearing down the shield, his back arched; and for a moment he slaked his fury with fang and talon. But on the instant I saw another spear driven clear through his body from side to side; and as the lion turned again the bright spear blades darting toward him were flashes of white flame. The end had come.[12]

When the deed was finished, two Nandi had been wounded and the lion lay pierced by ten or more spears. The whole scene greatly impressed Roosevelt, who called the Nandi "splendid savages . . . proud, cruel, fearless."[13]

Compared to the Nandi savages, however, Roosevelt seems vastly more destructive and considerably less connected to nature. Moreover, true to Western form in Africa, the president attempted to *hire* these Nandi hunters as beaters for his *own* hunt. They weren't interested unless they could kill the animals too, so no deal was struck; but Roosevelt failed to note the contradiction between his urge to dominate these men and his desire to be free himself in an imagined prehistoric Africa.[14]

For Americans, Roosevelt's famous safari occurred in the context of similar stories of African adventure. Americans had already heard many stories of trips to Africa in which man conquered beast. The famous missionary David Livingstone had a well-publicized hand-to-claw encounter with a lion in the mid–nineteenth century. The explorer Henry Morton Stanley shot game almost daily as he searched for Livingstone ("Dr. Livingstone, I presume"), crossed the continent, and opened the Congo River to European commerce and conquest. The British author H. Rider Haggard penned widely read African adventure stories such as *King Solomon's Mines* and *Mogambo,* in which the heroes were white big-game hunters.

After Roosevelt, there were more stories and more famous Americans who linked Africa with hunting in the American mind. Dozens of Edgar Rice Burroughs's Tarzan stories inspired young men from the 1920s onward to yearn for African jungle adventures.[15] And beginning in the 1920s the safari appeared in hit films such as *King Solomon's Mines* and the extensive Tarzan series. In the 1930s Ernest Hemingway described his version of the safari in *Green Hills of Africa* (1935) and in two short stories, "The Snows of Kilimanjaro" and "The Macomber Affair" (1936). The early 1950s were banner years for safari films, with the appearance of a Hollywood remake of Haggard's *King Solomon's Mines* (1950) and *Mogambo* (1953). The MGM on-location filming of *King Solomon's Mines* in East Africa entailed the largest safari since Roosevelt's, but it was outdone by the expedition for *Mogambo*. All in all, the stars (including Gregory Peck, Joan Bennett, Susan Hayward, Ava Gardner, Grace Kelly, and Clark Gable), the big movie releases, and the stories kept the safari and its glamour in the public eye.[16]

The white hunter in Africa became a minor American genre in the same way that the cowboy in the American West became a major one. Indeed, one could argue that about the time the American West had been conquered, Africa under colonial rule was opened up to white hunters. In a sense, the African safari became analogous to the conquest of the American West, because both demonstrated the Western urge to dominate man and nature. The similarity is only partial, however, because the celebrated hunters of the American West were solitary, were not wealthy, and did not need a caravan of assistants.

The Decline of the Great White Hunting Safari

In the American popular mind, the big-game safari was associated almost entirely with the British settler colony of Kenya, even though it was possible to hunt big game in many other places. As white power in Kenya receded after World War II, the glamour of the hunting safari declined. Bartle Bull's sympathetic history of the Kenya safari notes that:

> After the war everything seemed more intense, less carefree, a little more commercial, a little less romantic. There were fewer European clients, more Americans, all with less time than the old days. Thousands of Africans, after service in the war, took a different view of colonial relationships. Ambition crept into the African attitude. Kenya's whites were less confident of the future. Authority was suspect. One could not so easily take one's staff for granted, although life in camp was less changed than in town. As the population increased and agriculture spread, wild game and unspoiled bush were always a little harder to find.[17]

Bull mourns the passing of an era; Roosevelt would have understood completely. But the decline of the safari as Bull expresses it was not caused by a lack of animals but by an end to the conditions that made it possible to maintain the colonial illusion of power. In the quotation above, Bull identifies the conditions for the successful safari: dissatisfaction with the intensity of modern life, yearning for adventure and freedom from the domestic, confidence in the future, wild nature in abundance, and the subservience of other men. As white colonialism faded and modern life crept in, the illusion could not be maintained. Kenya's anticolonial agitation in the 1950s and its independence in 1963 physically disrupted the land and drastically reduced the influence of whites. More importantly, Kenyan independence, together with the eventual independence of all tropical African countries, took a psychological toll on whites and made the safari more like "just hunting" and less like the ultimate experience of dominance over man and nature.

From the 1970s, other factors have modified the safari experience. Continued modernization and high population growth in Africa have severely threatened many habitats and forced Africans to manage wildlife ever more carefully. The Kenyan government decided in 1977 to ban hunting entirely in order to preserve what wildlife remained. Such banning has become a contentious issue, however. Hunters and many conservationists argue that, when hunting is allowed, the profits from licenses can help finance conservation and development projects, which, among other things, convince ordinary Africans that animals are their cohabitants and benefactors rather than their competitors.

The 1984 global Convention on International Trade in Endangered Species of Wild Fauna and Flora, commonly known as CITES, recognized that hunting could be an acceptable way to conserve wildlife, but its restrictions on the international movement of some kinds of coveted trophies have caused many in Africa to criticize the convention as another Western attempt to keep Africans poor by preventing them from making a living. Such arguments are heard most strongly in southern Africa, where game management is relatively efficient. From the perspective of CITES, although some countries may be able to allow hunting *and* increase their wildlife populations, many cannot. For example, because it is impossible to differentiate between trade in ivory that is legally obtained in well-managed southern African game parks and trade in poached ivory from somewhere else on the continent, it is necessary to ban trade in *all* ivory to save the elephant.[18]

Smith Hempstone, who was U.S. ambassador to Kenya from 1989 to 1993, claims that all wildlife experts in Kenya favor restoring high-fee hunting, but they will not say so publicly because "they and their organizations depend financially on American and European tree-huggers, 'green' extremists who do not want to see a drop of blood shed, even if it means extinction of a species."[19] Hempstone, a hunter, may be right. Tanzania banned hunting in the 1980s but, after finding that game was still declining and that it needed the revenue from hunting licenses for conservation and development efforts, it reopened hunting. Zimbabwe has increased its game populations since independence in 1980 by allowing Africans to use their land to attract hunters, who pay for the experience. We should note, however, that the wildlife experts in Kenya whom Hempstone criticizes also know that the high profits from hunting (or from other sorts of tourism) do not necessarily go to ordinary Africans or to nature conservation.

It is still possible to go on a hunting safari in Africa. The client will probably still have a white guide—now called a "professional hunter" instead of a "white hunter"—but otherwise the surface experience is considerably different from the classic white man's safari of past decades. Hunting parties no longer go out with huge retinues, and Land Rover vehicles substitute for porters. Camps tend to be permanent and may consist of modern lodges rather than tents. The license fees for killing are extraordinarily high.[20] Most such hunting is now done in southern Africa, where safaris are closely regulated by governments and frequently undertaken on private property. The clientele is also different. Bartle Bull writes that "for most, [today's] safari is a holiday in which stress and hardship may not be desirable. Often it is easier for a professional hunter to set standards of moderately luxurious camping and undemanding hunting, which can then be adjusted either for the really spoiled or for the serious hunter."[21] There are a few places outside of southern Africa and Tanzania where hunting is possible. In Sudan, Congo (Kinshasa), and the Central African Republic, for example, hunters can sometimes make arrangements to fly into bush camps that we would consider extremely remote. Bull writes about a hunter who was able to pursue game in southern Sudan under conditions that he considered exceptional, because the human population had fled the area in a civil war in the 1960s and 1970s, and forest regrowth had allowed game to repopulate.[22] Such "luck" in finding abundant hunting grounds outside of game preserves is increasingly rare.

The Tourist Safari: Animals in Pictures

Photography has been a part of the hunting safari since at least the 1890s. Hunters love to capture themselves on film with their trophies. But the camera also produced a whole new kind of safari experience. Already in the late 1890s, the German naturalist C. G. Schilling is credited with undertaking the first African photo safari, in German East Africa (today's

Tanzania). Despite slow film speeds, heavy cameras, and terrible flash equipment, Schilling was determined to document the wildlife that he felt was already disappearing. In a more American vein, the wildlife photography of *National Geographic* is legendary, and its first African wildlife photos appeared soon after it began publishing in 1889. Also famous is the work of an American couple, Martin and Osa Johnson, noted for their early photographs and films in Kenya from 1924 to 1928. Their extraordinarily well-equipped safari (including two airplanes) recorded several hundred thousand feet of film for research purposes and produced a commercial film, *Simba,* first viewed in the United States in 1928.

Eventually, the nature film and the camera safari became American staples. It is now difficult to find a day when there is no African nature film on cable television, and most upper-middle-class and upper-class Americans know at least one person who has been on a photo safari in Africa. At a time of growing environmental consciousness, we might conclude that the photo safari and the nature film are positive developments for Africa. In a sense they are, because Africa's rich wildlife heritage is a global treasure that not only deserves preservation for the sake of maintaining the planet but also gives Africa the positive attention that it otherwise rarely receives in the West.

A look at advertisements for television programs and tourist safaris, however, reveals that their main attraction is not an understanding of nature but a sense of adventure and exoticism. The focus of tourist safaris tends to be on picture-perfect nature, interesting experiences, mild adventure, and comfort. Tourists are frequently promised that they will experience "native" or "tribal" customs. The focus of nature programs on television tends to be on the wildness of nature and the adventure of being near it or studying it. Certain animals get photographed again and again, particularly lions and elephants. Viewers are frequently assured that the film was made in the *best* place to see a particular animal and that what they are viewing is extraordinary.

Hunters often criticize photo-tourists and nature photographers. Again, Bull summarizes the hunter's point of view as he contrasts photographers with hunters:

> The photographer is concerned with light direction, a clear view of the animal and, above all, a retainable object for the future. The hunter or stalker must be concerned with wind direction and a protected approach. He is committed to the present. You can have a brilliant day's hunting with no trophy, and even no shooting, but the photographer must have a picture. The photographer benefits from a tamed, accessible animal that will appear wild, but the hunter wants truly wild, elusive game. Much of even the best game photography is done from vehicles, itself an abandonment of the intimacy of the chase.[23]

The point here is that photography tends to turn African game preserves into giant zoos where game is managed but where *real* wildness no longer exists. A recent public television program on South Africa illustrates this point. In this TV tour, an American couple is shown on safari in Londlozi, perhaps the most expensive and exclusive of Africa's game parks. At $500 a day, visitors feel that they have the right to experience something extraordinary. They are not disappointed. Night photos reveal leopards and lions that are so used to being in a Land Rover's spotlight that they disregard humans. It is even possible to sit in an open vehicle right next to the animals, providing a sense of being out in "real" African nature. The white guide notes that this represents "many, many years of work and a lot of respect on our part."[24] This kind of intimacy is shaped deeply by human management of nature. We could indeed ask whether this *is* natural.

The Safari from a Distance

On the ground, the hunting and tourist safaris can seem attractive and rewarding. But from a distance we can see the same patterns of Western experience in Africa discussed in earlier chapters. In both types of safari, the experience of Africa and nature is mediated by Western technology, commerce, and management techniques. Visitors arrive by air, approach by four-wheel drive vehicles, shoot with modern guns and ammunition, view with binoculars and high-tech cameras, and retreat to hot-water showers, food cooked on gas-fed stoves, beds covered with mosquito netting, and telephones. They are cared for by African employees who drive, cook, track, and clean. If they become ill, they are evacuated to modern hospitals in Africa or elsewhere.

The game is wild, but managed. Hunters are part of the management plan and must follow management rules. There is danger—hunters and tourists sometimes die from animal attacks—but it is managed danger, not the same danger faced by the African farmer or herder who is more vulnerable to nature's raw edges and is less equipped.

The hunter and the tourist go to Africa for similar reasons even though they scoff at each other's motives. The hunter claims that photographers cannot perceive what nature is really like because they are observers and not participants. The photographer replies that hunters are predators who upset nature's reality. Yet both imagine they can glimpse life as it was before humans became too numerous. Both kinds of visitors intend to stay in Africa for only a few days or weeks, and in this short time they attempt to experience life in fuller measure than they can back home. Both return with bragging rights, each bringing back material tokens of their conquest: the hunter, a trophy, and the photographer, a picture.

And what about the zoo, the animal amusement park (such as Disney's Animal Kingdom), the natural history museum, or animated films (such as *The Lion King*)? What is their relationship to the safari? On the ground, of course, there is little comparison. These experiences are much farther removed from nature than the safari. The animals in the museum are dead, the zoo and amusement park are caricatures of Africa, and *The Lion King* is mythical. Yet from a distance, again, where the details are less likely to clutter our overall view, the patterns of Western behavior are similar. African animals in these other places are also mediated by Western technology, commerce, and management techniques. Each experience is heavily technologized, requiring special equipment for presentation and access. Each requires large sums of money for maintenance and most allow access only upon payment.

The zoo and the amusement park safari are extreme cases of management, with human care substituted almost entirely for nature. The natural history museum, an artifact of Roosevelt's day, is very Western in its attempt to understand through science the workings of nature. We might even say that *The Lion King* gives children an introduction to management of African wildlife, since the movie is not about nature as it really is.

And each of these genres is heavily mixed with entertainment. There is something for everyone. The more intellectual patrons might like the museum; the more active, the zoo or amusement park; the children, *The Lion King*. The advertisements for all but the movie stress both education as well as entertainment, but entertainment is in the forefront even in the museum. Like the African safari, each focuses on personal pleasure to such an extent that it mistakes African nature.

The Lion Is King

The Disney animated movie *The Lion King* seems quite apart from the African safari because it does not attempt to depict real African animals and because it is clearly a folktale for children. The movie can, however, provide insight into the experience of the safari. In the movie, African nature is described as a "circle of life," an ecological web into which all living things fit. Carnivores eat herbivores, but herbivores eat grass fertilized by dead carnivores. Nature's interconnectedness is indeed a lesson that we need to learn. However, the action in the movie takes a somewhat different direction because (1) the Disney lions have friends that African lions would normally eat (*if* they lived in the same ecosystem, which is not true of lions and mandrills); (2) survival of the strongest is emphasized, recalling the evolutionist myth that led to the idea of the Dark Continent; and (3) lions are portrayed as the managers of the whole ecosystem. In fact, the movie specifically contrasts the "managerial styles" of a good and strong lion king with those of a bad one.

Many observers have noted that humans frequently use stories about nature to understand their own lives. In Western culture, Aesop used animals to teach about sour grapes and tortoiselike persistence. Fairy tales employ wolves that eat pigs and grandmothers, and bears that do not like blondes. Nursery rhymes feature spiders that frighten girls who eat curds and whey. But just as we use nature to think about who we are, we also use who we are to think about nature. Interestingly, African animals particularly lend themselves to our self-projection because, says biologist Frank Kuserk, the "'sociality' of animals in Africa is stronger than on any other continent."[25] That is, the large animals of Africa are more social than most large animals elsewhere, and therefore it is easier to read our own society into theirs.

The Lion King projects onto nature views of what society is like. For example, hyenas are depicted as poachers and Nazis. This is bad ecological theory, since the web-of-life concept would not portray hyenas in a negative fashion but merely as part of the web. The story also implies that nature is organized like a human kingdom. This teaches top-down management rather than bottom-up ecology.

Many ecologists complain about our fixation on "charismatic megafauna," those few large animals such as lions and elephants that attract our attention. These animals are not really as important to the web of life as we imagine. Perhaps we are projecting onto these large mammals our view of ourselves as key to nature's survival. One biologist writes:

> Biotic diversity is not linked to the distribution of elephants, rhinos, and other so-called charismatic megaherbivores. The massive investment in conservation campaigns directed at these species does more for the souls of the donors and the egos of the elephant experts than it does for biotic diversity, which is centered on less exciting communities of montane forests, Mediterranean heathlands, wetlands, lakes, and rivers.[26]

Biologists sometimes participate in this misdirection of attention, because they hope that attempts to save charismatic animals will lead us to save the habitats on which they depend.

Projecting our views on nature is common. For example, in the opening chapters of Genesis, nature is a paradisiacal garden (originally nature was in harmony), but because of human sin it became a place where humans had to toil, and then it became an ark necessitating management (was Noah the first park ranger?). Another common view is that civilization and nature are separate and that nature is something we can either "get back to" or "escape from." Or, Marshall Sahlins, an anthropologist, believes that we frequently impose on nature our view that capitalism is the social system most in tune with nature. For this reason, we tend to see nature itself as a large capitalist society where survival, profit, and management are the goals. We might say that *The Lion King* fits Sahlins's pattern.[27]

A safari rarely lasts more than a few days or weeks, and it would be hard to argue that in this short amount of time a tourist could learn much that is intimate about nature. If we want to learn about how nature operates, we would probably do better spending more quality time with nature in our own backyards. Therefore, it is quite likely that the tourist to Africa, and even the hunter, will interpret African nature based on preconceived notions. The safari confirms what we already know. We may feel that we are seeing the world as it was 10,000 years ago at the end of the Paleolithic era. We may feel that we are witnessing the balance of nature. We may have the illusion that we have momentarily become a part of nature. We may read the big predators as proof that nature operates in a "survival of the fittest" mode (a lion is a capitalist entrepreneur). We may see the lion as a manager as in *The Lion King,* and we may see our commanding position in the food chain as proof that nature is arranged hierarchically rather than in a web. We may even believe that we are seeing the last remnants of true nature, a leftover from before human colonization of the planet.[28]

The whole safari experience seems to be much more about ourselves than an attempt to learn about nature. If we take account of the larger structure of the experience—who can afford to go, how they get there, what they do, what they focus on, and what they think—we can see that it is part of the whole Western pattern of experiencing the world. And as such, it reconfirms what we already believe about Africa, as do zoos, natural history museums, animal amusement parks, nature TV, and even *The Lion King*.

Hunting Africa

My first reaction to my hunter student Richard was that, in his pursuit of a very personal and Western goal, he was going to participate in the Western domination of Africa. Even if killing a charging Cape buffalo is the ultimate experience of being alive, which I doubt, it is clear that we should not necessarily do it at Africa's or nature's expense. Moreover, the African hunting safari is clearly a Western experience, not a universal one, and in its contemporary form it still frequently mimics the efforts of Roosevelt's safari to gain dominion over Africans and animals.

In further investigating this question, however, I have come to a deeper appreciation of Richard's position as a hunter. Hunters get one thing right that many tourists seem to miss. They know that it is very dangerous to read our view of the structure of reality into nature. The Cape buffalo will kill the hunter who misreads nature. We need to "become part of nature" in order to survive. A short hunting safari in Africa cannot suffice to learn about African nature, but the impulse to be *in and of* nature seems correct. At the heart of the matter is the necessity not to be a spectator and not to turn nature into an object.

These ideas can be extended to the way safaris treat Africans. Whether for hunting, photography, or just sight-seeing, the modern safari tends to consider Africans as objects rather than as people. Although individual Africans may profit from the jobs and fees that result from safaris, Africans as people are only ancillary to the enterprise. Tourists and hunters arrive in Nairobi, Harare, Gaborone, or Johannesburg and get out of town to the game parks as quickly as possible. They interact with Africans only as employees: drivers, trackers, cooks, waiters, maids, and gift-shop salespersons. If there is contact with African culture, it is mostly through idealized re-creations of the African past in the form of dances, art, food, and "ritual."

And so there are parallels between the ways we tend to see African animals and how we view African people. Real African animals and real African people are not allowed to interfere with the tourist illusion of how nature and society ought to be. They do not hit us full in the face, causing us to question our relationships with African animals or people. In "safari Africa" we do not get involved with either animals or people in ways that challenge us to become partners on a shared planet.

In its 1997 Christmas catalog, Abercrombie and Fitch provides some suggestions for customers who want exotic places in which to use their adventure clothing. Presumably, if you can afford their clothing, you can at least afford to dream of such a trip. One of the trips suggested is a safari in Namibia:

> Namibia: A tame take on Africa. A trek through deepest, darkest Africa doesn't necessarily mean a mandatory case of diarrhea. For wildlife, food, and overall infrastructure at its most civilized, opt for Namibia over Kenya this Christmas. A former German colony and province of South Africa, Namibia is like an African state managed by the Swiss. Elephants appear on demand, baboons seem almost obedient, and the state parks are among the best on the continent.[29]

Abercrombie and Fitch recommends an exotic, entertaining experience that can be enjoyed without having to interact with stereotypical Africa. Or, rather, customers are promised that they *can* experience stereotypical "darkest Africa" without having to bear any pain. This is an improved Africa, one with well-managed animals and Africans. Of course, if you take such a safari, you will never be able to tell whether your stereotypes about Africa or animals had much basis in fact. You will likely understand *neither* Africa's sameness *nor* its difference.

10

Africa in Ads

This chapter presents a few examples of the way Africa is portrayed in print advertising. Africa also appears in many other places in popular culture, as we saw in Chapter 2, but print ads provide an easily accessible source to examine. I collected the ads reproduced below, as well as others, over only a few months' time. I had the help of a student and her mother, but none of us made any special effort looking for the ads. We found them in the magazines we subscribe to or read in doctors' offices. Because these were relatively easy to find, I presume that similar ads exist in many of the magazines that Americans read.

Africa is, of course, only one of the subjects that ad agencies treat in stereotypical ways. Indeed, advertising in general thrives on its ability to represent our culture's fantasies and myths about the world. Advertising is a dreamland where our hopes, fears, and illusions about reality and unreality appear. It is a place where we can look into the corners of the American mind.

The ads run by big corporations frequently aim to create name recognition or a positive image for the company or its products. Thus, an ad might only be trying to get our attention so we will read the company's name. Presumably, the next time we see the product and the name together we will take more interest because we already know the name. Or, an ad may evoke a certain emotion that the company wants us to feel when we see its name or its product.

The ad agency presumes that we do not read every ad and that we might only glimpse its ad in passing. Therefore, the ad must "grab" us, if only for a fraction of a second. The most universal subjects that will grab our attention are sex, children, and animals. Perhaps we are biologically programmed to respond to these subjects. Africa also seems to attract our eye, and often it is combined with sex, children, or animals.

Africa also conveys messages that enhance some companies' images. Look at the following ads and ask yourself what messages they convey.

How do these messages illustrate the ways we "use Africa to think with"? What is being said by or about Africa? Is it stereotypical? Does it promote a better understanding of Africa?

You might try to undertake your own analysis before you read the comments that accompany each ad. Sarah Soden (SS), the student mentioned above who helped locate these ads, also participated in writing commentaries on some of them.

THERE'S NO EASIER WAY TO GET FROM PEORIA TO PRETORIA.
Just dial 1 800 CALL ATT® and get from anywhere in the U.S. to anywhere in the world. You can charge your calls on MasterCard®, American Express®, Diners Club® or your AT&T Calling Card. AT&T makes international calling this easy.
AND
1·800 call ATT
GETS YOU FROM THE U.S. TO THE WORLD.
AT&T

Photo 1

Photo 2

Always wear your seat belt. Jeep is a registered trademark of Chrysler Corporation.
IF YOU CAN READ THIS
YOUR JEEP IS TOO CLOSE
Jeep
THERE'S ONLY ONE
If you want to get this close to nature, there's really only one way to do it. Drive a legendary Jeep 4x4.
For more information, call 1-800-925-JEEP or visit http://www.jeepunpaved.com on the Internet.

Photo 3

THE BEST PLACE TO SLEEP
Sears O'Pedic
When you're looking for the best place to sleep, just look for a Sears-O-Pedic ComfortCrafted™ mattress. Lie down on it. Feel the firm, yet gentle way it supports you in just the right places.
And you'll rest easier for years to come knowing that ComfortCrafted mattresses feature the only 25-year warranty in the world. Ask your salesperson for details.
Try a Sears-O-Pedic ComfortCrafted mattress for yourself at the Homelife Furniture Store from Sears. You won't find the best place to sleep anyplace else.
SEARS
HOMELIFE
FURNITURE STORE

Photo 4

The Franklin Institute Science Museum
SCHOOL FIELD TRIP
PLANNER
Spring 1996 • PreK-12
Special Exhibit
Ford Motor Company Presents
AFRICA
Your admission includes:
• Four floors of interactive exhibits
• Special exhibit...Ford Motor Company Presents Africa in the Mandell Center
• Free demonstrations
Plus...
Add an Omni or Planetarium show for one low group admission price
Winter Savings: Save $2 per student February 16 – March 22 • Details see page 7
Reservations: 215.448.1201

Photo 5

THE CIVILIZED WAY TO ANSWER
The Call of the Wild...
ON SAFARI IN AFRICA
BY PRIVATE LUXURY JET AND THE LEGENDARY BLUE TRAIN
South Africa • Zimbabwe • Botswana
Tanzania • Kenya • Morocco
Join us on our three-week African safari with peak-season departure: March 2, 1999.
HERE'S WHAT WE OFFER:
THE BIG PLANE
Travel from the U.S. and throughout your trip in our privately chartered L1011 wide-body jet. Its normal 362-seat configuration has been reduced to 83 extra-spacious, all first-class sleeper seats.
THE SMALL PLANES
Fly to the heart of remote game reserves via chartered small twin-engine aircraft. These versatile planes eliminate hours of travel on dusty roads, allow more time for game viewing and provide exceptional panoramic views.
THE TRAIN
Experience an overland rail journey aboard our exclusively chartered Blue Train, regarded as the height of five-star luxury train travel. Elegant passenger salon cars, dining and comfortable sleeper accommodations.
HOTELS, GAME LODGES AND TENTED CAMPS
Stay at the very best, like Cape Town's Mount Nelson Hotel, the classic Victoria Falls Hotel and La Mamounia in Marrakech. Game lodges such as Botswana's Chobe Game Lodge and Tanzania's Ngorongoro Serena Lodge. And several nights in a classic tented camp, the exclusively reserved Kichwa Tembo in Kenya's magnificent Masai Mara.
SPECIAL EVENTS
Savor Africa's most spectacular experiences: flightseeing over Victoria Falls and the Cape of Good Hope; wild-game viewing by hot-air balloon; sunset cruises on the Chobe and Zambezi rivers; exclusive receptions.
All-Inclusive Price
$36,800 per person, double occupancy
Single Supplement: $3,400
INTRAV PRIVATE JET ADVENTURES
Beyond First Class
For full details, call (800) 964-0500, or contact your travel agent.

Photo 6

Photo 7

STANLEY
PLODDED THROUGH
THE EQUATORIAL JUNGLE
RISKING malaria,
VENOMOUS SPIDERS
& ANKLE-BITING
PYGMIES JUST FOR THE
face-to-face GREETING.
"DR. LIVINGSTONE
I PRESUME?"
WOULDN'T
you RATHER BE
AT home?
VIDEO CONFERENCING
Presumably you would. Which is why Packard Bell Platinum™ series computers come equipped for video conferencing. Just add a video conferencing camera or camcorder and have face-to-face conversations via telephone or the Internet. The computers are powered with the Intel® Pentium processor and come with built-in, cable-ready TV, full 3-D graphics, Direct Internet Access and state-of-the-art hardware and software enhancements. So you can keep in touch with friends and colleagues in even the most remote corners of the world. All from the comfort of your home. Visit us at http://www.packardbell.com
intel inside pentium
Packard Bell
the world's #1 selling home computer

Photo 8

The sparkle from the exquisite yellow diamond startled the
sleeping lions, waking them. Cool and collected, our man reached for the
tranquilizer gun. Your escape from the jungle could be
far more treacherous. The tunnel or the bridge?
From our extraordinary collection of natural
fancy color diamonds comes this rare 11 carat beauty.
$195,000. For information call 212-758-6660.
fortunoff
Fifth Avenue
Westbury
Wayne
Woodbridge
Paramus

Photo 9

you either have it or you don't
Those who appreciate quality enjoy it responsibly

Photo 10

Phone-y Africans?[1]

Photo 1: The operative theme behind this ad is that "Peoria" and "Pretoria" happened to sound nice together. The fact that Pretoria is pictured in a radically different way than it exists in reality seems beside the point to the ad executives. It sounds good, and they are working on the assumption that the American audience will associate Pretoria with Africa. The executives also seem to be banking on the fact that we will view the ad through our preconceptions about rural Africa. Africa is *very* far away and *still* AT&T reaches it.

Peoria is also treated stereotypically. We could bet that most of its residents have never been near a cow. The ad is right, however, in associating the children with both the town and the telephone. These kids have certainly been to Peoria and they have certainly used a telephone. By contrast, Pretoria is so much farther from our consciousness that it's easy to assume that the reader will accept an even greater misrepresentation. Pretoria is a modern South African city populated by urbanites who are mostly white. The African children are *not* from Pretoria and probably have never been there. Depicting Pretoria as grassland populated by rural Africans makes AT&T look like it's wired to serve every rural professional and his cowphone worldwide. In reality, however, the kids in the Pretoria picture do not have access to the phones or other modern tools and conveniences of either Peoria or Pretoria, because of an oppressive history that is not mentioned.

So the big question is whether the ad executives created this piece with or without direct or researched knowledge of Pretoria. Did they just assume what Pretoria is like and build an ad campaign around it? Or did they intentionally distort Africa to serve their advertising purpose? What do you think?—*SS*

Smells Like Africa[2]

Photo 2: Combine a chic model, scummy hair, dirty clothes, and a leopard cub and what do you get? According to Ralph Lauren, you get a hot new fragrance for men. In the same vein as selling cars and beer by surrounding them with scantily clad women, the ad seems to say, "Apply this cologne and you will be a rugged, studly man braving the wilds of Africa, able to seduce women and tame native wildlife." But is this really what the ad conveys? Is it also an expression of neocolonial domination?—*SS*

Africa Disturbed[3]

Photo 3: Unlike the other elephant ad in this chapter, this Jeep ad actually makes a connection between Africa and the product. The small print on a bright yellow sign on the elephant's rump says, "If you can read this your Jeep is too close." Ha Ha. But how many people will actually drive their Jeep in an African game park or anywhere in the wilds? The ad tells us that "If you want to get this close to nature, there's really only one way to do it. Drive a legendary Jeep 4x4." In fact, there are few Jeeps in Africa (most safari vehicles are made by competitors), and people shouldn't be ruining the land with their vehicles. Besides, who wants to visit a game park that is so overmanaged that you can drive right up behind elephants bearing bumper stickers? And does the fact that this ad was on the back cover of *National Geographic* imply a scientific endorsement of disturbing animals with your Jeep?—*SS/CK*

An African Salesbeast[4]

Photo 4: So you're mattress shopping. Maybe you're even driving to Sears in your Jeep. Are you thinking about elephants at any point? No? Is there *any* connection between mattresses and elephants? No. And Sears, in all honesty, doesn't even try to make a connection. Sears-O-Pedic is announced as "the best place to sleep," but nothing in the ad implies that you should sleep on the mattress where it is. The animal is merely a prop holding the company's product. Why an elephant? Because Africa attracts our attention. Is this a useful conveyance?—*SS/CK*

Africa Is History, Naturally[5]

Photo 5: In 1996, the Franklin Institute Science Museum in Philadelphia hosted a temporary exhibition on Africa prepared by the Field Museum in Chicago. The exhibition was excellent, but it illustrates a problem in presenting Africa to American audiences. That is, although the Africa of our imagination and our interest is both wild and "traditional," today's Africa is more than 35 percent urban, and all Africans are part of the modern world.

The cover of this teacher's guide for school trips to the Franklin Institute gives no hint of the modern African world except for the nearly invisible out-of-date map of Africa that serves as a background. But it does provide many vivid symbols of a wild and rural Africa. The problem is not that there is no wildness and tradition in modern Africa, but that there is much more than these. Africa's wildness and tradition exist in a modern and global context. How will teachers learn to help students put Africa into perspective?

Natural history museums were established in the nineteenth century during the era of evolutionism. In addition to exhibits on the material universe, they undertook the study of so-called primitive peoples because these peoples were considered more a part of nature than of civilization. Today's natural history curators are quite aware of the problems posed by these older notions, yet they are to some degree prisoners of public expectations and of their own collections of objects, which were amassed in another era and which do not accurately represent modern Africa.

What images could be included to balance those already on this cover?—*CK*

Lifestyles of the Rich and Disgusting[6]

Photo 6: "The Civilized Way to Answer the Call of the Wild" is how Intrav Private Jet Adventures bills its African safaris. By Intrav's estimate, true civilization in Africa costs about $1,750 per person per day, or a grand total of almost $37,000 per person for three weeks. You'll pay more if you want single-occupancy lodging.

But with luxury transport and grand accommodations, how realistic an experience do such truly civilized people have? Ironically, they are saved from "dusty roads" but are privileged to spend several nights in a "classic tented camp"—"Ah, my dear, do you suppose they'll provide real water?"

The best part of the trip is that travelers will not have to actually experience Africa as Africans do, or perhaps even deal with Africa at all. The ad implies that "civilized" means a disconnection from most human reality. It also implies that Africa is *un*civilized. Fortunately, perhaps, travelers won't connect much with nature either, because according to the ad they will only "view" wildness.

This ad would be completely disgusting if it did not remind us that safari experiences costing vastly less also attempt to isolate travelers from Africans and unite them with an idealized nature. Are backpackers, students, or anyone else who travels economy class by choice or necessity considered as uncivilized as Africans?—*SS/CK*

The Spirit of Africa[7]

Photo 7: In the context of Jehovah's Witnesses, it makes perfect sense to question whether one ought to contact the spirit realm without Jesus as a guide. But to pick an African as the symbol of unholy contact with spirits perpetuates a stereotype among the worldwide readers of the nearly 16 million copies printed of this issue of *Awake!* The editor could have used an American or European practitioner of spirit possession, except that a Westerner would not have been so easily recognizable as such. The same mental associations do not apply. African systems of spirit contact are rarely so negative or dramatic as depicted here; they have in fact over time been beneficial for the well-being of hundreds of African societies. Moreover, Africans are aware that spirits and spirit practitioners can sometimes be harmful, and they take measures to protect themselves. In any case, Africa is hardly a continent of healers and diviners, because Christians and Muslims each outnumber the so-called traditionalists.

We could, of course, dismiss this as "just a religious tract," adding "what would you expect?" It illustrates, however, one way that stereotypical images of Africa are perpetuated.—*CK*

Don't Go There[8]

Photo 8: So there you are, innocently flipping through a magazine, when you're confronted with this ad, which you are sure, just sure, is wrong. It's a cute idea, but should they really have said "ankle-biting Pygmies"? Couldn't they have thought of something else? And what about the jungle, the disease, the ants, and the spiders? Packard Bell has unashamedly recreated the Dark Continent (with Latin American tarantulas!). But this Dark Continent is not in the past. It's still out there to frighten us, says Packard Bell.

"Wouldn't *you* rather be at *home?*" Is Packard Bell telling us that we can experience nothing and still know everything? Or perhaps the message is that we should only go places where there's a nice, safe, cushy hotel waiting at the end of the road, chocolates on the pillow preferred. With this attitude toward the world, is it any wonder that American interest in and knowledge of global affairs is at a low?[9]—*SS/CK*

Buying African Cheese[10]

Photo 9: In this ad, the diamond and Africa jump out at you, but the connection between the two is obscure. You have to read carefully the text at the top of the page. The sparkle of a man's diamond awakens ferocious sleeping lions in the African jungle, but he is quick-witted enough to escape. Presumably—the connection isn't explicit—if you buy the same diamond, it will awaken New York lions that are even more ferocious than the African ones. How adventuresome! And you, too, will get to feel that you have escaped from danger because, when compared to savage urban civilization, Africa is a picnic. Curiously, the message combines *both* Dark Continent and Wise Africa myths. Africa is bad, but not as bad as New York City.

Fortunoff probably thought quite a bit about how it could sell a rock like this to men. Usually, we associate diamond rings with women. But by combining the ring with a four-wheel-drive vehicle and Africa, its macho quotient is raised a few notches. If you buy this diamond, you are virile, because it will prove that you can provoke both lions and men and survive.

By the way, the mountain is Mount Kilimanjaro in Tanzania, and there are no "jungles" in the vicinity. The vehicle and ring are obviously added by computer, and the story is patently artificial. This ad is cheesy. Who "buys" this stuff, anyway?—*CK*

The Ads Must Be Crazy[11]

Photo 10: This ad is presumably a reference to *The Gods Must Be Crazy*, a movie that many Americans have seen. The plot turns on an empty Coke bottle that is tossed carelessly out of a small plane. The bottle lands in the camp of a small band of San, hunter-gatherers who live on the edges of the Kalahari Desert in southern Africa. The San are portrayed as stereotypical hunter-gatherers who are not used to having possessions. The Coke bottle causes dissension in the group over who will get to use it and for what. So, one man decides to throw it into the sea. Because the sea is a long way off, there is plenty of time for adventure and for showing many, many more stereotypes about Africa. This low-budget film is clever and funny (and mildly racist and strongly stereotyping) and has become a minor hit among video-store patrons.

The Chivas Regal ad seems to evoke the moment when the Coke bottle falls to earth and the movie begins. But what is the point? Does this ad imply that Africans should get rid of their full bottles of Chivas Regal? Will the bottle cause Africans trouble as the Coke bottle does in the movie? Surely these couldn't be the messages that Chivas Regal wishes to convey, could they? But perhaps, in fact, you shouldn't be thinking so hard. There *is* no point here except that you notice the product. Africa just helps you think about buying alcohol.

Part Four

New Directions

11

Race and Culture: The Same and the Other

Until only a few decades ago, the idea prevailed in Europe and America that some humans were more biologically evolved than others. The resulting racism, Dark Continent stereotypes, and evolutionism have been major themes of this book. Today, most Americans believe or want to believe that others are biologically the same as we are, yet few can explain the origins or significance of obvious differences among people and cultures. How is it that people can be so different and still be the same? We frequently see others doing such strange things that it is difficult for us to imagine that we all have the same basic biology.

Since this book deals with American attitudes toward a continent about which questions of race and culture have been prominent, it is important to discuss the underlying nature of our differences. What follows is not a detailed study but some ideas about directions we can pursue.

Race

When it comes to facts about the nature of race, much remains unclear. Scientists don't know for sure when or how races developed, and they are not entirely sure why. Nor can they prove that race plays no role in who we are. But science is like that. Whereas racism begins with belief, science begins with questions and doubt. Our best scientific knowledge with regard to the origins of modern races presumes that they developed over the past 100,000 years, as modern humans developed. Strong evidence suggests that *Homo sapiens* emerged first in Africa and then spread across the world, gradually differentiating into today's "races." This "Out of Africa" hypothesis, as it is called, is also known as the "Eve" hypothesis because the first genetic evidence supporting it came from the mitochondrial DNA of females.[1] We are unsure whether our early African ancestors replaced existing populations in Europe and Asia or whether they mixed with them, but new genetic evidence from China suggests that the different Asian physical types developed only in the past 60,000 years and out of a common center. This is consistent with the idea that all races came relatively recently from Africa.[2] But our original African ancestors were not the "blacks" we associate with sub-Saharan Africa today. Four thousand years ago, the so-called black people occupied only portions of West Africa, and the rest of the continent was inhabited by others. The present geographical distribution of blacks throughout sub-Saharan Africa has been very recent. Blacks are an offshoot of our early ancestors, just as whites and other peoples are. Limited evidence suggests that our early common ancestors were dark skinned but not black.

Why did we eventually differentiate into "races"? Evolutionary theory proposes that differentiation occurs for adaptive reasons, but it also notes that many genetic traits are adaptive neutral, meaning that they are neither particularly adaptive nor maladaptive. Whether adaptive-neutral traits persist or change is not important for the survival of a species, at least in the short run. Sometimes it is difficult to know whether a trait such as skin color is adaptive and, if it is, what its function is. Our best guess is that skin color is an adaptive trait, a result of biological reaction to the sun. Darker skin seems to protect us against skin cancer at the sun-drenched equator whereas lighter skin allows us to synthesize sufficient vitamin D closer to the sun-poor poles and thus protect ourselves from rickets, a potentially fatal bone disease. The fact that Eskimos, Inuits, and others living in the far north are darker than Scandinavians does not contradict this theory, because the former migrated from southern parts of Asia in relatively recent times and have presumably sustained themselves in the reduced sunlight by eating a fish diet rich in vitamin D.

In any case, skin color is not much of an indication of what we are. First of all, when we say that we "see" a particular skin color, we don't usually see what is in nature, but rather what our culture says is there. "Black" skin, for example, ranges from blue-black to all shades of brown to almost white, and so-called blacks display a wide variety of physical types. "White" skin ranges from white to pink, orange, and olive, and, likewise, "whites" include a whole range of body types. Moreover, someone who is considered black in the United States might be considered white in another culture. In fact, our whole system of race classification—Caucasoid, Mongoloid, Negroid, Pygmoid, and so forth—is a cultural artifact of the era in which Europeans were attempting to substantiate their own racial superiority.[3] Our limited categories literally blind us to the infinite differences within races and to the similarities across races.

If we actually make maps of different genetic factors, they rarely correspond to the races as we know them. Instead, our genetic traits, most of which are invisible, cross racial lines and are scattered among seemingly homogeneous populations. In short, the maps are quite jumbled.[4] Moreover, because of recent advances in molecular genetics, we have learned that the average genetic differences among individuals of different "races" are actually smaller than the average differences among individuals within the same race or even ethnic group. Here is one summary of our genetic similarities and differences:

> On average there's .2 percent difference in genetic material between any two randomly chosen people on Earth. Of that diversity, 85 percent will be found within any local group of people—say, between you and your neighbor. More than half (9 percent) of the remaining 15 percent will be represented by differences between ethnic and linguistic groups within a given race (for example, between Italians and French). Only 6 percent represents differences between races (for example, between Europeans and Asians). And remember—that's 6 percent of .2 percent. In other words, race accounts for only a minuscule .012 percent difference in our genetic material.[5]

To put it another way, the concept of race simply doesn't provide very much that is scientifically useful to us as we live our daily lives. Race helps *a little* in understanding why some individuals have certain physical features or are susceptible to certain diseases. But differences in most human traits can be more easily explained by one's family genetics and environment than by race. Thus race as we know it is "skin deep," a cultural myth and not a biological reality. Indeed, we are all Africans under our skin.

Given our obsession with race, it is ironic that genes account more for our sameness than for our difference. And our sameness is vast. One person who has spent his life thinking about human sameness, human behaviorist Desmond Morris, asks what similar traits the human animal displays worldwide. In his now-classic book *The Naked Ape,* Morris includes chapters on sex, child rearing, exploration, fighting, feeding, and comfort that provide ample evidence of the many fundamental traits shared by all humans.[6] His documentary television series *The Human Animal* covers similar topics and enjoys frequent reruns.[7] Morris's research demonstrates that our common human traits, including our attachment to groups (whether based on our race, our clan, or our friends), must certainly be a result of common biology.

Those who have attempted to test whether different races have different mental abilities have always failed to obtain meaningful results. What is required is a test that takes into account a person's physical and cultural environment, and such a test has yet to be devised. The problem is that humans are not only biological animals in the sense that Desmond Morris has described but they are also individually affected by environment (for example, nutrition and disease); history (for example, wars, slavery, and colonialism); and culture (for example, child-rearing practices and preferred kinds of logic). In addition, there are the idiosyncrasies of one's individual family and community to take into account. For these reasons, it would be virtually impossible to devise an intelligence test that would measure fairly across races. To do so would require an analysis that would take account of different environments, histories, cultures, and families. The task would be infinitely complex.

We have come to make two modern assumptions about human reality. First, because we know that there is more genetic difference among individuals of the same race than among individuals of different races, we assume that race is more a cultural than a biological construct. In other words, race does not really exist as a biological category. Second, because there is no way to test for mental differences, we assume that all humans operate with the same basic capacities. As far as I know, today's science can provide no absolute proof that these two assumptions are correct. Remember, however, that scientific inquiry begins with doubt, questioning its hypotheses. In the social sphere, it seems far safer to rely on the assumption of sameness, because this offers a way out of our dangerous racial perspectives, than to sink into the contentiousness of racial difference.

This is why those who study other cultures have generally concluded that there is no such thing as a primitive human being or even a primitive human culture. We assume that minds of similar capacity are working in all societies to solve the problems of life, and that the answers these minds arrive at will be similarly effective. On the other hand—and this is the hard part—we must not fall into the trap of believing that once we all recognize our biological sameness we will easily get along. It's a small world, but it is nonetheless a world marked by significant differences among cultures and peoples. We must take into account the influences of environment, history, and, most importantly, culture.

Culture

Other animals operate on instincts more than we do; our capacity for thinking and learning—that is, our ability to supplement and overcome our instincts through culture—is much greater than theirs. We rightly take pride in our ability to learn practically anything. Indeed, our cultural capacity is so great and so adaptive that, even though we are outclassed in terms of speed, agility, and strength by many of our competitors, we have colonized the entire globe and are reaching for the universe.

Our great capacity for culture depends on a number of our physical abilities including speech, bipedalism, and finely coordinated hands. Our cultural capacity is also shaped by our instincts, which encourage us, for example, to share with each other and live in groups. Some version of the golden rule is perhaps necessary in any human culture, but if we were not also programmed to cooperate, society as we know it would not be possible.

When it comes to culture, our crowning glory—literally—is our brains. Our capacity for culture is only possible because of two mental traits: thought and memory. Thinking is usually regarded as the more important of the two, because it helps us determine what works in a specific situation and gives us our prized imagination and sense of freedom. Chris Stringer and Robin McKie write that the key to the evolution of modern humans was our development of new ways of thinking. They note that "to a Neanderthal, a cave bear was a cave bear. To a modern human, it was not only a threat, or possibly a source of food, it was a god, an ancestor, and who knows what else."[8] The modern humans who emerged 40,000 to 60,000 years ago marked the beginning of a more "fluid and generalized" ability to think.[9] With our more developed brains, we could use ideas in one intellectual domain to think about ideas in another. We could eventually turn our hunting-and-gathering instincts toward job searching or grocery shopping. And we could turn our ability to keep track of what was going on among our neighbors toward storytelling, novel writing, and history writing. We could learn to use art, music, and religion to comment on who we are and how we want to live.

The other trait that is particularly significant in the development of human culture is memory, which deserves more attention if we are to understand the problems of race and culture. Each of us has complained that we cannot remember well, but in fact our whole world is largely created by memory. Let me give two simple examples. In Kenya, light switches move up for off and down for on, which is the opposite of switches in the United States. In Kenya, when I go to turn on a light I must stop and think. And thinking seems inappropriate and unnatural when it comes to a task that I do automatically all the time. I get momentarily confused and then annoyed. Another example is that cars in Kenya travel on the left. When I am a passenger in Kenya, I am sitting on the side of the car where I would be driving in the United States, but I have no steering wheel or brake pedal. Roads are narrow, cars pass frequently, and they come straight toward me. I am terrified. If I were to drive in Kenya, my body would take months to adjust to the point where I could trust my reflexes in the same way I do when driving in the United States.

These minor examples illustrate how dependent we are on memory. What would happen if we had no memory? What if we had to think about every small task we face such as how to brush our teeth, put on our clothes, get our breakfast, or cross a street? We would become exhausted from thinking or, more likely, we wouldn't even be able to think because we wouldn't remember what a toothbrush, or a shoe, or a street was. And what would happen if those around us were similarly incapacitated and forgetfully drove on the "wrong" side of the road?

It is not just in our daily actions that memory constructs our world. Humans learn their religion and develop their ideas through memory. We couldn't deal with the natural world without our memory. The societies we grow up in construct whole fields of memories that tell us what the world is and what it means. Although you might think that a tree is a tree, the ways trees are used and what trees mean differ from one *memory system* to the next, that is from one *culture* to the next. Our agriculture, our industry, our science all rely on our cultural memory systems. Even such fundamentals as our logical and emotional behavior are deeply shaped by memory, so that different cultures prefer different behaviors. And when we encounter something new, we tend to reach into our memories to find an analogy or metaphor that will allow us to categorize the new experience.

When it comes to action, the kind of memory we call *habit* is particularly important. Thankfully, most of our daily activities—turning on lights, crossing streets, brushing teeth—are governed by habit, so we can use our thinking ability to work on new ideas. And happily, people around us have similar habits, so we can predict ahead of time, more or less, what they are going to do. Habit is, in a sense, a cultural equivalent of instinct that allows humans to get along with each other, to build different worlds, and to adapt to many different kinds of environments. The capacity for habit helps us feel comfortable in our world. Indeed, we talk about our habits as "second nature," thoughts and actions we have learned so well that they feel instinctive.

But what happens when we meet a person or a whole society with different memories and habits? When humans are faced with the work of trying to deal with such difference, they try to make sense of it on several levels. Our conscious minds may think, "These people are OK. They are different only because they have learned different ways to look at the world. They have a different culture." But on an unconscious level our minds notice that we are not comfortable, that our habits are unable to keep us safe, and that every signal given by others has to be consciously evaluated. We feel threatened because even our smallest acts don't have the same results they do when we are with "our own kind."

This threat is not just a threat to our ideas, however. It is actually felt as a threat to our physical body because we have *become* our habits. In other words, our culture has come to feel *natural* even though it is learned. This is why living in or dealing with an unfamiliar culture commonly produces "culture shock," a physical sense of being unsettled and a desire to withdraw. This happens even to those who consciously want to be in the new culture. Life seems *un*natural and demands more thinking than we can tolerate, even leading some to fall into depression.

At this point, we experience a critical moment. If we are not aware of what is actually happening, we might wrongly conclude, consciously or unconsciously, that the other culture or persons actually have a different nature from ourselves because they belong to a different race or because they are witches, or animals, or monsters, or aliens. Or, we might conclude that others need us to show them how to act more naturally, more like we do. We even have similar responses to people in our *own* culture if we perceive that they are much different from us or if we have to interact intensely with them. Numerous problems occur, for example, when two people get married and neither has had much experience with the other's gender, subculture, family, or personality type. After an initial euphoria, the differences begin to cause wear and tear on the relationship.

On Being Human

We are not instinctively equipped to handle a great deal of difference even if we are naturally curious about how others live. Most of us do not mind being spectators of difference (via movies, novels, gossip columns, travel, and so on), but we do not wish to actually experience too much of it. Our instincts evolved to help us live in small communities, and most of us will subconsciously try to create for ourselves small circles of family and friends that make up a comfortable band or clan. One researcher estimates that the ideal biological size for human communities is about 150 people.[10] We tend "naturally" to be clannish (or tribal, or race-oriented, or national, or whatever).

We must somehow learn to deal with difference if we are going to survive in the world that is growing up around us. Fortunately, a significant feature of human beings is that our instincts are relatively weak, and through thinking and the influence of culture they can be channeled in new directions and even be overcome. When survival demands it, our cultural ability allows us to develop a "second nature" to deal with new environments. My presumption is that we will be happier and safer if we do not just *think* about how to deal with difference but actually develop the habit, the *memory,* of successful negotiations of otherness.

Learning to deal with difference can begin at a distance through reading, watching television, eating at restaurants, attending classes, and engaging in other experiences that are relatively easy to accept. But the deepest explorations necessitate placing ourselves in situations where we must physically experience the fact that others who also belong to the human race see the world in significantly different ways than we do. The first step is to teach our conscious minds what I discussed above—that for humans, culture becomes habit and habit feels natural even if it is not. The second step is to teach our unconscious minds, our memories, and our bodies to recognize the same thing. This second step is more difficult, and we may need to put ourselves in potentially painful situations to give our bodies the chance to adjust to difference.

Some people are born with little fear of cultural difference, and some families, communities, and societies are better at teaching members how to cope with and enjoy such difference. Most of us, however, have to learn about difference for ourselves. I was fortunate to learn at a young age that at least one kind of cultural difference was good, because my mother's parents were recent immigrants and spoke American English with a thick foreign accent. I was also lucky that my family was not openly racist, although I remember that they associated certain traits with certain races. It was not until I was in college, however, that I spoke in any seriousness with a person from another American subculture or from another world culture. Because I wanted to experience the world, I volunteered to room with a "foreign" student, as international students were called at that time. Life as a freshman with an older African roommate was rocky, to say the least. I recall that my roommate's assessment of my level of awareness was a sighing, "You just don't know!" He was right; I didn't. By the time I graduated, I was better at negotiating difference, but I felt the shock of difference again when I lived in Africa after some graduate study. For weeks after my arrival in Congo, where everyone was black, I felt *very* white, like a thousand-watt lightbulb.

There is an often-quoted Rogers and Hammerstein lyric from the musical *South Pacific* that says, "You've got to be carefully taught to hate." The song implies that those who are not taught to hate will naturally like others. My own experience shows that this view is much too simplistic. We also need to be trained to deal with and appreciate difference. The training begins at day care centers with feelings of separation and even panic, an early experience of culture shock. It continues as we go to school and eventually leave home—perhaps to college, to a job, or to marriage. All of this separation, this experience with difference, may be interpreted as pleasurable and exciting, but it is usually painful, too. Fortunately, most of us succeed in becoming full members of our communities, and, in doing so, we also become more comfortable with ourselves living in the wider world and interacting with it.

Americans are being asked to go even further in accepting difference as we mix with each other in our neighborhoods, organizations, and jobs and as our society is increasingly entwined in the affairs of other societies. But evidence suggests that we don't go nearly as far as we could in exploring either the difficulties or the benefits of difference. We usually do what is appropriate when the boss says, "This is your new coworker," but we rarely choose to go much further than the situation requires. In fact, we might say that for most of us the painful transitions toward living with difference—from our experiences in day care to those in our jobs—take place out of necessity rather than choice. After each transition we settle back down, living in and enjoying our new situation. Moving onward, toward *more* difference, may still be painful and remind us that our knowledge and skills are often shallow.

The rewards for putting ourselves in such potentially painful situations are great, however. Not only is there the excitement of difference but there are also the satisfying newfound skills of negotiating difference. It is indeed a pleasurable experience to "speak a new language," whether in the literal sense or in the sense of being able to cope comfortably in a different culture. But even more than this, learning to negotiate the difference of other cultures allows us to reflect more deeply on our own culture and selves, and on what it means to be human. Indeed, at its deepest levels we can discover that difference doesn't make as much difference as we once thought.

12

From Imagination to Dialogue

In the 1970s, I spent time researching the history of the Mangbetu people of northeastern Congo (Kinshasa). My best informant was a very old man named Iode Mbunza. Lame and frail, Iode was one of the brightest and gentlest men I have ever met. As a youth he had been interested in the history of his people, so he stayed home to listen to the elders when other young men went hunting. Iode knew stories. One evening, sitting around a fire, he told of a flying craft that had visited the Mangbetu in the 1930s, hovering briefly over the forest. People on the ground could see into the front window of the flying machine, where a white man stood reading a book. Astonished, I asked whether this had perhaps been a helicopter, and he assured me that it had not.[1]

Such a machine carrying white men over Central Africa in the 1930s is outside of my understanding, even if today someone might suggest it was a UFO. Iode himself was also unsure of the meaning of the event, but unlike myself, he had no problem imagining that what he remembered was true. He could easily conceive of the reality of such a craft because he knew only a little about white men, books, and machine technology. The strange white colonizers had brought the equally strange books and airplanes to Central Africa, so why not a white man reading a book in a hovering craft?

Contrast Iode's experience with that of Chief Batsakpide, a man I met in the same region in the late 1980s, after Iode and his generation had passed away. Chief Batsakpide, a young man of about thirty-five, had served in the Congolese air force and had studied aeronautical engineering in France. Well educated and with good employment prospects in urban Africa, he had nonetheless responded to the call of his people to be their leader. In a part of Africa most distant from cities, he was helping a population of about 4,000 cope with the changing world around them. As I had done with Iode, I sat with Chief Batsakpide around an evening fire. But instead of stories of inexplicable aircraft, he taught me Western astronomy and pointed out the many man-made satellites that streaked across the clear African sky.[2] The difference between the two Africans was striking.

Iode easily imagined a white man reading a book in a flying machine. Writing and operating machines were at the heart of the white man's power in colonial Africa. Iode also imagined that white colonizers had been cannibals and that whites in general had magic that made them powerful. Understandably, Iode interpreted *our* civilization from the perspective of his own. In contrast, Batsakpide, the aeronautical engineer trained in the West, was familiar with our technical culture and would never have imagined that we possessed levitating craft in the 1930s, that we are cannibals, or that we have powerful magic.

Most Americans have been more like Iode when it comes to thoughts about Africa. We have imagined what Africa is like by using limited knowledge and limited categories of reality. There is one major difference, however. Iode visualized us from a position of powerlessness, whereas Westerners have visualized Africa from a position of power. Iode imagined that whites acquired control through magic. We have imagined that we acquired control because Africa was primitive.

Evolutionism

The concept of *primitive* originated with the modern belief in evolutionism, which proposes that all things evolve along a single line and that some races and cultures are farther along that line than others. Evolutionism, a product of Western civilization, presumes that Westerners—especially white, male, upper-middle- and upper-class Westerners—are farthest along the line. This system uses the term *progress* to describe movement toward Western culture and Western ideals. Although Westerners themselves frequently disagree on the specific content of their ideals, there is an underlying Western belief that others *advance* as they become more Western. In other words, evolutionism assumes that there is only one reality and that its truth is best embodied in Western culture.

Evolutionism emerged in the West in the late eighteenth and early nineteenth centuries, as we discovered that the natural world had evolved and as we struggled to understand what that meant for us. If we evolved, was it only by chance that we became human? Was there no purpose to evolution? For most, this idea was unthinkable. Rather, evolution needed to be fit into larger schemata of meaning. For many, evolution was seen to be God's plan for working out His purpose; for others, it was nature's plan for perfecting life. In either case, however, Westerners easily imagined that there was a plan and that they were at the forefront of its realization.

In the evolutionists' eyes, others—including Africans—were less evolved. To state it another way, blacks were essentially whites at a much earlier stage of development. Here we see the critical role of *time* as the link between races.[3] Africans were seen as "living ancestors" who were present in this time yet representative of another time. Or they were seen as "perpetual children," not yet adults and therefore only marginally significant in contemporary time. In the nineteenth century, the root cause of African backwardness was considered to be their race. Most whites believed, for example, that Africans lacked philosophy because they lacked the biological capacity to produce philosophy. Over *time*—a very long time—blacks would evolve the ability to philosophize like whites, to create real art, and to rule themselves, but until that moment, the best that could be done was for white men to accept the burden of control and care, as one might do for children. In practice, of course, the White Man's Burden of taking care of Africans most frequently turned into the Black Man's Burden of suffering exploitation. Because Africans were presumed to represent a more primitive time, most Westerners, including most Americans, could easily accept African subjugation and overlook African contributions to history.

The idea of African racial inferiority dominated Western thinking until at least the 1960s and still has some currency in American and European society. As the twentieth century unfolded, however, the importance of race was challenged. Biologists emphasized that evolutionism is not the same as the scientific theory of *evolution*. Whereas evolutionism proposes that all forms of life lie along a single pathway, evolution proposes that life spreads out in a weblike fashion. And whereas evolutionism describes *progress* and assumes that all history is moving toward a single goal, evolution talks about *adaptation* and *interdependence*. The scientific theory of evolution does not assume that biological history has a goal but instead notes that the complete extinction of any and all species is a real possibility. In the twentieth century, biologists have also explored genetics and have concluded that all humans are indeed the same species.

Meanwhile, anthropologists began to live with and study non-Western peoples. They found that nonracial factors such as history, environment, and culture could explain the differences among Westerners, Africans, and others. And Western societies in general—having experienced two world wars, the loss of their colonies, civil and human rights movements, and the challenges of urban, industrial culture—became less certain that whiteness or Westernness alone conferred the capacity for solving human problems.

Increasingly, Americans have abandoned race as an explanation for why others are different. We have not, however, totally abandoned the idea of evolutionism. Race evolutionism has been largely replaced by cultural evolutionism. In its negative version, cultural evolutionism encourages us to imagine that African societies are "less developed" and should catch up to ours. Moreover, the modern development model has largely assumed that ordinary Africans have little to offer to development theory or practice and that it is up to us to help Africa modernize from the top down. We still frequently assume, for example, that Africans are woefully mired in static and irrational tribalism when we should realize that their lives have been dynamically shaped by colonialism, urbanization, technology, international markets, contemporary politics, and many other factors.

Cultural evolutionism also encourages positive myths and stereotypes of Africa. It is easy to believe, for example, that before Africans were corrupted by Western civlization, they led lives that were whole and even magnificent when compared to our lives today. Rural Africans, whom we imagine to be insulated from the West, are used as positive examples by critics of Western cultural patterns, whether of our excessive materialism and individuality, our medical science, our religion, or our imperialism. In this model, we can aspire to recuperate our essential goodness by studying African history and culture or by visiting isolated villages where the true, "unspoiled" Africa remains.

A Kind of Equality

Most Americans are still steeped in the kind of cultural evolutionism that overtly compares cultures to one another in terms of *progress*. That is, we openly presume that one society is ahead of or behind another. There is, however, still another way that some Americans mistake African culture. The events of the twentieth century have led an increasing number of us to believe that all cultures are equal. Many Americans now say that African cultures (and other cultures) are "not inferior, just different." My students frequently espouse this point of view. Perhaps this kind of perceived equality is helpful, because it attempts to give others space to be themselves. It is not, however, the solution to evolutionism.

In a discussion of the issue, anthropologist Bernard McGrane has noted that the "not inferior, just different" model has a long history. It was, he says, first worked out in the eighteenth century as a way to maintain Western feelings of superiority in the face of increasing knowledge about other cultures. As exchanges with non-Europeans intensified, Westerners had to cope with the fact that others saw reality in significantly different ways. But rather than engage others' ideas, a move that would have challenged Western culture, the "just different" explanation of other cultures arose. That is, if others were *not inferior,* then neither were they *superior,* just different. This reasoning allowed an intellectual distance that preserved Western cultural cohesiveness and feelings of superiority.[4]

Behind this earlier "just different" explanation of other cultures was the hidden assumption that others actually were inferior. "For the sake of good-conscience," says McGrane, eighteenth-century Westerners maintained the myth that all people, including those in other cultures, were equal.[5] At the same time, however, those who were ignorant of recently discovered Western notions about democracy, individualism, natural rights, private property, the free market, and the material nature of reality were considered inferior. Thus Westerners believed themselves to be the same as others, but with superior truths that allowed them to look down on others and justify their domination.

In the twentieth century, say McGrane and many other critics, the anthropologists who largely formed our modern notions of culture took a similar position. That is, although these anthropologists abandoned racism and argued that other cultures were equal, they *acted* as though Western culture was superior. Anthropologists learned *about* others but did not believe that others could make valid comments about the nature of reality or, especially, about us. "Equal, just different" was another way to avoid real discussions with others about the meaning of life. In the words of McGrane, such a view of equality is "not a moral nor an intellectual victory but rather a great trivialization of the encounter with the Other."[6] This seems a bit harsh, considering the significant contributions anthropologists made to destroying Dark Continent myths, but the point must be considered seriously.

We can use this perspective to examine how Americans think about Africa today. After learning to avoid Dark Continent and Wise Africa images of Africa, we still might imagine Africans to be "equal, just different." We might be "objective" and seriously study Africa to learn about its various environments, histories, customs, politics, and economics. In learning about Africa, we might even become sympathetic toward African problems and act to be helpful. But our viewing Africa objectively and helping Africans does not necessarily mean that we take Africa's differences seriously. If we treat Africa objectively—that is, as an object—it continues to isolate us from Africa, because we still specify the categories of study, set the agendas for interaction and help, and define what constitutes progress.

Moreover, thinking in the "just different" mode allows us to say that Africans should live their way while we live ours. This sort of cultural individualism would seem to imply respect for African cultures, but ultimately it does not. We do not really mean that others can do whatever they want. As in the eighteenth century, contemporary Western culture insists that there are certain universal rules of reality that can be deduced from nature. In a sense, our proposing that African cultures are "equal, just different" is analogous to South African whites proposing that Africans who had political and cultural autonomy in their "homelands" also had equality. In this extreme example, the realities of interaction and exploitation are easy to see. In the broader world context, the fiction of the "separate but equal" arguments may be less clear. Nevertheless, the reality is that the cultures of Africa are neither separate from our own nor equal in their power to control their own destinies.

The "equal, just different" understanding of African cultures attempts to put us in the same time, without acknowledging the fact that we *share* the same history and space.

An African Dialogue

Today, it is still difficult for Americans not to stereotype Africa in one way or another. Our most dominant stereotype is that Africa is culturally "behind" us, but the Wise Africa and "equal, just different" myths also have significant followings. Even those who consciously attempt to see Africa in more accurate terms find it difficult to locate everyday sources of information that are not already embued with these stereotypes. What we know comes from teachers, newspapers, television programs, movies, magazines, and books that frequently tell us about an Africa that substantiates our myths, positive or negative. It usually takes a great deal of conscious effort to find material with which to construct whole pictures of Africa and Africans.

Africa is also vulnerable to stereotypical interpretations. It has no powerful group of advocates to challenge our myths. Moreover, events in Africa frequently lend themselves to stereotypical interpretations, and of all the continents, sub-Saharan Africa seems the most culturally distant from us. This is true for both its rural and urban populations. Africa's diseases, famines, poverty, wars, corruption, weak governments, and other problems can be easily mistaken as indications of African backwardness rather than as evidence of the continent's complex history, in which we ourselves participated. In contrast, Africa's hospitality, communality, and other positive features can easily be construed as the true soul of Africa if one ignores the more problematic aspects of African cultures.

It is true that Africans are generally different from ourselves. But African cultures are not remnants of primitive cultures that survived into the present, and they are not some version of our culture at a different stage of development. Neither are they "equal, just different."

Africans share the same biology, era, and planet as ourselves. Rather than using Africa's difference as a tool to separate and control Africans, we can use their difference as an opportunity to deepen our understanding of what difference means. Africa clearly represents for us the fundamental fact that *all* people are different. We all occupy essentially the same time and space and yet we see the world in separate ways. Even *within* our own culture or family, there are distinct perceptions of reality.

Africa's difference is important to us because it helps to define ourselves and the world we live in. It is worth taking seriously. We should not try to minimize the difference by assuming that Africans are basically just like us. Nor should we exaggerate it by believing Africans are different *kinds* of humans. And we should not try to evaluate or dominate African difference by assuming that Africans would be better off if only they were more like us. Finally, we should not search for the "admirable qualities" of Africans in isolation from their other qualities.

The first step to understanding African difference is to "listen" to African cultures and attempt to discover Africa in its own words and in its own context. We should work at understanding how Africans conceive of reality and how that reality has been shaped by their environments and histories. In other words, we must allow Africans to be our teachers. We need to learn African languages, find African friends, read African novels, eat African food, listen to African music, and live in African cities and villages.

Such attempts to understand "Africa" will be difficult. It is not easy to venture beyond our own comfortable corners of the world. And such attempts will be limited. I do not know of anyone, including myself or any African, whom I would trust to define what Africa represents, because sub-Saharan Africa is a huge region with nearly forty countries, a thousand or more separate cultures, and hundreds of millions of people. One person can only begin to understand a small corner of the continent.

Americans need both detail and context for Africa. When I tell people I am interested in Africa, they frequently inform me that they know someone who has lived in Africa, but cannot name the country or even the region where the person lived or lives. Others have asked me what the capital of Africa is, or whether I know their friend who went to Africa. Learning to distinguish among Africans and African countries and societies will help us to see Africans as real people, people who share our time and place, and, paradoxically, will make it more difficult to imagine that we have found the Real Africa. In fact, we will ultimately conclude that there *is* no one real Africa, just as there is no one real America.

Although Americans may never completely succeed in understanding Africa's difference or, for that matter, anyone's difference, we can learn to take our differences seriously through continuing dialogue. Dialogue with others implies both self-respect and other-respect, both listening and talking. It is the essence of life with others and, not coincidentally, of education. Through dialogue we can exchange ideas about the meaning and use of our common time and place. Dialogue implies *answer*-ability and *response*-ability. In a sense, dialogue puts people under mutual control. It recognizes that we have a claim on each other's actions, because we share our time and place.

Dialogue can help us avoid two significant dangers: universalism and isolationism. *Universalism* claims that we know the truth and that all true and good people should live according to that truth. Universalism leads to a hierarchical construction of the world and promotes control over others. Evolutionism is one form of universalism. At the other end of the spectrum, *isolationism* claims that everyone should be able to live however they choose, which is an impossibility on our shrinking planet and which will lead to wars over cultural differences and dwindling resources. Dialogue, however, promotes *transversality,* the recognition that truth, so far as it exists for humans, lies somewhere between universalism and isolationism, between absolutism and relativism. Transversality affirms that we share the same time and place, that we are equal *and* different, and that our individual and collective well-being are interdependent.[7]

Living in a world of engagement with Africans and African difference will complicate our lives and challenge many of our cherished values. It will necessitate the added effort of learning about others and the difficulty of sharing decisionmaking and resources. But the benefits will be great. Africans will escape from their damaging mistaken identities, both primitive and wise. They will be able to find the tools they need to accomplish *their* goals rather than ours. And together we will begin to develop the skills and attitudes needed to live peacefully in our ever smaller neighborhood.

Notes

Chapter 1

1. Julian Nundy, "France Haunted by Rwanda Genocide," *Telegraph Group Limited,* April 14, 1998. Available: <http://www.telegraph.co.uk/>.

2. Gary Althen, *American Ways* (Yarmouth, ME: Intercultural Press, 1988), 89.

3. Carol Beckwith and Angela Fisher, "Royal Gold of the Asante Empire," *National Geographic,* October 1996, 36–47. I see the problem as not so much the work of Beckwith and Fisher as *National Geographic*'s use of photographs without context. For comments on Beckwith and Fisher's larger body of work, see Michael D. Lemonick, "Lost Africa," *Time,* September 2, 1996, 52.

Chapter 2

1. Astair Zekiros with Marylee Wiley, *Africa in Social Studies Textbooks,* Bulletin no. 9550 (Madison: Wisconsin Department of Public Instruction, 1978), 4. An article by Wiley contains most of the same ideas and is easier to locate: "Africa in Social Studies Textbooks," *Social Education* 46 (November-December 1982): 492–497, 548–552.

2. Burton F. Beers, *World History: Patterns of Civilization* (Englewood Cliffs, NJ: Prentice-Hall, 1993).

3. Egerton O. Osunde, Josiah Tlou, and Neil L. Brown, "Persisting and Common Stereotypes in U.S. Students' Knowledge of Africa: A Study of Preservice Social Studies Teachers," *The Social Studies* 87, no. 3 (May-June 1996): 120–121.

4. Elaine Windrich, "Media Coverage of the Angolan War," *Africa Today* (spring 1992). Available: <http://www.EBSCOhost.com>.

5. *Morning Call* (Allentown, PA), November 3, 1996, 2.

6. Carole J. L. Collins and Steven Askin, "In the Dark About Africa," *Utne Reader,* May-June 1995, 17, 20, 22; and Robert D. Kaplan, "The Coming Anarchy," *Atlantic Monthly,* February 1994, 44–76. An article in *Vanity Fair* is also critical of Kaplan: Christopher Hitchens, "African Gothic," *Vanity Fair,* November 1994, 92–117.

7. James B. Steward, "The Smart Traveler," *SmartMoney,* October 1996, 169.

8. Philip Gourevitch, "Wondering Where the Lions Are," *Outside,* October 1996, 74. Philip Gourevitch is an informed observer of Africa. The promotion for his article uses stereotypes to hype what is actually a fair critique of the safari experience.

9. Bernard Block, "Romance and High Purpose: *The National Geographic,*" *Wilson Library Bulletin* 68 (January 1994): 333–337.

10. Robert Caputo, "Zaire River," *National Geographic,* November 1990, 5–35; Peter Reinthal, "The Living Jewels of Lake Malawi," *National Geographic,* May 1991, 42–51.

11. Charles E. Cobb Jr. and Robert Caputo, "Eritrea Wins the Peace," *National Geographic,* June 1996, 82–105.

12. Charles E. Cobb Jr., "The Twilight of Apartheid: Life in Black South Africa," *National Geographic,* February 1993, 66–93.

13. Robert Caputo, "Tragedy Stalks the Horn of Africa," *National Geographic,* August 1993, 99–100.

14. To give credit where it is due, a 1997 article on Central Africa provides a generally accurate analysis of the history of the civil wars in Rwanda and Burundi. Its major shortcoming is that it is too brief. Thus, for example, while it mentions foreign involvement since independence, it does not explain the nature and extent of that involvement. Most readers would be unable to decipher the implications of the article's points because they know little about postindependence international influence and competition in Africa. Mike Edwards, "In Focus: Central Africa's Cycle of Violence," *National Geographic,* June 1997, 124–133.

15. Colin Palmer, "African Slave Trade: The Cruelest Commerce," *National Geographic,* September 1992, 62–91.

16. Carol Beckwith and Angela Fisher, "Fantasy Coffins of Ghana," *National Geographic,* September 1994, 120–130.

17. Donnarae MacCann and Olga Richard, "Through African Eyes: An Interview About Recent Picture Books with Yulisa Amadu Maddy," *Wilson Library Bulletin* 69 (June 1995): 41; and Pete Watson and Mary Watson, *The Market Lady and the Mango Tree* (New York: Tambourine Books, 1994).

18. Philip R. DeVita and James D. Armstrong, *Distant Mirrors: America As a Foreign Culture* (Belmont, CA: Wadsworth, 1993). In one more example, National Public Radio's *Morning Edition* of August 14, 1998, discussed the bombings of U.S. embassies in Nairobi and Dar es Salaam and described the reactions of "the natives" of those two countries. The word was used correctly and was not meant to be pejorative, but how often are the residents of France and England referred to as "the natives"?

Chapter 3

1. Djibril Tamsir Niane, *Sundiata: An Epic of Old Mali,* trans. G. D. Pickett (London: Longman, 1965), 1–2.

2. Frank M. Snowden Jr., *Blacks in Antiquity: Ethiopians in the Greco-Roman Experience* (Cambridge, MA: Belknap, 1970), 176.

3. Ibid., 217.

4. Ibid., 105–107.

5. Gerhard von Rad, *Genesis: A Commentary* (Philadelphia: Westminster Press, 1959), 131–135; and Walter Brueggemann, *Genesis: A Bible Commentary for Teaching and Preaching* (Atlanta: John Knox, 1982), 89–91.

6. Acts 8: 26–40; see, for example, Gerhard Krodel, *Acts* (Philadelphia: Fortress, 1981), 37–38; and Johannes Munck, *The Acts of the Apostles,* revised by William F. Albright and C. S. Mann (Garden City, NY: Doubleday, 1967), 77–79.

7. Snowden, *Blacks in Antiquity,* 196–205.

8. Maghan Keita, "Africa Backwards and Forwards: Interpreting Africa and Africans in Pre- and Post-Modern Space" (paper presented at the Sixth Annual African Studies Consortium Workshop, University of Pennsylvania, Philadelphia, October 2, 1998). Keita also notes that our modern lack of awareness of this favorable treatment of Africans during the medieval period parallels our lack of knowledge about the ancient Greek debt to black Egypt. That is, our ignorance is due to late-eighteenth- and nineteenth-century considerations of Africans in terms of racial inferiority. Keita plans to publish a book-length study on this subject.

9. Michael Adas, *Machines As the Measure of Men: Science, Technology, and Ideologies of Western Dominance* (Ithaca: Cornell University Press, 1989), 22.

10. Philip D. Curtin, *The Image of Africa: British Ideas and Action, 1780–1850* (Madison: University of Wisconsin Press, 1964), 10.

11. Ibid., 35. A comprehensive history of the idea of race is available in Ivan Hannaford, *Race: The History of an Idea in the West* (Washington, DC: Woodrow Wilson Center Press, 1996). For selected readings by Enlightenment thinkers, see Emmanuel Chukwudi Eze, ed., *Race and the Enlightenment: A Reader* (Oxford: Blackwell, 1997).

12. Curtin, *Image of Africa,* 123–139; and David Jenkins, *Black Zion: Africa, Imagined and Real, As Seen by Today's Blacks* (New York: Harcourt Brace Jovanovich, 1975), 69. See also Christopher Fyfe, *A History of Sierra Leone* (London: Oxford University Press, 1962).

13. Jenkins, *Black Zion,* 73–88.

14. See, for example, J. Gus Liebenow, *Liberia: The Evolution of Privilege* (Ithaca: Cornell University Press, 1969); and Tom W. Shick, *Behold the Promised Land: A History of Afro-American Settler Society in Nineteenth-Century Liberia* (Baltimore: Johns Hopkins University Press, 1977).

15. See, for example, Curtin, *Image of Africa,* 138, 239.

16. Adas, *Machines As the Measure,* 22.

17. Ibid., 71, 79–95.

18. For an extended discussion of this subject, see William Stanton, *The Leopard's Spots: Scientific Attitudes Toward Race in America, 1815–1859* (Chicago: University of Chicago Press, 1960).

19. Curtin, *Image of Africa,* 364.

20. Ibid., 479–480. There were somewhat different theoretical patterns among the various European colonizers. The French, for example, seemed less racist and began to talk about *association* with Africans rather than conversion or trusteeship. They also permitted the African *évolués* of the four communes of Senegal (small areas that the government in Paris had declared a part of France) to retain their French citizenship. On the whole, however, all European colonizers thought of Africans as racial inferiors and excluded Africans from power.

21. Mungo Park, *Travels into the Interior Districts of Africa* (New York: Hippocrene Books, 1983).

22. Patrick Brantlinger, "Victorians and Africans: The Genealogy of the Myth of the Dark Continent," in *"Race," Writing, and Difference,* ed. Henry Louis Gates Jr. (Chicago: University of Chicago Press, 1985), 217.

23. Rudyard Kipling, "The White Man's Burden," in *Collected Verse* (New York: Doubleday, 1907), 215–217. The complete poem has seven verses. In the Philippines, Americans tended to conceptualize themselves as older siblings rather than as parents, but the effect was similar. Leon Wolff, *Little Brown Brother: How the United States Purchased and Pacified the Philippine Islands at the Century's Turn* (Garden City, NY: Doubleday, 1961).

24. Henry Morton Stanley, *Through the Dark Continent* (New York: Harper, 1878).

25. Theodore Roosevelt, *African Game Trails: An Account of the African Wanderings of an American Hunter-Naturalist* (New York: Syndicate Publishing Company, 1910), 94.

Chapter 4

1. Joseph Conrad, *Heart of Darkness,* Norton Critical Editions, ed. Robert Kimbrough, 3rd ed. (New York: Norton, 1988), 35, 37.

2. Chinua Achebe, "An Image of Africa: Racism in Conrad's *Heart of Darkness,*" in *Heart of Darkness,* by Joseph Conrad, Norton Critical Editions, ed. Robert Kimbrough, 3rd ed. (New York: Norton, 1988), 251–262.

3. Robert Caputo, "Zaire River," *National Geographic,* November 1990, 30.

4. Ibid., 30.

5. Theodore Roosevelt, *African Game Trails: An Account of the African Wanderings of an American Hunter-Naturalist* (New York: Syndicate Publishing Company, 1910), 2.

6. Lewis Henry Morgan, *Ancient Society* (New York: Henry Holt, 1878; reprint, Cambridge, MA: Belknap, 1964).

7. Gaetano Casati, *Ten Years in Equatoria and the Return with Emin Pasha,* vol. 2 (London: Frederick Warne, 1891), 114.

8. Roosevelt, *African Game Trails,* x.

9. Ibid., 2.

10. Enid Schildkrout and Curtis A. Keim, *African Reflections: Art from Northeastern Zaire* (Seattle: University of Washington Press, 1990).

11. Ibid., 143–147; and Curtis A. Keim, "*Artes Africanae:* The Western Discovery of 'Art' in Northeastern Congo," in *The Scramble for Art in Central Africa,* ed. Enid Schildkrout and Curtis A. Keim, 109–132 (Cambridge: Cambridge University Press, 1998).

12. Georg Schweinfurth, *Artes Africanae: Illustrations and Descriptions of Productions of the Industrial Arts of Central African Tribes* (Leipzig: F. A. Brockhaus, 1875), vii.

13. Georg Schweinfurth, *The Heart of Africa: Three Years' Travels and Adventures in the Unexplored Regions of Central Africa from 1868 to 1871,* trans. Ellen E. Frewer, vol. 2 (New York: Harper, 1874), 46.

14. Sigmund Freud, "The Savage's Dread of Incest," in *The Basic Writings of Sigmund Freud* (New York: The Modern Library, 1939), 807.

15. Ibid.

16. See, for example, Octave Mannoni, *Prospero and Caliban: The Psychology of Colonization* (London: Methuen, 1956).

17. See, for example, Michael Adas, *Machines As the Measure of Men: Science, Technology, and Ideologies of Western Dominance* (Ithaca: Cornell University Press, 1989).

18. For an extended discussion of the relationship between evolutionary science and social theory in the twentieth century, see Carl N. Degler, *In Search of Human Nature: The Decline and Revival of Darwinism in American Social Thought* (New York: Oxford University Press, 1991).

19. Lewis Thomas, *Harvard Magazine*. This quotation was given to me by a friend. I apologize to readers because I was unable to locate its exact source.

20. Dennis Hickey and Kenneth C. Wylie, *An Enchanting Darkness: The American Vision of Africa in the Twentieth Century* (East Lansing: Michigan State University Press, 1993), 20–21.

21. Stanley Burnham, *America's Bimodal Crisis: Black Intelligence in White Society*, 3rd ed. (Athens, GA: Foundation for Human Understanding, 1993), 49–56. (The first edition was published in 1985.)

22. Ibid., 57–63.

Chapter 5

1. Hillary Rodham Clinton, *It Takes a Village: And Other Lessons Children Teach Us* (New York: Simon and Schuster, 1996).

2. David Roberts, "Mali's Dogon: Below the Cliff of Tombs," *National Geographic*, October 1990, 100–127.

3. Ibid., 126.

4. Katherine Dettwyler, *Dancing Skeletons: Life and Death in West Africa* (Prospect Heights, IL: Waveland, 1994), 62.

5. Dennis Hickey and Kenneth C. Wylie, *An Enchanting Darkness: The American Vision of Africa in the Twentieth Century* (East Lansing: Michigan State University Press, 1993), 111–112.

6. Ibid., 93–125.

7. Franklin Institute Science Museum, "School Field Trip Planner," spring 1996 (Philadelphia: Franklin Institute Science Museum).

8. Wyatt MacGaffey, "'Magic,' or as We Usually Say, 'Art': A Framework for Comparing European and African Art," in *The Scramble for Art in Central Africa*, ed. Enid Schildkrout and Curtis A. Keim (Cambridge: Cambridge University Press, 1998), 230.

9. See, for example, Christopher Steiner, *African Art in Transit* (New York: Cambridge University Press, 1994).

10. Perhaps the least exploitative way to buy and sell African objects is demonstrated by "alternative trade" organizations such as SERRV International, which sells products from the developing world in the United States to support producer cooperatives and charities in Africa and elsewhere. SERRV has more than 2,200 outlets around the country and an Internet catalog service: <http://www.serrv.org/>. The organization advertises that its "mission is to promote the social and economic progress of people in developing regions of the world by marketing their products in a just and direct manner." SERRV, a program of the Church

of the Brethren, imports handicrafts and other products from 160 artisan groups in thirty-seven countries.

11. Theodore Sturgeon, "Shore Leave," *Star Trek,* Paramount Pictures, original broadcast, December 29, 1966.

12. Shakaland is discussed in Carolyn Hamilton, *Terrific Majesty: The Powers of Shaka Zulu and the Limits of Historical Invention* (Cambridge: Harvard University Press, 1998), 187–205.

13. Many resources are available to the adventure traveler, especially in southern Africa. Interesting choices include several travel guides published by Lonely Planet (Hawthorn, Victoria, Australia): David Else, *Trekking in East Africa,* 2nd ed. (1998); Hugh Finlay, *Africa on a Shoestring,* 8th ed. (1998); Hugh Finlay and Geoff Crowther, *East Africa* (1997); and Alex Newton, *West Africa: A Lonely Planet Travel Survival Kit,* 3rd ed. (1995). See also Richard Trillo, *West Africa: The Rough Guide,* 2nd ed. (London: Rough Guides, 1995). On the Internet, two sites that deal with backpacking in southern Africa are <http://www.backpacking.co.za/milestxt.html> and <http://www.backpackafrica.com>.

14. Pam Ascanio, *White Men Don't Have Juju: An American Couple's Adventure Through Africa* (Chicago: Noble Press, 1992). Commenting on American aid workers and embassy people in Bamako, Mali, Ascanio writes: "They bragged about their extravagant living allowance because Bamako was a hardship post. They also showed us their cellars filled with tax-free, duty-exempt food, and name brand products, shampoos, and toothpaste from home. 'Thank God, we've got everything we need,' they said, 'and we don't have to deal with the local population.' This was their badge of courage" (121).

15. I once co-led a tour with these expert guides though Senegal, the Gambia, Mali, and Côte d'Ivoire. There are, today, other opportunities for intentional travel. For example, Travel Senegal! (a tour operator) advertises tours to Senegal "For Adventurous Travelers Only!" They provide "specialized small tours to Senegal, West Africa, for photographers, musicians, artists, writers, educators and those interested in West African Arts and Culture." Actually, the tours are arranged by a couple in Alaska, Sher and Bruce Schwartz, who provide this service as a way to help a Senegalese friend connect with interested Americans. Their friend, Pacoo Mane, is a musician who speaks English well and is skilled in arranging city tours, homestays in both urban and rural settings, visits to artists and schools, cooking and music lessons, and the like: "Mane's friendly, poised and insightful disposition is a delight to work with. He's an excellent guide for non French-speaking travelers and he understands well how to work harmoniously between both African and American cultures. Senegalese are warm and welcoming people. Guide books say that Senegal is the safest West African country to travel in, and we believe it. During our adventures there we have never felt physically threatened. Traveling to Senegal is an unforgettable experience filled with adventure, wonderment and insights into a culture much different from our own. Senegal is a poor country and unemployment is high. Our experience with Pacoo Mane has been a very positive one. We feel that he is reputable and honest. We would like to see him be successful, and so we have created a web site to entice those like ourselves who dream of going to French-speaking West Africa, but who don't have the contacts to do it. Travel Senegal! is an excellent opportunity

especially for photographers to capture the essence of the country." The Travel Senegal! World Wide Web page advertises a bit of the exotic Africa—visit "the bush," "explore sacred grounds," "capture the essence of the country"—but they clearly attempt to introduce tourists to ordinary, dignified African life. Sher Schwartz and Bruce Schwartz, *Travel Senegal!* Available: <http://www.senegaltravel.com/>.

16. These perspectives have been gleaned from conversations with a number of study-tour guides who prefer to remain anonymous.

17. Charlie Hauck, "Alarmed by Burglars," *Home Improvement,* American Broadcasting Company, original broadcast, May 14, 1996.

18. Indiana Botanic Gardens, promotional flyer, spring 1998.

19. Walter Chin, "Kenya: The Maasai," *Sports Illustrated,* special issue, winter 1998, 66.

20. "Kenya: You Could Look It Up," *Sports Illustrated,* special issue, winter 1998, 62.

21. Ibid.

22. Dympna Ugwu-Oju, *What Will My Mother Say: A Tribal African Girl Comes of Age in America* (Chicago: Bonus Books, 1995).

23. Tepilit Ole Saitoti, *The Worlds of a Maasai Warrior: An Autobiography* (New York: Random House, 1986).

24. Anonymous, interview by author, Bethlehem, PA, May 20, 1998.

25. Anonymous, interview by author, Philadelphia, July 18, 1998.

26. Malidoma Patrice Somé, *Of Water and the Spirit: Ritual, Magic, and Initiation in the Life of an African Shaman* (New York: Putnam, 1994). Also see an article by Somé, "Rights of Passage: If Adolescence Is a Disease, Initiation Is a Cure," *Utne Reader,* July-August 1994, 67–68. Adapted from an article in *In Context* (winter 1993).

27. Malidoma Patrice Somé, *Nature, Magic, and Community: The Way of the Dagara,* Wisdom of Africa Series (Pacific Grove, CA: Oral Tradition Archives, 1993), audiocassette. See also Malidoma Patrice Somé, *The Healing Wisdom of Africa: Finding Life Purpose Through Nature, Ritual, and Community* (New York: Putnam, 1998). An interesting contrast to Somé's autobiography is the autobiography of James Hall, an American who became a healer in Swaziland: James Hall, *Sangoma: My Odyssey into the Spirit World of Africa* (New York: Putnam, 1994).

28. Wanja Njuguna, "Cultural Ambassador on Peace Mission," *Daily Nation* (Nairobi), August 9, 1996, 2.

29. Mutahi Mureithi, "Genuine Interest in Our Culture or Mere Fascination?" *Daily Nation* (Nairobi), August 9, 1996, 2. For a critique of Western myths about the Maasai, see Paul Spencer, *The Pastoral Continuum: The Marginalization of Tradition in East Africa* (New York: Oxford University Press, 1998).

30. Ibid.

31. From the perspective of understanding Africa (rather than American attitudes toward Africa), a more interesting view of Surum might be to think about the way he has combined Africa and America. Surum married a white American woman and maintains homes in both Kenya and the United States. The advertisement for the videotape notes that "Tom also shares what he has learned of America with young Maasai. While he partakes of the bounty of American life, includ-

ing Armani suits, a luxury car, and credit cards, he is still strongly attached to his tribe and its traditions." Surum himself is good evidence that those traditions are changing rapidly. Filmakers Library. Available: <http://www.filmakers.com/ANTHRO.html>.

32. George Packer, *The Village of Waiting* (New York: Vintage, 1988), 284–291.

33. Useful general studies on African-American attitudes toward Africa up to the 1960s and 1970s include Tunde Adeleke, *UnAfrican Americans: Nineteenth-Century Black Nationalists and the Civilizing Mission* (Lexington, KY: University Press of Kentucky, 1998); Harold R. Isaacs, *The New World of Negro Americans* (New York: John Day, 1963); David Jenkins, *Black Zion: Africa, Imagined and Real, As Seen by Today's Blacks* (New York: Harcourt Brace Jovanovich, 1975); Bernard Makhosezwe Magubane, *The Ties That Bind: African-American Consciousness of Africa* (Trenton, NJ: Africa World Press, 1987); and Okon Edet Uya, ed., *Black Brotherhood: Afro-Americans and Africa* (Lexington, MA: Heath, 1971).

34. Isaacs, *New World*, 105–113. There are a number of examples of African Americans who traveled to Africa in the precolonial and colonial eras. In Central Africa, for example, the missionary William Sheppard worked among the Kuba in the late nineteenth century. See David A. Binkley and Patricia J. Darish, "'Enlightened But in Darkness': Interpretations of Kuba Art and Culture at the Turn of the Twentieth Century," in *The Scramble for Art in Central Africa*, ed. Enid Schildkrout and Curtis A. Keim (Cambridge: Cambridge University Press, 1998), 37–62. Another African American, George Washington Williams, made a tour of Congo in 1890 and wrote an open letter to King Leopold that outlined the atrocities being committed there. Williams's biographer, John Hope Franklin, notes that "of all the 1890 observers and critics of Leopold's rule . . . only Williams saw fit to make his unfavorable views widely known immediately." John Hope Franklin, *George Washington Williams: A Biography* (Chicago: University of Chicago Press, 1985), 262–263.

In the era leading up to the American civil rights movement of the 1960s, several African-American writers are known for their travels to Africa. Perhaps the most famous is Richard Wright, whose book *Black Power: A Record of Reactions in a Land of Pathos* (New York: Harper, 1954) discusses his mixed reactions to being in Africa. Most Europeans resisted allowing African Americans into their colonies, because their presence implied too great a measure of black independence. See Sylvia M. Jacobs, ed., *Black Americans and the Missionary Movement in Africa* (Westport, CT: Greenwood Press, 1982).

35. See, for example, Uya, *Black Brotherhood*.

36. John Hope Franklin, *From Slavery to Freedom: A History of Negro Americans*, 4th ed. (New York: Alfred A. Knopf, 1974), 367.

37. William R. Scott, *The Sons of Sheba's Race: African-Americans and the Italo-Ethiopian War, 1935–1941* (Bloomington: Indiana University Press, 1993), 2–22.

38. Ibid., 23.

39. Ibid., 21–22.

40. Ibid., 192–207.

41. Carter Godwin Woodson, *The Mis-education of the Negro* (Trenton, NJ: Africa World Press, 1998); and *The Negro in Our History*, 11th ed. (Washington, DC: Associated Publishers, 1966).

42. In the last years of his long life, Du Bois became disillusioned with the American situation, and in 1961 he moved to newly independent Ghana.

43. There are exceptions. For example, two recent accounts by African Americans portray the continent in a relatively negative light: Eddy Harris, *Native Stranger: A Black American's Journey into the Heart of Africa* (New York: Simon and Schuster, 1992); and Keith Richburg, *Out of America: A Black Man Confronts Africa* (New York: Basic Books, 1997).

44. There are many opinions, pro and con, on Afrocentrism. For a discussion by the originator of the idea see Molefi Kete Asante, *The Afrocentric Idea* (Philadelphia: Temple University Press, 1987). For largely favorable assessments, see Dhyana Ziegler, ed., *Molefi Kete Asante and Afrocentricity: In Praise and in Criticism* (Nashville, TN: James C. Winston, 1995). Two discussions that are critical, but useful in the context of general American stereotypes about Africa, are Hickey and Wylie, *An Enchanting Darkness,* 1–6, 308–318; and Gary B. Nash, Charlotte Crabtree, and Ross E. Dunn, *History on Trial: Culture Wars and the Teaching of the Past* (New York: Alfred A. Knopf, 1998), 117–122.

45. This missionary image persists. I recently heard rural Africans referred to as "innocent" by a well-intentioned Christian pastor.

46. Bob Hilliard, "Civilization (Bongo, Bongo, Bongo)," musical composition from *Angel in the Wings,* lyrics by Bob Hilliard and music by Carl Sigman (New York: Edwin H. Morris, 1947).

Chapter 6

1. James Perry, *Living Africa: A Village Experience,* 35 min. (Bloomington: Indiana University Television, 1983), videotape.

2. For a discussion of the civilizing mission in the first half of the twentieth century, see Michael Adas, *Machines As the Measure of Men: Science, Technology, and Ideologies of Western Dominance* (Ithaca: Cornell University Press, 1989), 199–270.

3. For a summary of structural adjustment thinking, see Amy L. Sherman, "Rethinking Development: A Market-Friendly Strategy for the Poor," *Christian Century,* December 9, 1992, 1130–1134. A somewhat more scholarly summary can be found in Michael Roemer and Steven C. Radelet, "Macroeconomic Reform in Developing Countries," in *Reforming Economic Systems in Developing Countries,* ed. Dwight H. Perkins and Michael Roemer (Cambridge: Harvard Institute for International Development, 1991), 55–80.

4. Ake, *Democracy and Development,* 118–119.

5. Dwight H. Perkins, "Economic Systems Reform in Developing Countries," in *Reforming Economic Systems in Developing Countries,* ed. Dwight H. Perkins and Michael Roemer (Cambridge: Harvard Institute for International Development, 1991), 45.

6. INFACT. Available: <http://www.infact.org/aboutinf.html>. The WHO/UNICEF International Code of Marketing of Breastmilk Substitutes was adopted by Resolution 34.22 of the World Health Assembly.

7. Baby Milk Action. Available: <http://www.gn.apc.org/babymilk/>.

8. Pierre Pradervand, *Listening to Africa: Developing Africa from the Grassroots* (New York: Praeger, 1989), 178.

9. Ali Mazrui, "A Clash of Cultures," episode 8 of *The Africans: A Triple Heritage,* 58 min. (Boston: WETA; London: British Broadcasting Corporation, 1986), videotape.

10. Organization for Economic Cooperation and Development, news release, June 18, 1998. Available: <http://www.africapolicy.org>.

11. Ibid.

12. For an introductory discussion of women in African development efforts, see April A. Gordon, "Women and Development," in April A. Gordon and Donald L. Gordon, *Understanding Contemporary Africa,* 2nd. ed. (Boulder: Lynne Rienner, 1996), 249–272.

13. Joseph Hanlon, "Strangling Mozambique: International Monetary Fund 'Stabilization' in the World's Poorest Country," *Multinational Monitor* 17, nos. 7–8 (July-August 1996). Available: <http://www.essential.org/monitor/hyper/mm0796.06.html>. Hanlon has also written a book on this subject: *Peace Without Profit: How the IMF Blocks Rebuilding in Mozambique* (Portsmouth, NH: Heinemann, 1996).

14. See, for example, Peter T. Bauer, "Creating the Third World: Foreign Aid and Its Offspring," *Encounter,* April 1988, 66–75; and James A. Dorn, Steve H. Hanke, and Alan A. Walters, eds., *The Revolution in Development Economics* (Washington, DC: Cato Institute, 1998).

15. The literature on participatory development is expanding rapidly. Among the many interesting examples, Stan Burkey's *People First: A Guide to Self-Reliant, Participatory Rural Development* (Atlantic Highlands, NJ: Zed Books, 1993) seems most complete. Burkey has many years of training experience in Africa. Pradervand, *Listening to Africa,* provides many hopeful examples of ordinary Africans helping themselves plus a sense of the cultural problems Africans must overcome. Many works on participatory development have been written by practitioners, who tend to see grassroots efforts as the only real solution to development. Among the more academic treatments of this topic are Barbara Thomas-Slayter and Dianne E. Rocheleau, *Gender, Environment, and Development in Kenya: A Grassroots Perspective* (Boulder: Lynne Rienner, 1995). A large number of organizations are working to promote participatory development efforts. For example, the American Council for Voluntary International Action—"a coalition of over 150 U.S.-based non-profits working to promote human dignity and development around the world"—can be found at <http://www.interaction.org/>. Likewise, the Institute for Food and Development Policy is at <www.foodfirst.org>.

16. Ian Askew, *Community Participation in Family Planning* (Exeter, England: University of Exeter, Institute of Population Studies, 1984), quoted in Burkey, *People First,* 205.

17. Thierno H. Kane, "Alternative Development Strategies in Africa: A Challenge to Grass-Root Initiatives," *Development* 2 (1994): 48.

18. Mennonite Central Committee, 21 South 12th Street, P.O. Box 500, Akron, PA 17501; tel.: (717) 859-1151; <http://www.mbnet.mb.ca/mcc/index.html>; and Heifer Project International, P.O. Box 808, Little Rock, AR 72203; tel.: (800) 422-0474; <http://www.heifer.org>.

19. Frans J. Schuurman, ed., *Beyond the Impasse: New Directions in Development Theory* (Atlantic Highlands, NJ: Zed Books, 1993).

20. Andrea Cornwall and Rachel Jewkes, "What Is Participatory Research?" *Social Science Medicine* 41, no. 12 (1995): 1669.

21. The "Economic Partnership with Africa" proposed by the Bill Clinton administration is not really a partnership. Although it might be helpful to some Africans, it is mainly an effort designed to give the United States an edge in competition with Europe. It provides no new aid for health care or education and targets only those countries in which the United States has an economic interest.

22. Thierry G. Verhelst, *No Life Without Roots: Culture and Development*, trans. Bob Cumming (Atlantic Highlands, NJ: Zed Books, 1990), 62–63.

23. Ibid., 63.

24. Pradervand, *Listening to Africa*, 204.

25. Weaver, Rock, and Kusterer, *Broad-Based Sustainable Development*, 272–277.

26. The American Institute of Philanthropy and the National Charities Information Bureau help potential donors evaluate the finances of nonprofit NGOs. The AIP is located at 4579 Laclede Avenue, Suite 136, St. Louis, MO 63108; tel.: (314) 454-3040, and publishes the quarterly *Charity Rating Guide*. The NCIB has an extensive Internet site at <http://www.give.org/index.cfm> and produces several publications that suggest guidelines for giving.

Chapter 7

1. Egerton O. Osunde, Josiah Tlou, and Neil L. Brown, "Persisting and Common Stereotypes in U.S. Students' Knowledge of Africa: A Study of Preservice Social Studies Teachers," *The Social Studies* 87, no. 3 (May-June 1996): 120.

2. Stanley Burnham, *America's Bimodal Crisis: Black Intelligence in White Society*, 3rd ed. (Athens, GA: Foundation for Human Understanding, 1993), 50.

3. Peter Forbath, *The River Congo* (New York: Harper and Row, 1977), 368.

4. David Levering Lewis, *The Race to Fashoda: European Colonialism and African Resistance in the Scramble for Africa* (New York: Weidenfeld and Nicolson, 1987), 32.

5. Ibid.

6. Caught in a snowstorm while crossing the Sierra Nevada in the winter of 1846–1847, a party of more than eighty immigrants to California became stranded, and nearly half starved to death. Some who survived did so by eating the dead.

7. William W. Arens, *The Man-Eating Myth: Anthropology and Anthropophagy* (New York: Oxford University Press, 1979).

8. Philip Boucher, *Cannibal Encounters: Europeans and Island Caribs, 1492–1763* (Baltimore: Johns Hopkins University Press, 1992).

9. Marvin Harris, *Cannibals and Kings: The Origins of Cultures* (New York: Random House, 1977), 147–166.

10. Georg Schweinfurth, *The Heart of Africa: Three Years' Travels and Adventures in the Unexplored Regions of Central Africa from 1868 to 1871*, vol. 2, trans. Ellen E. Frewer (New York: Harper, 1874), 92–93.

11. Enid Schildkrout and Curtis A. Keim, *African Reflections: Art from Northeastern Zaire* (Seattle: University of Washington Press, 1990), 33–36.

12. Schweinfurth, *Heart of Africa,* 2: 55.

13. Bob Thaves, "Frank and Ernest," Newspaper Enterprise Association, April 27, 1979.

14. Bob Thaves, "Frank and Ernest," Newspaper Enterprise Association, February 27, 1979.

15. Roger Lell, *Postmodern Cannibalism* (Durham, NC: Roger Lell, 1995). Reprinted with permission of the author.

Chapter 8

1. I thank colleagues who participated in an Internet discussion on *tribe* in September and October 1997. I have benefited from their comments and bibliographic contributions. The entire discussion is available at <http://www.h-net.msu.edu/~africa/>. *Africa News* also prepared a special issue in 1990 on the meaning of *tribe* in Africa. It is available at <http://www.africanews.org/info/tribe.html>. The Africa Policy Information Center has published a background paper on the meaning of *tribe:* Chris Lowe, "Tribe," *Africa Policy Information Center Background Paper,* no. 10 (New York: Africa Policy Information Center, 1997). This paper is available at <http://www.africapolicy.org>.

2. William A. Haviland, *Cultural Anthropology,* 9th ed. (New York: Harcourt Brace Jovanovich 1999), 346–351. Many but not all introductory anthropology textbooks treat *tribe* in a similar way. Some avoid the term and some, like Haviland, warn students that it is a contested category. Frequently, anthropologists also specify that a tribe traces its ancestry to a single common ancestor. Sometimes, definitions include chiefdoms and tribes in a single category. Marshall Sahlins, for example, calls the chiefdom the "most developed expression" of the tribe. Marshall Sahlins, *Tribesmen* (Englewood Cliffs, NJ: Prentice-Hall, 1968), 20–21.

3. For a discussion of the tribal organization of ancient Israel, see Norman K. Gottwald, *The Tribes of Yahweh: A Sociology of the Religion of Liberated Israel, 1250–1050 B.C.E.* (Maryknoll, NY: Orbis, 1979).

4. John Iliffe, *A Modern History of Tanganyika* (Cambridge: Cambridge University Press, 1979), 324.

5. Ibid., 331–337.

6. For examples, see ibid., 321–322, 326–327.

7. See, for example, Morton H. Fried, "On the Concepts of 'Tribe' and 'Tribal Society,'" *Transactions of the New York Academy of Sciences* 28, no. 4 (fall 1966): 527–540; and chapters in June Helm, ed., *Essays on the Problem of Tribe* (Seattle: University of Washington Press and American Ethnological Society, 1968).

8. See, for example, Morton H. Fried, "The Myth of Tribe," *Natural History,* April 1975, 12–20.

9. See, for example, Aidan Southall, "The Illusion of Tribe," in *The Passing of Tribal Man in Africa,* ed. Peter Gutkind (Leiden: E. J. Brill, 1970), 28–50; and Immanuel Wallerstein, "Ethnicity and National Integration in West Africa," *Cahiers d'Études Africaines* 1, no. 1 (1960): 129–139.

10. John Paden and Edward Soja, *The African Experience,* 2 vols. (Evanston, IL: Northwestern University Press, 1970).

11. For an overview of English-language perspectives on the idea of *tribe* in Africa, see Carola Lentz, "'Tribalism' and Ethnicity in Africa: A Review of Four Decades of Anglophone Research," *Cahiers des Sciences Humaines* 31, no. 2 (1995): 303–328.

12. Fried, "The Myth of Tribe," 14.

13. "First Nations" and "First Peoples" are increasingly popular alternatives to "Native Americans," presumably because the word *native* does not carry sufficient dignity or force.

14. The National Public Radio program *All Things Considered*, generally a source that treats Africa well, reported that the first known case of AIDS occurred before 1960 in the Belgian Congo in a "Bantu tribesman." Such categorization and overgeneralization is problematic for both of these words. National Public Radio, *All Things Considered*, February 3, 1998.

15. Anthony Appiah, "African Identities," in *Constructions Identitaires: Questionnements Théoriques et Études de Cas*, ed. Bogumil Jewsiewicki and Jocelyn Létourneau, Actes du Célat, no. 6 (Quebec: Célat, 1992), 58.

Chapter 9

1. Children's Television Workshop, *Sesame Street*, broadcast by WLVT, Bethlehem, PA, September 3, 1998.

2. Jeff Cooper, *To Ride, Shoot Straight, and Speak the Truth* (Paulden, AZ: Gunsite Press, 1990), 310.

3. José Ortega y Gasset, *Meditations on Hunting* (New York: Scribner, [1943] 1972).

4. Peter Matthiessen writes about his search for the few elephants left in West Africa in *African Silences* (London: Harvill, 1991).

5. Theodore Roosevelt, *African Game Trails: An Account of the African Wanderings of an American Hunter-Naturalist* (New York: Syndicate Publishing Company, 1910), ix.

6. Ibid., 20–23.

7. Marshall Everett, *Roosevelt's Thrilling Experiences in the Wilds of Africa Hunting Big Game* (Chicago: J. T. Moss, 1909), 60–61.

8. Bartle Bull, *Safari: A Chronicle of Adventure* (London: Penguin, 1992), 179–180. For another account of Roosevelt's safari and of the safari experience in general, see Kenneth M. Cameron, *Into Africa: The Story of the East African Safari* (London: Constable, 1990).

9. Roosevelt, *African Game Trails*, 288–289.

10. Bull, *Safari*, 182.

11. Ibid., 195–196, 257.

12. Roosevelt, *African Game Trails*, 409.

13. Ibid., 410.

14. Ibid., 414.

15. For an interesting discussion of Tarzan, see Marianna Torgovnick, *Gone Primitive: Savage Intellects, Modern Lives* (Chicago: University of Chicago Press, 1990), 42–72.

16. Bull, *Safari,* 281.

17. Ibid., 297.

18. For an Internet site that offers mostly pro-hunter views, see Wildnet Africa at <http://wildnetafrica.co.za/cites/>.

19. Smith Hempstone, *Rogue Ambassador: An African Memoir* (Sewanee, TN: University of the South Press, 1997), 242.

20. In South Africa, for example, impalas go for only $300, but leopards are $2,750 plus an $850 baiting fee. Prices for white rhino and buffalo are only available "on request." Zulu Nyala Safaris, available at <http://africanadrenalin.co.za/zulunyala/tro_zul.htm>.

21. Bull, *Safari,* 318.

22. Ibid., 322.

23. Ibid., 162.

24. Public Broadcasting Service, "South Africa," *Going Places,* original broadcast, May 18, 1998.

25. Frank Kuserk, interview by author, Bethlehem, PA, April 28, 1998.

26. Brian J. Huntly, "Conserving and Monitoring Biotic Diversity: Some African Examples," in *Biodiversity,* ed. Edward O. Wilson and Frances M. Peter (Washington, DC: National Academy Press, 1988), 258–259.

27. Marshall Sahlins, *The Use and Abuse of Biology: An Anthropological Critique of Sociobiology* (Ann Arbor: University of Michigan Press, 1976), xv.

28. For a critique of the Western management perspective in wildlife conservation and research, see Jonathan S. Adams and Thomas O. McShane, *The Myth of Wild Africa: Conservation Without Illusion* (New York: Norton, 1992).

29. Abercrombie and Fitch, *Christmas Catalog,* 1997, 73.

Chapter 10

1. AT&T, "There's No Easier Way to Get from Peoria to Pretoria," *Gourmet,* August 1997, 49.

2. Saks Fifth Avenue, "Safari: The Men's Fragrance by Ralph Lauren," *Gourmet,* March 1995, 16.

3. Jeep, "If You Can Read This Your Jeep Is Too Close," *National Geographic,* October 1996, back cover.

4. Sears Homelife Furniture Store, "The Best Place to Sleep," *Better Homes and Gardens,* August 1995, 25.

5. Franklin Institute Science Museum, "School Field Trip Planner: Pre K–12," spring 1996. Philadelphia: Franklin Institute Science Museum.

6. Intrav Private Jet Adventures, "The Civilized Way to Answer the Call of the Wild," *New York Times,* July 19, 1998, 16.

7. Watchtower Bible and Tract Society, "Should You Contact the Spirit Realm?" *Awake!* November 2, 1996, front cover.

8. Packard Bell, "Ankle-Biting Pygmies," *Parenting,* December 1996–January 1997, 246–247.

9. See, for example, Raymon A. Eve and Bob Price, "Geographic Illiteracy Among College Students," *Youth and Society* 25, no. 3 (March 1994): 408–427.

10. Fortunoff, "The Tunnel or the Bridge?" *Vanity Fair,* November 1998, 167.

11. Chivas Regal, "You Either Have It or You Don't," *Newsweek,* combined issue, December 29, 1997, and January 5, 1998, 91.

Chapter 11

1. See, for example, Chris Stringer and Robin McKie, *African Exodus: The Origins of Modern Humanity* (New York: Henry Holt, 1997).

2. J. Y. Chu, et al., "Genetic Relationship of Populations in China," *Proceedings of the National Academy of Sciences, USA* 95 (September 1998): 11763–11768.

3. For an extended discussion of the origins of race thinking in the Western world, see Ivan Hannaford, *Race: The History of an Idea in the West* (Washington, DC: Woodrow Wilson Center Press, 1996).

4. See, for example, Jared Diamond, "Race Without Color," *Discover,* November 1994, 83–89; and Stephen Jay Gould, "Why We Should Not Name Human Races: A Biological View," in *Ever Since Darwin: Reflections in Natural History* (New York: Norton, 1977), 231–236.

5. Paul Hoffman, "From the Editor: The Science of Race," *Discover,* November 1994, 4.

6. Desmond Morris, *The Naked Ape: A Zoologist's Study of the Human Animal* (New York: McGraw-Hill, 1967), 127–128. See also Morris' *The Human Animal: A Personal View of the Human Species* (New York: Crown, 1994).

7. Desmond Morris, *The Human Animal,* prod. Mike Beynon, 6 tapes, 50 min. each (Alexandria, VA: Time-Life Video, 1995), videotape.

8. Stringer and McKie, *African Exodus,* 212.

9. Ibid.

10. Robin Dunbar, "The Chattering Classes: What Separates Us from the Animals," *The Times* (London), February 5, 1994, quoted in Stringer and McKie, *African Exodus,* 208–209.

Chapter 12

1. Iode Mbunza, interview by author, Namagogole, Congo (Kinshasa), September 29, 1976.

2. Batsakpide-Mandeandroi, interview by author, Nyoala, Congo (Kinshasa), September 1, 1988.

3. Many authors discuss evolutionism and the way it creates both racial and cultural hierarchies. Readers wishing to pursue the subject should first consult Johannes Fabian's *Time and the Other: How Anthropology Makes Its Object* (New York: Columbia University Press, 1983). Fabian discusses the evolutionary hierarchies of twentieth-century anthropologists in terms of concepts of time.

4. Bernard McGrane, *Beyond Anthropology: Society and the Other* (New York: Columbia University Press, 1989), 55–76, 129.

5. Ibid., 129.

6. Ibid.

7. The concept of *transversality* has been employed by a number of modern philosophers. Ideas about transversality and the responsibility of dialogue and care are explicated in the work of philosophers Hwa Yol Jung and Calvin O. Schrag. See Hwa Yol Jung, "Bakhtin's Dialogical Body Politics," in *Bakhtin and the Human Sciences: No Last Words,* ed. Michael Mayerfeld Bell and Michael Gardiner (Thousand Oaks, CA: Sage, 1998), 95–111; Hwa Yol Jung, "Review Essay: Calvin O. Schrag, *The Self After Postmodernity,*" *Philosophy and Social Criticism* 24, no. 6 (1998): 133–140; Hwa Yol Jung, "The *Tao* of Transversality As a Global Approach to Truth: A Metacommentary on Calvin O. Schrag," *Man and the World* 28 (1995): 11–31; and Calvin O. Schrag, *The Resources of Rationality: A Response to the Postmodern Challenge* (Bloomington: Indiana University Press, 1992).

Works Cited

Abercrombie and Fitch. *Christmas Catalog*. 1997.

Achebe, Chinua. "An Image of Africa: Racism in Conrad's *Heart of Darkness*." In *Heart of Darkness*, by Joseph Conrad, Norton Critical Editions, ed. Robert Kimbrough, 3rd ed., 251–262. New York: Norton, 1988.

Adams, Jonathan S., and Thomas O. McShane. *The Myth of Wild Africa: Conservation Without Illusion*. New York: Norton, 1992.

Adas, Michael. *Machines As the Measure of Men: Science, Technology, and Ideologies of Western Dominance*. Ithaca: Cornell University Press, 1989.

Adeleke, Tunde. *UnAfrican Americans: Nineteenth-Century Black Nationalists and the Civilizing Mission*. Lexington, KY: University Press of Kentucky, 1998.

Ake, Claude. *Democracy and Development in Africa*. Washington, DC: Brookings Institution, 1996.

Althen, Gary. *American Ways*. Yarmouth, ME: Intercultural Press, 1998.

American Council for Voluntary International Action. Available: <http://www.interaction.org/>.

Appiah, Anthony. "African Identities." In *Constructions Identitaires: Questionnements Théoriques et Études de Cas,* ed. Bogumil Jewsiewicki and Jocelyn Létourneau, 53–61. Actes du Célat, no. 6. Quebec: Célat, 1992.

Arens, William W. *The Man-Eating Myth: Anthropology and Anthropophagy*. New York: Oxford University Press, 1979.

Asante, Molefi Kete. *The Afrocentric Idea*. Philadelphia: Temple University Press, 1987.

Ascanio, Pam. *White Men Don't Have Juju: An American Couple's Adventure Through Africa*. Chicago: Noble Press, 1992.

AT&T. "There's No Easier Way to Get from Peoria to Pretoria." *Gourmet,* August 1997, 49.

Baby Milk Action. Available: <http://www.gn.apc.org/babymilk/>.

Batsakpide-Mandeandroi. Interview by author. Nyoala, Congo (Kinshasa), September 1, 1988.

Bauer, Peter T. "Creating the Third World: Foreign Aid and Its Offspring." *Encounter,* April 1988, 66–75.

Beckwith, Carol, and Angela Fisher. "Fantasy Coffins of Ghana." *National Geographic,* September 1994, 120–130.

______. "Royal Gold of the Asante Empire." *National Geographic,* October 1996, 36–47.

Beers, Burton F. *World History: Patterns of Civilization*. Englewood Cliffs, NJ: Prentice-Hall, 1993.

Binkley, David A., and Patricia J. Darish. "'Enlightened But in Darkness': Interpretations of Kuba Art and Culture at the Turn of the Twentieth Century." In *The*

Scramble for Art in Central Africa, ed. Enid Schildkrout and Curtis A. Keim, 37–62. Cambridge: Cambridge University Press, 1998.

Block, Bernard. "Romance and High Purpose: *The National Geographic.*" *Wilson Library Bulletin* 68 (January 1994): 333–337.

Bonzai Rhino Tours and Safaris. Available: <http://www.index.co.za/bonzai/bonzai/index.html>.

Boucher, Philip. *Cannibal Encounters: Europeans and Island Caribs, 1492–1763.* Baltimore: Johns Hopkins University Press, 1992.

Brantlinger, Patrick. "Victorians and Africans: The Genealogy of the Myth of the Dark Continent." In *"Race," Writing, and Difference,* ed. Henry Louis Gates Jr., 185–222. Chicago: University of Chicago Press, 1985.

Brueggemann, Walter. *Genesis: A Bible Commentary for Teaching and Preaching.* Atlanta: John Knox, 1982.

Bull, Bartle. *Safari: A Chronicle of Adventure.* London: Penguin, 1992.

Burkey, Stan. *People First: A Guide to Self-Reliant, Participatory Rural Development.* Atlantic Highlands, NJ: Zed Books, 1993.

Burnham, Stanley. *America's Bimodal Crisis: Black Intelligence in White Society,* 3rd ed. Athens, GA: Foundation for Human Understanding, 1993.

Cameron, Kenneth M. *Into Africa: The Story of the East African Safari.* London: Constable, 1990.

Caputo, Robert. "Zaire River." *National Geographic,* November 1990, 5–35.

_____. "Tragedy Stalks the Horn of Africa." *National Geographic,* August 1993, 88–120.

Casati, Gaetano. *Ten Years in Equatoria and the Return with Emin Pasha.* Vol. 2. London: Frederick Warne, 1891.

Chin, Walter. "Kenya: The Maasai." *Sports Illustrated,* special issue, winter 1998, 66–72, 74.

Chivas Regal. "You Either Have It or You Don't." *Newsweek,* combined issue, December 29, 1997, and January 5, 1998, 91.

Chu, J. Y., et al. "Genetic Relationship of Populations in China." *Proceedings of the National Academy of Sciences, USA* 95 (September 1998): 11763–11768.

Clinton, Hillary Rodham. *It Takes a Village: And Other Lessons Children Teach Us.* New York: Simon and Schuster, 1996.

Cobb, Charles E., Jr. "The Twilight of Apartheid: Life in Black South Africa." *National Geographic,* February 1993, 66–93.

Cobb, Charles E., Jr., and Robert Caputo. "Eritrea Wins the Peace." *National Geographic,* June 1996, 82–105.

Collins, Carole J. L., and Steven Askin. "In the Dark About Africa." *Utne Reader,* May-June 1995, 17, 20, 22.

Conrad, Joseph. *Heart of Darkness.* Norton Critical Editions, ed. Robert Kimbrough, 3rd ed. New York: Norton, 1988.

Cooper, Jeff. *To Ride, Shoot Straight, and Speak the Truth.* Paulden, AZ: Gunsite Press, 1990.

Cornwall, Andrea, and Rachel Jewkes. "What Is Participatory Research?" *Social Science Medicine* 41, no. 12 (1995): 1667–1676.

Curtin, Philip D. *The Image of Africa: British Ideas and Action, 1780–1850.* Madison: University of Wisconsin Press, 1964.

Degler, Carl N. *In Search of Human Nature: The Decline and Revival of Darwinism in American Social Thought*. New York: Oxford University Press, 1991.
DeLancey, Virginia. "The Economies of Africa." In *Understanding Contemporary Africa,* ed. April A. Gordon and Donald L. Gordon, 2nd ed., 91–128. Boulder: Lynne Rienner, 1996.
Dettwyler, Katherine. *Dancing Skeletons: Life and Death in West Africa*. Prospect Heights, IL: Waveland, 1994.
DeVita, Philip R., and James D. Armstrong. *Distant Mirrors: America As a Foreign Culture*. Belmont, CA: Wadsworth, 1993.
Diamond, Jared. "Race Without Color." *Discover,* November 1994, 83–89.
Dorn, James A., Steve H. Hanke, and Alan A. Walters, eds. *The Revolution in Development Economics*. Washington, DC: Cato Institute, 1998.
Edwards, Mike. "In Focus: Central Africa's Cycle of Violence." *National Geographic,* June 1997, 124–133.
Else, David. *Trekking in East Africa,* 2nd ed. Hawthorn, Victoria, Australia: Lonely Planet, 1998.
Eve, Raymon A., and Bob Price. "Geographic Illiteracy Among College Students." *Youth and Society* 25, no. 3 (March 1994): 408–427.
Everett, Marshall. *Roosevelt's Thrilling Experiences in the Wilds of Africa Hunting Big Game*. Chicago: J. T. Moss, 1909.
Eze, Emmanuel Chukwudi, ed. *Race and the Enlightenment: A Reader*. Oxford: Blackwell, 1997.
Fabian, Johannes. *Time and the Other: How Anthropology Makes Its Object*. New York: Columbia University Press, 1983.
Filmakers Library. Available: <http://www.filmakers.com/ANTHRO.html>.
Finlay, Hugh. *Africa on a Shoestring,* 8th ed. Hawthorn, Victoria, Australia: Lonely Planet, 1998.
Finlay, Hugh, and Geoff Crowther. *East Africa*. Hawthorn, Victoria, Australia: Lonely Planet, 1997.
Forbath, Peter. *The River Congo*. New York: Harper and Row, 1977.
Fortunoff. "The Tunnel or the Bridge?" *Vanity Fair,* November 1998, 167.
Franklin Institute Science Museum. "School Field Trip Planner: Pre K–12." Spring 1996. Philadelphia: Franklin Institute Science Museum.
Franklin, John Hope. *From Slavery to Freedom: A History of Negro Americans,* 4th ed. New York: Alfred A. Knopf, 1974.
______. *George Washington Williams: A Biography*. Chicago: University of Chicago Press, 1985.
Freud, Sigmund. "The Savage's Dread of Incest." In *The Basic Writings of Sigmund Freud*. New York: The Modern Library, 1939.
Fried, Morton. *The Evolution of Political Society: An Essay in Political Anthropology*. New York: Random House, 1967.
______. "The Myth of Tribe." *Natural History,* April 1975, 12–20.
______. "On the Concepts of 'Tribe' and 'Tribal Society.'" *Transactions of the New York Academy of Sciences* 28, no. 4 (fall 1966): 527–540.
Fyfe, Christopher. *A History of Sierra Leone*. London: Oxford University Press, 1962.

Gordon, April A. "Women and Development." In *Understanding Contemporary Africa,* ed. April A. Gordon and Donald L. Gordon, 2nd ed., 249–272. Boulder: Lynne Rienner, 1996.

Gottwald, Norman K. *The Tribes of Yahweh: A Sociology of the Religion of Liberated Israel, 1250–1050 B.C.E.* Maryknoll, NY: Orbis, 1979.

Gould, Stephen Jay. "Why We Should Not Name Human Races: A Biological View." In *Ever Since Darwin: Reflections in Natural History*. New York: Norton, 1977.

Gourevitch, Philip. "Wondering Where the Lions Are." *Outside,* October 1996, 74–77.

Grant, Anthony. "Where the Wild Things Are: Touring in South Africa." *Student Travels Magazine,* spring 1998, 31–32.

Hall, James. *Sangoma: My Odyssey into the Spirit World of Africa*. New York: Putnam, 1994.

Hamilton, Carolyn. *Terrific Majesty: The Powers of Shaka Zulu and the Limits of Historical Invention*. Cambridge: Harvard University Press, 1998.

Hanlon, Joseph. *Peace Without Profit: How the IMF Blocks Rebuilding in Mozambique*. Portsmouth, NH: Heinemann, 1996.

______. "Strangling Mozambique: International Monetary Fund 'Stabilization' in the World's Poorest Country." *Multinational Monitor* 17, nos. 7–8 (July-August 1996). Available: <http://www.essential.org/monitor/hyper/mm0796.06.html>.

Hannaford, Ivan. *Race: The History of an Idea in the West*. Washington, DC: Woodrow Wilson Center Press, 1996.

Harris, Eddy. *Native Stranger: A Black American's Journey into the Heart of Africa*. New York: Simon and Schuster, 1992.

Harris, Marvin. *Cannibals and Kings: The Origins of Cultures*. New York: Random House, 1977.

______. *Cultural Anthropology*, 3rd ed. New York: Harper Collins, 1991.

Hauck, Charlie. "Alarmed by Burglars." *Home Improvement*. American Broadcasting Company. Original broadcast, May 14, 1996.

Haviland, William A. *Cultural Anthropology*, 9th ed. New York: Harcourt Brace Jovanovich, 1999.

Helm, June, ed. *Essays on the Problem of Tribe*. Seattle: University of Washington Press and American Ethnological Society, 1968.

Hempstone, Smith. *Rogue Ambassador: An African Memoir*. Sewanee, TN: University of the South Press, 1997.

Hickey, Dennis, and Kenneth C. Wylie. *An Enchanting Darkness: The American Vision of Africa in the Twentieth Century*. East Lansing: Michigan State University Press, 1993.

Hilliard, Bob. "Civilization (Bongo, Bongo, Bongo)." Musical composition from *Angel in the Wings*. Lyrics by Bob Hilliard, music by Carl Sigman. New York: Edwin H. Morris, 1947.

Hitchens, Christopher. "African Gothic." *Vanity Fair,* November 1994, 92–117.

Hoffman, Paul. "From the Editor: The Science of Race." *Discover,* November 1994, 4.

Huntly, Brian J. "Conserving and Monitoring Biotic Diversity: Some African Examples." In *Biodiversity,* ed. Edward O. Wilson and Frances M. Peter, 248–260. Washington, DC: National Academy Press, 1988.

Iliffe, John. *A Modern History of Tanganyika*. Cambridge: Cambridge University Press, 1979.

Indiana Botanic Gardens. Promotional flyer, spring 1998.

INFACT. Available: <http://www.infact.org/>.

Institute for Food and Development Policy. Available: <http://www.foodfirst.org>.

Intrav Private Jet Adventures. "The Civilized Way to Answer the Call of the Wild." *New York Times*, July 19, 1998, 16.

Isaacs, Harold R. *The New World of Negro Americans*. New York: John Day, 1963.

Jacobs, Sylvia M., ed. *Black Americans and the Missionary Movement in Africa*. Westport, CT: Greenwood Press, 1982.

Jeep. "If You Can Read This Your Jeep Is Too Close." *National Geographic*, October 1996, back cover.

Jenkins, David. *Black Zion: Africa, Imagined and Real, As Seen by Today's Blacks*. New York: Harcourt Brace Jovanovich, 1975.

Jung, Hwa Yol. "The *Tao* of Transversality As a Global Approach to Truth: A Metacommentary on Calvin O. Schrag." *Man and the World* 28 (1995): 11–31.

______. "Bakhtin's Dialogical Body Politics." In *Bakhtin and the Human Sciences: No Last Words*, ed. Michael Mayerfeld Bell and Michael Gardiner, 95–111. Thousand Oaks, CA: Sage, 1998.

______. "Review Essay: Calvin O. Schrag, *The Self After Postmodernity*." *Philosophy and Social Criticism* 24, no. 6 (1998): 133–140.

Kane, Thierno H. "Alternative Development Strategies in Africa: A Challenge to Grass-Root Initiatives." *Development* 2 (1994): 48–49.

Kaplan, Robert D. "The Coming Anarchy." *Atlantic Monthly*, February 1994, 44–76.

Keim, Curtis A. "*Artes Africanae:* The Western Discovery of 'Art' in Northeastern Congo." In *The Scramble for Art in Central Africa*, ed. Enid Schildkrout and Curtis A. Keim, 109–132. Cambridge: Cambridge University Press, 1998.

Keita, Maghan. "Africa Backwards and Forwards: Interpreting Africa and Africans in Pre- and Post-Modern Space." Paper presented at the Sixth Annual African Studies Consortium Workshop, University of Pennsylvania, Philadelphia, October 2, 1998.

Keith, Nelson W. *Reframing International Development: Globalism, Postmodernity, and Difference*. Thousand Oaks, CA: Sage, 1997.

"Kenya: You Could Look It Up." *Sports Illustrated*, special issue, winter 1998, 62.

Kipling, Rudyard. "The White Man's Burden." In *Collected Verse*, 215–217. New York: Doubleday, 1907.

Knoblauch, Edward. Contribution to H-Africa (a listserv resource for Africanists). Available: <http://www.h-net.msu.edu/africa>.

Krodel, Gerhard. *Acts*. Philadelphia: Fortress, 1981.

Kuserk, Frank. Interview by author. Bethlehem, PA, April 28, 1998.

Lell, Roger. *Postmodern Cannibalism*. Durham, NC: Roger Lell, 1995.

Lemonick, Michael D. "Lost Africa." *Time*, September 2, 1996, 52–56.

Lentz, Carola. "'Tribalism' and Ethnicity in Africa: A Review of Four Decades of Anglophone Research." *Cahiers des Sciences Humaines* 31, no. 2 (1995): 303–328.

Lewis, David Levering. *The Race to Fashoda: European Colonialism and African Resistance in the Scramble for Africa*. New York: Weidenfeld and Nicolson, 1987.

Liebenow, J. Gus. *Liberia: The Evolution of Privilege*. Ithaca: Cornell University Press, 1969.

Lowe, Chris. "Tribe." *Africa Policy Information Center Background Paper*. No. 10. New York: Africa Policy Information Center, 1997. Available: <http://www.africapolicy.org>.

MacCann, Donnarae, and Olga Richard. "Through African Eyes: An Interview About Recent Picture Books with Yulisa Amadu Maddy." *Wilson Library Bulletin* 69 (June 1995): 41–45, 141.

MacGaffey, Wyatt. "'Magic,' or as We Usually Say, 'Art': A Framework for Comparing European and African Art." In *The Scramble for Art in Central Africa*, ed. Enid Schildkrout and Curtis A. Keim, 217–235. Cambridge: Cambridge University Press, 1998.

Magubane, Bernard Makhosezwe. *The Ties That Bind: African-American Consciousness of Africa*. Trenton, NJ: Africa World Press, 1987.

Mannoni, Octave. *Prospero and Caliban: The Psychology of Colonization*. London: Methuen, 1956.

Matthiessen, Peter. *African Silences*. London: Harvill, 1991.

Maybury-Lewis, David. *Millennium: Tribal Wisdom and the Modern World*. New York: Viking-Penguin, 1992.

Mazrui, Ali. "A Clash of Cultures." Episode 8 of *The Africans: A Triple Heritage*. 58 min. Boston: WETA; London: British Broadcasting Corporation, 1986. Videotape.

Mbunza, Iode. Interview by author. Namagogole, Congo (Kinshasa), September 29, 1976.

McGrane, Bernard. *Beyond Anthropology: Society and the Other*. New York: Columbia University Press, 1989.

"Missionaries and Cannibals." Available: <http://www.ndsu.nodak.edu/~juell/cs724/prog3.txt>.

Morgan, Lewis Henry. *Ancient Society*. New York: Henry Holt, 1878. Reprint, Cambridge, MA: Belknap, 1964.

Morris, Desmond. *The Naked Ape: A Zoologist's Study of the Human Animal*. New York: McGraw-Hill, 1967.

______. *The Human Animal: A Personal View of the Human Species*. New York: Crown, 1994.

______. *The Human Animal*. Prod. Mike Beynon. 6 tapes, 50 min. each. Alexandria, VA: Time-Life Video, 1995. Videotape.

Munck, Johannes. *The Acts of the Apostles*. Revised by William F. Albright and C. S. Mann. Garden City, NY: Doubleday, 1967.

Mureithi, Mutahi. "Genuine Interest in Our Culture or Mere Fascination?" *Daily Nation* (Nairobi), August 9, 1996, 2.

Nash, Gary B., Charlotte Crabtree, and Ross E. Dunn. *History on Trial: Culture Wars and the Teaching of the Past*. New York: Alfred A. Knopf, 1998.

National Charities Information Bureau. Available: <http://www.give.org/index.cfm>.

Newton, Alex. *West Africa: A Lonely Planet Travel Survival Kit*, 3rd ed. Hawthorn, Victoria, Australia: Lonely Planet, 1995.

Niane, Djibril Tamsir. *Sundiata: An Epic of Old Mali.* Translated by G. D. Pickett. London: Longman, 1965.

Njuguna, Wanja. "Cultural Ambassador on Peace Mission." *Daily Nation* (Nairobi), August 9, 1996, 2.

Nundy, Julian. "France Haunted by Rwanda Genocide." *Telegraph Group Limited,* April 14, 1998. Available: <http://www.telegraph.co.uk/>.

Organization for Economic Cooperation and Development. News release, June 18, 1998. Available: <http://www.africapolicy.org>.

Osunde, Egerton O., Josiah Tlou, and Neil L. Brown. "Persisting and Common Stereotypes in U.S. Students' Knowledge of Africa: A Study of Preservice Social Studies Teachers." *The Social Studies* 87, no. 3 (May-June 1996): 119–124.

Ortega y Gasset, José. *Meditations on Hunting.* New York: Scribner, [1943] 1972.

Packard Bell. "Ankle-Biting Pygmies." *Parenting,* December 1996–January 1997, 246–247.

Packer, George. *The Village of Waiting.* New York: Vintage, 1988.

Paden, John, and Edward Soja. *The African Experience.* 2 vols. Evanston, IL: Northwestern University Press, 1970.

Palmer, Colin. "African Slave Trade: The Cruelest Commerce." *National Geographic,* September 1992, 62–91.

Park, Mungo. *Travels into the Interior Districts of Africa.* New York: Hippocrene Books, 1983.

Perkins, Dwight H. "Economic Systems Reform in Developing Countries." In *Reforming Economic Systems in Developing Countries,* ed. Dwight H. Perkins and Michael Roemer, 11–53. Cambridge: Harvard Institute for International Development, 1991.

Perry, James. *Living Africa: A Village Experience.* 35 min. Bloomington: Indiana University Television, 1983. Videotape.

Pradervand, Pierre. *Listening to Africa: Developing Africa from the Grassroots.* New York: Praeger, 1989.

Public Broadcasting Service. "South Africa." *Going Places.* Original broadcast, May 18, 1998.

Rad, Gerhard von. *Genesis: A Commentary.* Philadelphia: Westminster Press, 1959.

Reinthal, Peter. "The Living Jewels of Lake Malawi." *National Geographic,* May 1991, 42–51.

Richburg, Keith. *Out of America: A Black Man Confronts Africa.* New York: Basic Books, 1997.

Roberts, David. "Mali's Dogon: Below the Cliff of Tombs." *National Geographic,* October 1990, 100–127.

Roemer, Michael, and Steven C. Radelet. "Macroeconomic Reform in Developing Countries." In *Reforming Economic Systems in Developing Countries,* ed. Dwight H. Perkins and Michael Roemer, 55–80. Cambridge: Harvard Institute for International Development, 1991.

Roosevelt, Theodore. *African Game Trails: An Account of the African Wanderings of an American Hunter-Naturalist.* New York: Syndicate Publishing Company, 1910.

Sahlins, Marshall. *Tribesmen.* Englewood Cliffs, NJ: Prentice-Hall, 1968.

———. *The Use and Abuse of Biology: An Anthropological Critique of Sociobiology.* Ann Arbor: University of Michigan Press, 1976.

Saitoti, Tepilit Ole. *The Worlds of a Maasai Warrior: An Autobiography*. New York: Random House, 1986.

Saks Fifth Avenue. "Safari: The Men's Fragrance by Ralph Lauren." *Gourmet*, March 1995, 16.

Schildkrout, Enid, and Curtis A. Keim. *African Reflections: Art from Northeastern Zaire*. Seattle: University of Washington Press, 1990.

Schrag, Calvin O. *The Resources of Rationality: A Response to the Postmodern Challenge*. Bloomington: Indiana University Press, 1992.

Schultz, Emily A., and Robert H. Lavenda. *Cultural Anthropology: A Perspective on the Human Condition*, 3rd ed. Mountain View, CA: Mayfield, 1995.

Schuurman, Frans J., ed. *Beyond the Impasse: New Directions in Development Theory*. Atlantic Highlands, NJ: Zed Books, 1993.

Schwartz, Sher, and Bruce Schwartz. *Travel Senegal!* Available: <http://www.senegaltravel.com/>.

Schweinfurth, Georg. *The Heart of Africa: Three Years' Travels and Adventures in the Unexplored Regions of Central Africa from 1868 to 1871*. Vol. 2. Translated by Ellen E. Frewer. New York: Harper, 1874.

______. *Artes Africanae: Illustrations and Descriptions of Productions of the Industrial Arts of Central African Tribes*. Leipzig: F. A. Brockhaus, 1875.

Scott, William R. *The Sons of Sheba's Race: African-Americans and the Italo-Ethiopian War, 1935–1941*. Bloomington: Indiana University Press, 1993.

Sears Homelife Furniture Store. "The Best Place to Sleep." *Better Homes and Gardens*, August 1995, 25.

SERRV International. Available: <http://www.serrv.org/>.

Service, Elman R. *Primitive Social Organization*. New York: Random House, 1962.

Sherman, Amy L. "Rethinking Development: A Market-Friendly Strategy for the Poor." *Christian Century*, December 9, 1992, 1130–1134.

Shick, Tom W. *Behold the Promised Land: A History of Afro-American Settler Society in Nineteenth-Century Liberia*. Baltimore: Johns Hopkins University Press, 1977.

Snowden, Frank M., Jr. *Blacks in Antiquity: Ethiopians in the Greco-Roman Experience*. Cambridge, MA: Belknap, 1970.

Somé, Malidoma Patrice. *Nature, Magic, and Community: The Way of the Dagara*. Wisdom of Africa Series. Pacific Grove, CA: Oral Tradition Archives, 1993. Audiocassette.

______. *Of Water and the Spirit: Ritual, Magic, and Initiation in the Life of an African Shaman*. New York: Putnam, 1994.

______. "Rights of Passage: If Adolescence Is a Disease, Initiation Is a Cure." *Utne Reader*, July-August 1994, 67–68. Adapted from an article in *In Context* (winter 1993).

______. *The Healing Wisdom of Africa: Finding Life Purpose Through Nature, Ritual, and Community*. New York: Putnam, 1998.

Southall, Aidan. "The Illusion of Tribe." In *The Passing of Tribal Man in Africa*, ed. Peter Gutkind, 28–50. Leiden: E. J. Brill, 1970.

Soyinka, Wole. *The Open Sore of a Continent*. New York: Oxford University Press, 1996.

Spencer, Paul. *The Pastoral Continuum: The Marginalization of Tradition in East Africa*. New York: Oxford University Press, 1998.

Stanley, Henry Morton. *Through the Dark Continent*. New York: Harper, 1878.
Stanton, William. *The Leopard's Spots: Scientific Attitudes Toward Race in America, 1815–1859*. Chicago: University of Chicago Press, 1960.
Steiner, Christopher. *African Art in Transit*. New York: Cambridge University Press, 1994.
Steward, James B. "The Smart Traveler." *SmartMoney*, October 1996, 169.
Stringer, Chris, and Robin McKie. *African Exodus: The Origins of Modern Humanity*. New York: Henry Holt, 1997.
Sturgeon, Theodore. "Shore Leave." *Star Trek*. Paramount Pictures. Original broadcast, December 29, 1966.
Thomas-Slayter, Barbara, and Dianne E. Rocheleau. *Gender, Environment, and Development in Kenya: A Grassroots Perspective*. Boulder: Lynne Rienner, 1995.
Torgovnick, Marianna. *Gone Primitive: Savage Intellects, Modern Lives*. Chicago: University of Chicago Press, 1990.
Trillo, Richard. *West Africa: The Rough Guide*, 2nd ed. London: Rough Guides, 1995.
Ugwu-Oju, Dympna. *What Will My Mother Say: A Tribal African Girl Comes of Age in America*. Chicago: Bonus Books, 1995.
Uya, Okon Edet, ed. *Black Brotherhood: Afro-Americans and Africa*. Lexington, MA: Heath, 1971.
Verhelst, Thierry G. *No Life Without Roots: Culture and Development*. Translated by Bob Cumming. Atlantic Highlands, NJ: Zed Books, 1990.
Wallerstein, Immanuel. "Ethnicity and National Integration in West Africa." *Cahiers d'Études Africaines* 1, no. 1 (1960): 129–139.
Watchtower Bible and Tract Society. "Should You Contact the Spirit Realm?" *Awake!* November 2, 1996, front cover.
Watson, Pete, and Mary Watson. *The Market Lady and the Mango Tree*. New York: Tambourine Books, 1994.
Weaver, James H., Michael T. Rock, and Kenneth Kusterer. *Achieving Broad-Based Sustainable Development: Governance, Environment, and Growth with Equity*. West Hartford, CT: Kumarian Press, 1997.
Wildnet Africa. Available: <http://wildnetafrica.co.za/cites/>.
Wiley, Marylee. "Africa in Social Studies Textbooks." *Social Education* 46 (November-December 1982): 492–497, 548–552.
Windrich, Elaine. "Media Coverage of the Angolan War." *Africa Today* (spring 1992). Available: <http://www.EBSCOhost.com>.
Wolff, Leon. *Little Brown Brother: How the United States Purchased and Pacified the Philippine Islands at the Century's Turn*. Garden City, NY: Doubleday, 1961.
Woodson, Carter Godwin. *The Negro in Our History*, 11th ed. Washington, DC: Associated Publishers, 1966.
______. *The Mis-education of the Negro*. Trenton, NJ: Africa World Press, 1998.
World Bank. Available: <http://www.worldbank.org>.
Wright, Richard. *Black Power: A Record of Reactions in a Land of Pathos*. New York: Harper, 1954.
Yansané, Aguibou Y. "The Development of Development Thinking in Africa: The Theory Revisited." In *Development Strategies in Africa: Current Economic, Socio-*

political, and Institutional Trends and Issues, ed. Aguibou Y. Yansané, 3–62. Westport, CT: Greenwood Press, 1996.
Zekiros, Astair, with Marylee Wiley. *Africa in Social Studies Textbooks*. Bulletin no. 9550. Madison: Wisconsin Department of Public Instruction, 1978.
Ziegler, Dhyana, ed. *Molefi Kete Asante and Afrocentricity: In Praise and in Criticism*. Nashville, TN: James C. Winston, 1995.
Zulu Nyala Safaris. Available: <http://africanadrenalin.co.za/zulunyala/tro_zul.htm>.

Index